Rent and Its Discontents

Transforming Capitalism

Series Editors:
Ian Bruff, University of Manchester; Julie Cupples, University of Edinburgh; Gemma Edwards, University of Manchester; Laura Horn, University of Roskilde; Simon Springer, University of Victoria; Jacqui True, Monash University

This book series provides an open platform for the publication of path-breaking and interdisciplinary scholarship which seeks to understand and critique capitalism along four key lines: crisis, development, inequality, and resistance. At its core lies the assumption that the world is in various states of transformation, and that these transformations may build upon earlier paths of change and conflict while also potentially producing new forms of crisis, development, inequality, and resistance. Through this approach the series alerts us to how capitalism is always evolving and hints at how we could also transform capitalism itself through our own actions. It is rooted in the vibrant, broad and pluralistic debates spanning a range of approaches which are being practised in a number of fields and disciplines. As such, it will appeal to sociology, geography, cultural studies, international studies, development, social theory, politics, labour and welfare studies, economics, anthropology, law, and more.

Titles in the Series

Rent and Its Discontents

A Century of Housing Struggle

Edited by
Neil Gray

ROWMAN &
LITTLEFIELD
INTERNATIONAL

London • New York

Published by Rowman & Littlefield International Ltd
Unit A, Whitacre Mews, 26-34 Stannary Street, London SE11 4AB
www.rowmaninternational.com

Rowman & Littlefield International Ltd. is an affiliate of Rowman & Littlefield
4501 Forbes Boulevard, Suite 200, Lanham, Maryland 20706, USA
With additional offices in Boulder, New York, Toronto (Canada), and Plymouth (UK)
www.rowman.com

British Library Cataloguing in Publication Data
A catalogue record for this book is available from the British Library

ISBN: HB 978-1-7866-0574-0
     PB 978-1-7866-0575-7

Library of Congress Cataloging-in-Publication Data

Names: Gray, Neil, 1970- editor.
Title: Rent and its discontents : a century of housing struggle / edited by Neil Gray.
Description: London ; New York : Rowman & Littlefield International, [2018] | Series:
   Transforming capitalism | Includes bibliographical references and index.
Identifiers: LCCN 2018022461 (print) | LCCN 2018025389 (ebook) |
   ISBN 9781786605764 (Electronic) | ISBN 9781786605740 (cloth : alk. paper) |
   ISBN 9781786605757 (pbk.)
Subjects: LCSH: Public housing—Rent—Great Britain—History. |
   Housing policy—Great Britain—History. | Housing—Great Britain—History.
Classification: LCC HD7288.78.G7 (ebook) | LCC HD7288.78.G7 R46 2018 (print) |
   DDC 363.5/850941—dc23
LC record available at https://lccn.loc.gov/2018022461

Contents

Acknowledgements

I want to thank the *Transforming Capitalism* series editors, Ian Bruff, Julie Cupples, Gemma Edwards, Laura Horn, Simon Springer and Jacqui True, for supporting the publication of this book. Thanks also to Tom Slater who initially suggested the series, and to series editor Julie Cupples who ran with the idea. Much gratitude to all the contributors for timely submissions and commitment to the project, and especially to Hamish Kallin for also contributing the cover artwork. Special thanks to Bechaela Walker, Cian O'Callaghan, Hamish Kallin, Joey Simons and Mick Byrne for engaged feedback on my own contributions, and to my partner Bechaela and son Gene, for patience and support. I also want to thank editors and friends from *Variant* and *Mute* magazines, who have provided many opportunities for me to develop my thinking and writing on urbanization and the housing question over the years.

This book is dedicated to the memory of Jenni Marrow of Pennywell/Muirhouse Edinburgh, a committed housing activist who taught me, and many others, a great deal about housing and tenant organization.

Acknowledgements

Abbreviations

ACORN	Association of Community Organizations for Reform Now
AHFPA	Association of House Factors and Property Agents
ALMO	Arm's Length Management Organization
ASH	Architects 4 Social Housing
BSP	British Socialist Party
BTL	Buy-to-Let scheme
CARP	Carpenter against Regeneration Plans
CDO	Collateral Debt Obligation
CSO	Central Statistics Office (Ireland)
CWU	Communication Workers Union
DAFT	An Irish property website
DCH	Defend Council Housing
DCLG	Department for Communities and Local Government
DTA	Dublin Tenants Association
DTC	Dundee Trades Council
EPTAG	Edinburgh Private Tenants' Action Group
FOQM	Friends of Queens Market
GFC	Great Financial Crisis
GLA	Greater London Authority
GLC	Greater London Council
GMB	General British Union
GWHA	Glasgow Women's Housing Association
HA	Housing Association
HAT	Housing Action Trust
HAP	Housing Assistance Payment (Ireland)
HMG	His or Her Majesty's Government
HMO	Houses in Multiple Occupation

HOCCHG	House of Commons Council Housing Group
IAP	Integrated Area Plans
IEA	Institute of Economic Affairs
IHN	Irish Housing Network
ILP	Independent Labour Party
IMPACT	A public service trade union in Ireland
JFWU	Jute and Flax Workers Union
LSVT	Large Scale Voluntary Transfer
LHFA	Landlords' and House Factors' Association
LR	Living Rent
LRC	Labour Representation Committee (Dundee)
LVT	Land Value Tax
MBS	Mortgage-Backed Security
MSP	Member of the Scottish Parliament
NAMA	National Asset Management Agency (Ireland)
NHHC	National Homeless and Housing Coalition (Ireland)
NUS	National Union of Students (Scotland)
PAH	*Plataforma de Afectados por la Hipoteca* (Platform for People Affected by Mortgages)
PDH	Principal Dwelling House
PFI	Private Finance Initiative
PPP	Public Private Partnership
PRS	Private Rented Sector
REIT	Real Estate Investment Trust
RHN	Radical Housing Network
RMT	The National Union of Rail, Maritime and Transport Workers
RPZ	Rent Pressure Zone
RSL	Registered Social Landlord
RTA	Residential Tenancies Act (Ireland)
RTB	Residential Tenancies Board (Ireland)
RTB	Right-to-Buy (scheme)
RTE	Raidió Teilifís Éireann (Ireland's national television and radio broadcaster)
SCWG	Scottish Co-operative Women's Guild
SDF	Social Democratic Federation
SIPTU	Services, Industrial, Professional and Technical Union (Ireland)
SIV	Structured Investment Vehicle
SLHC	Short-Life Housing Co-Operative
SNP	Scottish National Party
SOHCA	Scottish Oral History Centre Archive
SPP	Scottish Prohibition Party
SQUASH	Squatters' Action for Secure Homes

STUC	Scottish Trades Union Council (Youth Committee)
TELCO	The East London Citizens Organization
UCL	University College London
UCU	University and College Union
US	United Suffragists
WHU	West Ham United Football Club
WPC	Women's Peace Crusade
WSF	Workers' Suffrage Federation
WSPU	Women's Social and Political Union

Preface

Housing and Direct Action

Seán Damer

The fact that housing, particularly public housing, has a profoundly political dimension is often obscured by seemingly more evident and dramatic political issues, such as Brexit, immigration or the Scottish independence referendum in the contemporary era. For example, the anomalous and important position of rent strikes in historical and sociological analysis was first flagged up fully forty-five years ago by Bert Moorhouse and his colleagues (Moorhouse et al. 1972). Since then, there has been a plethora of studies investigating both the empirical and theoretical dimensions of such strikes in Britain and Ireland; these are fully documented in this book. These studies fall into two schools of thought, broadly speaking. The first derives from elements of the Marxist tradition and argues that rent strikes are an integral part of the class struggle, are profoundly embedded in working-class culture and agency and are to be interpreted with reference to the politics of the social reproduction of the labour power of that class. The second is a revisionist stance which argues that rent strikes constitute a phenomenon quite distinct from class struggle and are to be interpreted as some form of 'social movement'. I have criticized this latter position as both reactionary and wholly illegitimate (Damer 2000a).

Where the two schools agree is in the importance of the 1915 Glasgow Rent Strike, also discussed at length in the present volume. The disagreement is in the *interpretation* of this dramatic event. My interpretation, and that of the contributors to this book, is that this strike was an integral part of the struggle of the Clydeside working class. It was organized within that class, initially as a defence against rapacious wartime rent hikes by local property owners and factors; it was led by local working-class men and women; and it was theorized by these leaders as a critical element of the contemporary class struggle. Most unusually within the British Left, this strike overcame divisions of gender, skill, religion and ethnicity within the Clydeside working class and forged it into a formidable fighting force. The result, the passing of the 1915 Rent Restrictions Act, was arguably the most significant working-class victory of the twentieth century. This wartime struggle led directly to the postwar Clydebank Strike, which lasted from 1920 to 1927 (see Damer 2000a). This curiously understudied strike caused profound reverberations at both the local and national levels and ensured the retention of the principle of rent control well after the events of 1915.[1]

Yet, it is more than a century since the 1915 Rent Strike, and perhaps its dramatic success has camouflaged the fact that there were rent strikes all over the country in both the interwar and postwar years; these receive a welcome summary in this book. However, Margaret Thatcher's notorious 'Right-to-Buy' policy of 1980 changed the picture of housing in the United Kingdom drastically, signalling the beginning of the end of what used to be called 'council housing', or public housing for the working class as owned and managed by local authorities. Such housing, now called 'social housing'—a misnomer if there ever was one—is currently in the hands of housing associations. Initially, there was some hope that such associations would be more democratic and sensitive to the housing needs of working-class tenants than, say, the historically authoritarian and paternalistic Corporation of Glasgow (later Glasgow City Council) because tenants were to be represented on the management committees. However, as some of the chapters in this book demonstrate, this hope has not been realized. The principal reasons are that the associations have been starved of central government funding, on the one hand, and tenants' representatives are prevented from overt criticism by company law, on the other, such that the tenant management committee's powers are effectively illusory. This raises the question of what a tenants' politics, including rent strikes and other forms of direct action, might look like in the contemporary situation because there is common agreement that the housing situation in both Britain and Ireland is in crisis. This book systematically analyses these issues in a welcome departure from the standard 'social policy' literature on social housing. It is a book whose time has come.

NOTE

1. The outraged reaction of the Clydeside bourgeoisie can be judged from the *minutes* of the Glasgow Factors & Property Owners Association, now available in the Glasgow University Archives at UGD 342 1/4. These minutes were not available to me when I did my original research into the Clydebank Rent Strike.

REFERENCES

Damer, Seán. 2000a. "'The Clyde Rent War!' The Clydebank Rent Strike of the 1920s." In *Class Struggle and Social Welfare*, edited by Michael Lavalette and Gerry Mooney, 71–95. London: Routledge.

Moorhouse, Bert, Mary Wilson and Chris Chamberlain. 1972. "Rent Strikes—Direct Action and the Working-Class." *Socialist Register* 9(9): 133–56.

Introduction

Rent Unrest: From the 1915 Rent Strikes to Contemporary Housing Struggles

Neil Gray

Britain and Ireland are in the grip of an entrenched and escalating housing crisis. This book exposes the causes and consequences of that crisis, revealing its more permanent character, and showing how tenants and residents have been challenging it. The book was inspired by the centenary of the 1915 Rent Strikes in Glasgow, which played a decisive role in establishing rent controls in Britain for the first time and ultimately forcing the government to introduce public housing provision in 1919. It re-examines this formative moment of tenant organization in light of new empirical research and new theoretical understandings, exploring its relevance through a largely hidden continuum of tenant struggles following 1915 and through multiple contemporary case studies from the most significant housing struggles in Britain and Ireland today. The primary focus is on the particular context of Britain and Ireland,[1] but given the depth of the housing crisis across multiple borders, these studies will resonate with those attempting to comprehend and contest housing tyranny internationally.

Here, I provide a brief historical overview of rent unrest in Britain and Ireland, focusing initially on the 1915 Rent Strikes in Glasgow but also on the many, largely hidden, tenant and resident struggles in the sphere of social reproduction before, during and after 1915. Such a summary is politically vital because the labour movement and related trade unions have often viewed the housing question as merely secondary to workplace struggles in the sphere of direct production (see Moorehouse et al. 1972; Sklair 1975; Englander 1983; Bradley 2014). Yet, as Bunge (1977) observes, it is precisely on the 'second front' of social reproduction that the everyday life of the working class (in all its diverse dimensions) is located. Exploring this blind spot is all the more crucial because the capacity for radical change in the workplace has been deeply undermined by industrial decomposition and automation in Britain and Ireland, and housing is now more central to contemporary forms of capital accumulation than ever (Harvey 2012; Aalbers and Christophers 2014; Madden and Marcuse 2016; Gray, this volume).

Providing a material basis for this argument, I outline the prominent role of housing in what has been an epochal transformation from industrialization to urbanization since the early 1970s (Lefebvre 2003 [1970]; Harvey 1985, 2012; Christophers 2011), in conjunction with a resurgent financialized rentier economy (Hudson 2006a, 2010; Vercellone 2010; Harvey 2012; Fields and Uffer 2016). Yet merely describing this systemic context would be of limited political value if it did not allow us to comprehend the central importance of housing as a field of immanent political struggle (see Fields 2015, 2017; Gray, this volume). As Harvey (2012, 65) contends: 'If the capitalist form of urbanization is so completely embedded in and foundational for the reproduction of capitalism, then it also follows that alternative forms of urbanization must necessarily become central to any pursuit of a capitalist alternative.' The need for such a challenge is underscored here by an examination of contemporary housing conditions and the stark injustice and inequality that has become normalized through the hyper-commodification of housing in the last few decades. In conclusion, I outline the plan of this book and its potential utility for tenant movements in Britain, Ireland and beyond.

GLASGOW 1915:
'A MASS CONCERN WITH THE FACTS OF EVERYDAY LIFE'

[W]ithout the 1915 Rent Strike in Glasgow, there would have been no 1915 Rents and Mortgage Restrictions Act, and without the 1915 Act, there would have been no 1919 Housing and Town Planning Act.

—Damer (1980, 103)

The 1915 Rent Strikes in Glasgow are now widely acknowledged as a decisive event in a wider national struggle that shaped both the British tenants' movement and British housing policy dramatically (Damer 1980; Melling 1983; Castells 1983; Englander 1983), with few historical events exhibiting such a close causal link between urban struggle and state intervention. The crucial historical impetus for forcing the establishment of the Housing and Town Planning Act 1919 (the 'Addison Act')—which made state provision of housing a right 'for the first time in history'—was undoubtedly the rent strikes and the rent restrictions act it impelled (Castells 1983, 27; Damer 1980, 103). The Increase of Rent and Mortgage Interest (War Restrictions)

Act 1915, besides immediately ameliorating a vicious rent burden for tenants, established rent controls in Britain for the first time (fixed at prewar levels) and made the revival of speculative building unprofitable for decades (Damer 1980). With contemporary tenant and resident movements in Britain and Ireland showing signs of a long overdue resurgence, probably the greatest lesson from the 1915 rent strikes is that the threat and practice of collective tenant organization and direct action is a prerequisite condition for radical housing transformation, and indeed, any wider claims for the 'right to the city' (see Gray 2017).

The First World War generated a massive influx of people to work in Glasgow's munitions industry, exacerbating an already acute and well-documented housing crisis. By 1914, the city had the highest population density in Britain, with 'colossal' profits being extracted from slum housing by rentier landlords in near monopoly conditions (Damer 1980, 81; Melling 1983) and evictions taking place on an unprecedented scale in the British context (Englander 1981). Compounding these affronts, under the 'Law of Urban Hypothec' Scottish landowners were permitted to seize the property of those who were unable to pay the sharply escalating rent (Damer 1980; Melling, 1983). Even at the end of the nineteenth century, it was self-evident to housing campaigners that private enterprise could not and would not solve the housing problem, and agitation on the housing question became widespread in Glasgow and across Britain in the early twentieth century (Damer 1980; Melling 1983; Englander 1983; Grayson 1996).

Following the formal constitution of local and national tenant organizations from the 1890s, municipalization of housing became a primary objective in Glasgow (Damer 1980). By 1898, the Independent Labour Party (ILP) had ten members on Glasgow's Town Council, where tenant grievances were expressed on a range of issues throughout the 1910s. In 1911, the Glasgow Labour Party was founded, with housing a 'central plank' of their activity (Damer 1980, 90). In 1913, the Scottish Federation of Tenants' Associations was formed by the Social Democratic Federation (SDF), following agitation over rent increases. The Glasgow Trades' Council was also very active, and most significantly, the Glasgow Women's Housing Association (GWHA) was established in 1914 through the auspices of the ILP Housing Committee and the Glasgow Women's Labour Party (Damer 1980; Melling 1983; Smyth 1992). The composition of the rents movement was marked by gender and party diversity with mutual cooperation between different strategies and tendencies: women led on the ground in the sphere of social reproduction; the ILP, at that time a very broad church, performed an important 'networking' and coordinating function; and workers in the shipyards and munitions industries offered vital support (Damer 1980; Melling 1983; Foster 1990).

The key events in the 1915 rent strikes have been described in depth elsewhere (Damer 1980; Melling 1983; Castells 1983; Smyth 1992), necessitating only a brief summary here. In Spring 1915, following several recent rent hikes, up to 25 percent in some districts, groups of tenants in Govan began to refuse the rent increases (Damer 1980), ultimately leading to an estimated 25,000 tenants on rent strike across Glasgow by November 1915 (Melling 1983, 107). As noted, evictions for non-payment of rent were a major issue in Glasgow in this period (Englander 1981), and the harassment and ejectment of women and children while male soldiers were at war was a central rallying point because tenants and the labour movement associated high rents with 'unpatriotic' wartime profiteering. The eviction of serving soldiers' families in Govan and Shettleston—in April and June 1915, respectively—was capitalized on by the rents movement to generate a strategic 'patriotic' uproar that served as vital propaganda for the movement. 'RENT STRIKE: WE ARE NOT REMOVING' and 'WE ARE NOT PAYING INCREASED RENT' notices targeting landlord tyranny by 'THE PRUSSIANS OF PARTICK' were plastered over thousands of windows across the city (Melling 1983; Smyth 1992; Currie, this volume). Factory and shipyard gate meetings and mass public meetings addressed by Marxist revolutionaries such as John McLean incited workers to direct action, while public meetings were held throughout the city by the official Labour movement with the goal of parliamentary reform via petitions and deputations to the City Chambers.

A celebrated incident occurred in October 1915 when a group of women attacked a factor's clerk[2] with bags of peasemeal (pea flour) and chased him from the street after an eviction attempt in Govan (see Currie, this volume). By November 1915, around 20,000 people were on rent strike in Glasgow, including five Labour councillors (Damer 1980, 1990; Melling 1983; Castells 1983; Smyth 1992). Rent strikes are reported to have occurred in the districts of Govan, Partick, Parkhead, Pollokshaws, Pollok, Cowcaddens, Kelvingrove, Ibrox, Govanhill, St. Rollox, Townhead, Springburn, Maryhill, Fairfield, Blackfriars (Gorbals) and Woodside (Damer 1980, 93), indicating the mass character of the movement and illustrating how rent was seen as a general problematic rather than a mere secondary concern behind the workplace. Following a massive women-led demonstration on St. Enoch Square in October 1915, the decisive flashpoint came when eighteen rent-striking munitions workers were put on trial on November 17 at the Small Debts Court (Damer, 1980; Melling, 1983; Foster 1990). Thousands of men and women marched to the court, with a demonstration of 10,000 to 15,000 workers and tenants demanding a wartime rent freeze and that all defendants be released on threat of general strike. The next day it was formally announced that a rent-restriction bill would be passed in Parliament. On November 28, the Rents and Mortgage Interest (War Restrictions) Bill was introduced at the

House of Commons, receiving Royal Assent and becoming law on December 25, 1915 (Damer 1980; Melling 1983; Smyth 1992).

THE COLLECTIVE POWER OF ORGANIZED TENANTS' MOVEMENTS: HISTORICAL RENT UNREST IN GLASGOW AND BEYOND

The 1915 Glasgow Rent Strikes are deservedly renowned, but rent strikes were widespread before, during and after the war throughout Britain. More generally, housing contestation has been a continual, if often overlooked, feature of political activity across Britain since the 1880s. In Scotland alone, Dundee was another 'storm centre' of housing struggle in 1915 (see Cox, this volume), and it is rarely mentioned that contemporary rent strikes were also enacted with varying degrees of intensity and scale in Aberdeen, Kircaldy and Leith (Edinburgh) on the east coast of Scotland (Petrie 2008); Mid-Lanark, Clydebank, Greenock, Cambuslang and Hamilton on the west coast; and Annan and Gretna in the south (see Cox, this volume; Petrie 2008). As Seán Damer stresses, such militant anti-landlord struggles cannot be detached from the historical enmity built up by the violence of eviction and displacement in the Highland Clearances of Scotland and enforced preventable famine and land wars in Ireland in the nineteenth century. This hatred of landlords provided a volatile and unruly proletarian presence in cities like Glasgow, whose slums were multiplied by dispossessed Highland and Irish workers in the nineteenth and early twentieth centuries (1997, 35–36).

As Englander (1983) observes, prewar rent strikes and rent agitation occurred throughout England between 1912 and 1914. He cites Wolverhampton, Birmingham, Leeds, Bradford, Liverpool and several districts in London as key examples, with such struggles escalating in 1915 during wartime (see also Ginsburg 1979; Grayson 1996; Bradley 2014). There were genuine and well-documented fears within government circles that such disputes, especially in areas of munitions production, where the fiercest struggles occurred (Englander 1983, 195), could potentially transform themselves into a unified challenge to government authority across Britain (Swenarton 1981; Englander 1983; Foster 1990; Glynn 2009). Englander (1983) surveys numerous examples of rent strikes and rent unrest in England in this period, including, but not limited to: Newcastle, Barrow-in-Furness, Manchester, Liverpool, Warrington, Birmingham, West Bromwich, Burton-on-Trent and Luton. In London alone, Shoreditch, Bethnal Green, Hammersmith, Camberwell, Tooting and Woolwich were all active centres of rent resistance. Yet for all this militant class organization across Britain, it is widely agreed that it was ultimately the scale, intensity and strategic power of the Glasgow Rent

Strikes that was the decisive factor in forcing state intervention and formal rent restrictions (Damer 1980; Castells 1983; Englander 1983; Melling 1983). But if the 1915 Rent Act was undoubtedly of great political significance, it did not ultimately solve the housing question. Crucially, rents did not *decrease* (which was a compelling necessity at the time) but were only restricted from rising above prewar levels; housing supply remained negligible (at a time when overcrowding and slum conditions were rife); and evictions remained frequent (Englander 1983).

It is crucial to recognize today that the retention of rent restriction gains and the slow development of housing reform in Britain after the war were dependent on the sustained threat of militant working-class organization and antagonism rather than state benevolence (see Gray, this volume). In the US context, Madden and Marcuse (2016, 119–20) show how the 'myth of the benevolent state' masks the fact that state action in the housing sector has always been premised on supporting the accumulation of private profit while channelling 'system-challenging' housing demands into 'system-maintaining' forms. Similar constraints have faced radical or progressive housing movements in Britain and Ireland, with any housing reform requiring concerted direct action and campaigning from tenant groups, often but not always, in isolation from the labour movement and trade unions who tend to fixate on the workplace. In Scotland, the Independent Labour Party (ILP), at that time a relatively militant party affiliated to, but independent from, the Labour Party, pushed for municipal housing for all workers, skilled or unskilled, throughout the 1920s (Horsey 1990). In the same period, as Damer (2000a) has shown, the largely under-acknowledged Clydebank Rent Strike (1920–1927) formed a sustained and significant campaign involving thousands of tenants against rent increases, and for municipal housing at a time when the depression had sapped much of the militancy and bargaining capacity from Clydeside's industrial workers. Innovatively marrying direct-action tactics and legal activity, the campaign prevented persistent attempts to decontrol and raise rents, while blocking multiple evictions in Clydebank between 1920 and 1927. The significance of the Clydebank Rent Strikes remains to be fully acknowledged, yet without them, Damer (1997, 94) contends: 'rent control would have been removed by the mid-1920s.

Englander (1983) documents how tenants in Barrow, Newcastle, Birkenhead and Workington agitated for 'special area' status in 1917 to avoid housing evictions in munitions areas and how tenants in areas of heavy industry in the Scottish Clyde Valley—Airdrie, Coatbridge, Hamilton, Motherwell, Wishaw and Mid-Lanarkshire—organized against housing shortages and overcrowding in the same year. Additionally, he observes, Rosyth, Coventry, Woolwich and Dudley all maintained rent strikes and rent unrest in the 1917–1918 period. Rent struggles in the interwar years have been given less attention, but Englander cites the Scottish Labour Housing Association, Glasgow Council of Tenants' Associations, the War Rents League, Birmingham & District Tenants' Federation and the Stepney Tenants' Defence League as active bodies in the period. There were also significant rent strikes in Birmingham and Leeds in the 1930s (Ginsburg 1979; Bradley 2014), and Englander (1983, 306) cites an article in the *News Chronicle*, suggesting that 60,000 tenants throughout Britain were on rent strike in June 1938.

For the government, the 1915 rent restrictions were an emergency measure hastily enacted to quell and mediate tenant and worker agitation to maintain munitions production in wartime and reassert control over the housing question. From their position, the repeal of rent controls would be undertaken at the first available opportunity in peacetime (Damer 1980; Englander 1983). Yet, continued rent agitation in the interwar period made this return to the prewar status quo an intractable problem for the government in the immediate and long term, with rent restrictions only being substantially repealed with the Housing Act 1988. Housing unrest was also central to defending and maintaining public housing gains from the postwar period to the present era (see Bradley 2014; Grayson 1996; Johnstone 1992, 2000; Moorhouse at al. 1972; Sklair 1975). This history embraces rent strikes in St. Pancras, London (1959–1961); East London (1968–1970); Kirkby, Merseyside (1972–1973); the Gorbals, Glasgow (1976–1982); and more recently the University College London (UCL) 'Cut the Rent' strikes over exorbitant student accommodations bills. It also includes a series of under-acknowledged but successful challenges to 'housing stock transfer' from public housing (or 'council housing') to housing associations (HAs) by ballot (see Robbins 2002; Mooney and Poole 2005; Watt 2009a; Watt, this volume), which still await their chronicler. There is not the space here for a full account of these postwar struggles and campaigns, but Johnstone (1992), Grayson (1996) and Bradley (2014) provide excellent summaries elsewhere.

RETHINKING THE RENT STRIKES

We are fortunate to have some compelling and well-researched accounts of the 1915 rent strikes, yet these were largely produced in the early 1980s, with little substantive new research being undertaken since. This is therefore a deeply opportune moment to reassess the rent strikes and their ongoing significance with reference to subsequent transformations in housing policy and housing experience: the Conservative Party's infamous 'Right-to-Buy' (RTB) scheme enacted in 1980; the repeal of rent restrictions in the 1988 Housing Act; and the inception of large-scale 'stock transfer' programs beginning in the late 1980s. Notably, tenant-purchase schemes comparable to

RTB were introduced in Ireland as early as the Housing Act 1966, with more local authority homes being sold to sitting tenants than being constructed during the 1970s. Moreover, rent controls were abolished in 1982, six years before Britain (McCabe 2011, 31–32). RTB was the most substantial of all British privatization schemes during the 1980s, and the privatization, commodification and financialization of housing—alongside numerous programmes of large-scale social housing demolition and welfare retraction of an enormous magnitude—have been central to the political economy of Britain since then (in Ireland, since the 1970s). Such transformations in the political economy of housing necessitate a significant reappraisal of the perennial housing question.

The recent centenary in 2015 of the rent strikes produced widespread interest and numerous public events in Glasgow, including a welcome reconsideration of women's involvement in the rent strikes (Burness 2015; Orr 2015), and the 'Remember Mary Barbour' campaign, which successfully campaigned for a statue in honour of one of the principal leaders of the rent strikes, one of only four statues of women in Glasgow.[3] Yet the centenary has generated little in the way of original new *housing analysis* and has been marked by a somewhat nostalgic register that has made little attempt to relate the rent strikes to the contemporary housing question. By contrast, this volume deploys an interdisciplinary approach—using analyses from housing studies, urban studies, history, sociology, geography, gender studies and activist/scholar-activist positions—that aims to reinterpret the rent strikes in ways that might inform and incite contemporary housing mobilization in relation to wider transformations in urban political economy. This involves a mix of contributions, revisiting historical housing movements and documenting contemporary housing struggles from below—often from an engaged position within those struggles—and more theoretical interventions which contend that the housing question must necessarily be placed at the forefront of contemporary political struggles given the centrality of housing to the national political economies of Britain and Ireland. Such a diverse range of contributions allows for several points of entry into the housing question, revealing the continuity and relevance of housing contestation across both time and space.

As Jameson (1991, 5) once noted, of all the arts 'architecture is the closest constitutively to the economic, with which, in the form of commissions and land values, it has a virtually unmediated relationship'. It should come as no surprise then that much, but certainly not all, housing research and journalism has been compromised by proximity to this economic nexus (see Kallin and Slater, this volume). In mainstream debates, housing has tended to be treated as a separate specialized domain for experts like developers, architects, planners and economists, eschewing a perspective on housing as a wider political-economic problem that is riddled with class, race and gender conflict (Madden and Marcuse 2016). As Johnstone (2000, 140) observes in an earlier attempt to reclaim the hidden history of tenants' movements, historians and 'housing experts' have typically regarded the development of progressive housing policy as 'part of a legislative and administrative process somehow separate from broader social and economic struggles which inevitably take place within class divided societies'. This perpetuation of the 'myth of the benevolent state' (Madden and Marcuse 2016) is compounded by the fact that housing struggles historically—typically undertaken by tenants and residents without institutional funding or support—have been poorly recorded, discussed and analysed as a result of a lack of institutional support from the labour movement and trade unions (Moorhouse et al. 1972; Sklair 1975; Bradley 2014). Political focus has routinely been placed on typically male workplace relations at the expense of predominantly women-led community and tenant organizations (Grayson 1996, 6), with tenants' movements in Britain and Ireland far too often being hidden from history.

Challenging the actions and discourse of powerful government agencies, construction and landlord lobbies, estate agents and media discourse, and more troublingly the aporias of the labour movement, associated trade unions and certain strands of academic research necessitates an unapologetically critical, partisan and situated response. Most of the contributors in this volume are distinguished by their housing activism or support of housing activism, their membership of tenant and resident organizations and their critical academic and journalistic work around the housing question. All seek a more equitable, radical approach to the housing question, taking their cue from a fundamental need to address the processes of capital accumulation, hypercommodification and state retrenchment that have led to the current housing crisis—an exacerbated moment in a much longer continuum of housing crises—and the everyday needs and desires of tenants and residents at the sharp end of housing privatization. This embedded critical activist and scholar-activist approach is a crucial and necessary corrective to what Kallin and Slater (this volume) call 'agnotology': the strategic production of ignorance. Yet, to gain wider political traction, this subjective side of the housing question must necessarily be premised on a deeper understanding of the structural changes in the economy which have placed urbanization and housing at the centre of Britain and Ireland's political economy.

THE URBANIZATION OF CAPITAL AND THE RETURN OF THE RENTIER

Grasping the current housing crisis in its material reality and its full amplitude requires comprehending a long-term transformation of capitalism from industrialization to urbanization since the early 1970s, a shift most presciently diagnosed by the French Marxist urban theorist, Henri Lefebvre. With an emerging global economic crisis and militant workers' demands blocking profitability in industry, he argues, capital 'found new inspiration in the conquest of space . . . in real estate speculation, capital projects (inside and outside the city), the buying and selling of space. And it did so on a worldwide scale' (Lefebvre 2003 [1970], 155). Central to this transition for Lefebvre is a process of 'capital switching' from the primary sector of industry and manufacturing to the secondary sector of land, real estate, housing and the built environment (Harvey 1985; Beauregard 1994; Gotham 2009; Christophers 2011). In a key section of *The Urban Revolution*, Lefebvre (2003 [1970], 160) explains how the secondary sector provides capitalism with a crucial 'buffer' in times of industrial slowdown and economic depression.

> As the principal circuit . . . begins to slow down, capital shifts to the second sector, real estate. It can even heppen that real-estate speculation becomes the principal source for the formation of capital, that is, the realization of surplus value.

Such processes have clearly not been universal because they are premised on particular historical, material and institutional contexts in Western Europe. Moreover, tracing capital switching in the built environment is extremely complex given the expanded role of financial intermediaries and data-protection laws related to private companies (Christophers 2011). Yet grasped as a *general tendency*, the process of capital switching certainly resonates at an empirical and subjective level in the British context. Crucially, Lefebvre (2003 [1970], 160) conceives of such processes as being intimately bound up with socioeconomic crisis, noting how classical economists and critics of political economy alike have long understood that overinvestment in real estate is an 'unhealthy situation' for capital. As Harvey (1985) observes, following Lefebvre, when capitalist production edges towards periodic crises of overaccumulation, capital routinely switches from the primary circuit to the secondary circuit as a means to absorb capital and labour surpluses and avoid crisis. But such capital switching is also crisis switching. Real estate investment tends to dampen investment in the productive economy, becoming 'fixed' in land and property when it really requires constant movement and flow for the continual realization of surplus value (Harvey 1985, 2012; Weber 2002; Christophers 2011; Madden and Marcuse 2016). With the central role that housing and urbanization increasingly play in the national political economies of most major Western countries—in symbiosis with the proliferation of forms of rent and the exacerbated financialization of housing and property markets (Aalbers and Christophers 2014; Fields and Uffer 2016; Vercellone

2010)—the link between capital switching and socioeconomic crisis has only become clearer over time (Hudson 2010; Christophers 2011; Harvey 2012).

As Hudson (2010, 419) contends, the interrelated processes of financialization and rentier capitalism form a 'counter-Enlightenment' that has usurped the predictions of Marx and the classical economists of the nineteenth century, who thought that rentier interests would be subordinated to the needs of industrial capitalism in the long run. Even proto-capitalists like Adam Smith and Stuart Mill, Hudson observes, argued that rent is a parasitic 'unearned increment' (2010, 429), a monopoly price based on extraction rather than productive investment, garnering economic rent for the financier or capitalist by virtue of simply 'owning something' (Hudson 2006b, 40). Yet, far from the 'euthanasia of the rentier' that Keynes envisaged in the 1930s, rentier activity is central to contemporary capital-accumulation strategies, reproducing and magnifying socioeconomic inequality via incessant cyclical forms of looting from the wider economy.

The point here is not to extol the virtues of the halcyon days of industry and manufacturing, which came with their own forms of exploitation and injustice,[4] but to illustrate that the rentier economy puts money in the hands of even fewer people than the 'productive' economy. Rentier income is invested back into real estate or ownership rights, inflating prices for assets and making further speculation more attractive to investors. These rental incomes are an unproductive 'free lunch' gouged from the economy at large, forcing an ever-higher proportion of wages to be spent on rent and basic social subsistence (Hudson 2006a, 2010). While the rentier economy cuts across the entirety of socioeconomic relations, Hudson (2006a) shows that most rentier wealth is generated by rent-yielding property, with real estate the economy's largest asset and land accounting for most of the gains in real estate valuation. Hudson is referring primarily to the United States, but as Glynn notes (this volume), dwellings also accounted for £5.5 trillion, or 62 percent of the UK's total net worth in 2015 according to the Office for National Statistics (ONS). The results of this restructuring of the economy for rentier interests have been all too evident in the housing market: the 'subprime' housing crisis, housing commodification and privatization, the travails of 'generation rent', spiralling house prices, mortgage debt, gentrification, foreclosure, eviction, displacement, homelessness and overcrowding.

THE CONTEMPORARY HOUSING CRISIS

For most oppressed people there is always a housing crisis; and most people are oppressed within the deeply unequal global relations of capitalism. As Madden and Marcuse (2016, 10) observe, housing crisis is a predictable, consistent outcome of capitalist spatial development: housing is not produced and distributed for the purpose of dwellings for all; it is produced and distributed as a commodity to enrich the few. Housing crisis is not the result of the system breaking down but of the system working as intended.

But what marks this particular post-2008 crisis moment out is how middle-class homeowners and investors have become subject to the crisis-laden vicissitudes of the housing market, and in relation to the previous section, the sheer extent of speculative capital liquidity operating in the housing market. The most important housing tendencies in Britain and Ireland over the last decade have been the virtual decimation of public and social housing, the rapid expansion of the private-rented sector (PRS), the liberalization and financialization of mortgage markets and the end of the 'homeownership dream' for many people. The ideology of homeownership and its potential attainment appeared to be intact and secure pre-2008, but the bursting of the property bubble and resultant austerity policies has made homeownership unattainable for many in 'Generation Rent' (Robertson 2015; Byrne, this volume). The shift to private renting—disingenuously mis-sold as a lifestyle choice by letting agents and advertisement agencies—involves an increased transfer of wealth from low-income households to housing-market investors. The former are denied the formation of housing-asset wealth through ownership, and the latter are increasingly driven by financialized dynamics, with global financial institutions targeting the private rental sector to profit from the postcrisis context via such agents as private equity firms and real estate investment trusts (REITs) (see Beswick et al. 2016; Fields and Uffer 2016; Fields 2017; Robbins 2017).

The dramatic shift in housing tenures from public to private has led to a shift in the politics of housing. Rent increases, household debt and evictions have become key issues alongside security of tenure, housing standards, overcrowding and homelessness. Historically, the PRS in Britain decreased from 88 percent of total housing provision in 1914 to as little as 14 percent in 1974 (Stafford 1976, 3), seeming to confirm, albeit it in gradual form, Keynes' 'euthanasia of the rentier' thesis. Yet successive reforms in public and social housing since then—especially the Right-to-Buy Act, the repeal of rent controls in 1988 and mass 'housing stock transfer' from public housing to HAs from the late 1980s—have reversed that process through widespread housing privatization (Ginsburg 2005; Watt 2009a; Hodkinson and Robbins, 2013). More than 1.8 million local authority homes (council homes) have been sold through RTB in England alone since 1980 (Murie 2015). Once renowned for its public housing provision, social-housing construction has dwindled massively, and social-rented tenancies in Britain now account for just 16 percent of the housing stock, of which local-authority housing makes up only half (Robbins 2017, xix). In Ireland, where social housing accounted for between 52 and 65.2 percent of total Irish housing construction in the 1930s, 1940s and 1950s, less than 10 percent is now local-authority or voluntary association housing (Byrne and Norris 2017).

The definition of 'social housing' and 'affordable housing' has been deliberately distorted through government redesignation (Robbins 2017; Watt, this volume). 'Affordable rent' now means up to 80 percent of market rent in England and Wales, and 'intermediate housing'—homes for sale and rent including 'shared equity', 'part-buy' and 'market rent'—has increasingly come to be recognized as 'social housing' but is far removed from the notion of public housing that was accepted for most of the twentieth century (the term *social housing* is itself obfuscatory, compounding public housing with HAs and a whole host of intermediate rental and purchase forms). In England, for the year 2016–2017, only 8.2 percent of HA housing construction completions were for social rent, with 61 percent of starts and 48 percent of completions built outside the Affordable Housing Programme (AHP), without any government investment (National Housing Federation 2017). HAs, once heralded as a community empowering solution to the housing question, are no more likely to solve the British housing crisis than the private market.[5]

Meanwhile, terms like *mixed tenure* and *mixed communities*, supposedly predicated on planning more sustainable, cohesive, fairer and 'affordable' neighbourhoods, have long been understood by critics as a Trojan horse for introducing more private housing into poorer neighbourhoods (Lees 2008; Glynn 2009; Robbins 2017; Watt, this volume). There is no evidence to back up the benefits of imposing mixed communities through such policies. If anything, imposed mixing of communities and tenures tends to exacerbate socioeconomic divisions rather than mitigate them (Lees 2008; Robbins 2017, 3). In the British context, it is a sick joke among housing activists that 'mixing' never introduces social rented housing into predominantly private housing neighbourhoods but always private tenure into predominantly social-rented neighbourhoods. In Ireland, where social housing is markedly more limited, a dramatic decrease in social-housing funding and output between 2008 and 2014 (88 and 91.5 percent, respectively), alongside the deepening financialization of social housing, means that the tenure has more recently functioned to exacerbate the boom-and-bust dynamics of the Irish housing market rather than acting as a counterbalance within it (Byrne and Norris 2017). It remains to be seen whether new social-housing models in Ireland, sorely lacking at present, could address the dominance of homeownership and the PRS, but the British experience provides a cautionary tale.

Overall, such processes have involved a fundamental direct and indirect tenure switch from public to private or intermediate housing, with the latter in reality entailing a privatization process.[6] In Glasgow, the birthplace of UK rent restrictions, social-rented housing decreased from 70 to 36 percent of citywide housing provision overall between 1975 and 2015, and the PRS, widely acknowledged as the worst of all possible tenures, increased from 5 to 20 percent, more than doubling in the last decade alone (Glasgow City Council 2017). In the United Kingdom overall, 20 percent of all housing is now in the PRS, exceeding the 18 percent of housing in the social-housing sector (Robbins 2017). Similarly, Ireland's PRS, which has doubled in size within a decade, now represents 20 percent of all households. Rents have spiralled by 60 percent in Dublin since 2010 and are now 15 percent higher than at the peak of the boom (Byrne, this volume), which, lest we forget, resulted in a massive property-led crash and brutal austerity programmes post-crash (O'Callaghan et al. 2014; Byrne, this volume).

In the 1950s, British residents typically spent 10 percent or less of their income on rent (Robbins 2017, 27), but the average tenant in England now spends almost 50 percent of their take-home pay on rent; a figure that rises to more than 70 percent in London (Osborne 2015) where the average monthly rent on a new tenancy in July 2016 was over £1,500 (Jones 2016). Following the 2008 global financial crisis, wages have been either frozen or extremely limited, with any minimal gains offset by higher living costs, especially related to housing. This gives substantive credence to Bunge's (1977) contention that a 'double-front' of resistance is required in both productive and reproductive spheres. The toxic social results of the transition from public to private housing in Britain and Ireland in terms of affordability, debt, poverty, health, security, building conditions, overcrowding, homelessness and evictions are detailed unsparingly in this volume and by numerous commentators, charities and even local authorities. Yet, the recent Housing and Planning Act 2016 will only exacerbate these already profound problems, which found their culmination in the criminal negligence that led to the tragedy of the Grenfell Tower fire disaster in London in June 2017, when seventy-one tenants lost their lives. Chronic underinvestment, neglect and deregulation of social housing are widely regarded as the culpable factors in the tragedy, and such desperate housing conditions, often ignored until something like Grenfell happens, stoke understandable rage. The contributors in this book share that rage; what concerns us most here is how tenants, residents and social movements are transforming that rage into coherent transformative forms of critique and housing organization.

PLAN OF THE BOOK

This book has a three-part structure, comprising four chapters in each part. Part I, 'History against the Grain', revisits and rethinks the 1915 rent strikes, with a focus on questions of social reproduction, class agency and the strengths and limits of previous accounts. Overall, it records and affirms a tenant's 'history-from-below', contending that proletarian men, women and children, often but not always operating outside the control of formal Left organizations, were primary, not secondary, agents in the prewar, wartime and interwar tenants' movements in Britain. Part II, 'Reports from the Housing Frontline', provides a series of situated, participatory accounts, self-reflexively exploring the composition, strategies, development and concrete articulations of some of the most significant housing movements across a multiplicity of tenures in Britain and Ireland today. Part III, 'Rethinking the Housing Question: Theories, Aims, Tactics and Strategies for Today', takes a step back to examine and deconstruct the political, discursive and economic factors contributing to the current housing crisis, and at a wider level of abstraction, to explore the potential strategic, theoretical and practical direction of contemporary housing movements.

In the first two chapters of Part I, the role of women in the rent strikes is explored and documented in depth in the prewar and interwar eras, respectively. In chapter 1, Pam Currie situates the rent strikes within a wider tendency of women's activism, from the suffrage campaigns and emergent socialist movements of the prewar period through to the food protests and Women's Peace Crusade in the latter years of the war. She suggests, in contradiction to previous discussions on the subject, that there is a direct line of continuity between prewar suffrage campaigns and the rent strikes and, moreover, that these campaigns were clearly separated by social class (with the rent strikes being led by a broad faction of working-class women). She also contrasts the quasi-religious and reductive characterization of female rent strikers—'woman-as-mother' doing her patriotic duty by defending hearth and home—with the actuality of female activists' militancy, class consciousness and participation in the public sphere.

In chapter 2, Annmarie Hughes and Valerie Wright explore what the rent strikers did after 1915 in a discussion on the implications of the rent strikes for women in the interwar period. Arguing that women's involvement in housing disputes has been consistently marginalized at the expense of male workplace studies, they contend that the pragmatic 'politics of the kitchen' espoused by many working-class women from their situated material conditions in the interwar years has been largely ignored because such issues have been pejoratively considered 'domestic'. They consider the ways in which women were involved with the housing question throughout interwar Scotland and how a 'politics of the kitchen' was employed to create a space in political discourse for women to participate. 'Against the grain' of mainstream historiography, they argue that much can be learned from women's hitherto largely ignored housing and social-reproductive struggles in the interwar years.

In chapter 3, Tony Cox explores the 1915 rent strikes in Dundee, opening up the discussion of rent strikes beyond the exemplar case of Glasgow. Edwardian Dundee, he observes, was dominated by jute industry barons and rack-renting landlords, where wages were among the lowest in Britain, yet rents in many tenement flats were equivalent to those in London. During the First World War, Dundee witnessed the eruption of mass struggles against toxic working and living conditions, with rent strikes sweeping across the city in 1915. Examining the causes and consequences of these rent strikes, he deviates from previous accounts, contending that they were primarily organized informally at the street level, with women and adolescent workers leading the way, often in opposition to formal representatives of the labour movement.

In chapter 4, I take a broader, more theoretical view of the 1915 rent strikes in Glasgow, situating them within wider concerns over social reproduction and rent, concerns that have historically been obscured by the theoretical and practical separation of productive and reproductive spheres. Contesting a prevalent, but by no means unchallenged (see Bunge 1977; Damer 2000a; Harvey 2012) tendency within Marxism to see housing struggle as a 'secondary' contradiction behind the 'primary' contradiction of workplace struggles (inaugurated by Engels' *The Housing Question* in 1872), I reconsider the ongoing relevance of women-led housing and social-reproductive struggles by 1915 rent strikers in the context of a resurgent rentier economy and the marked tendency towards the urbanization of capital since the 1970s. Deploying the autonomist Marxist method of 'class composition'—which considers subjective political organization in dialectical relation with the objective factors of capitalist development—I employ a 'spatial composition' analysis to show how the rent strikes can be seen as part of a continuum of struggles around housing, rent and social reproduction that has only become more relevant over time.

In chapter 5, which begins Part II, Vickie Cooper and Kirsteen Paton discuss the resurgence of everyday evictions in the twenty-first century, paying particular attention to forms of collective tenant organization resisting these punitive processes. They describe how large-scale evictions are driven by the market in tandem with government policy and practice in a context where housing is increasingly viewed as a global financial product, and austerity is enacted as an eviscerating process of welfare reduction and debt transfer to the individual. Such economic and social policies have forced thousands of households into rent arrears, leading to the widespread rollout of state-led evictions. In response, they document how anti-eviction alliances in England have responded to these processes as part of a wider mobilization of collective anti-austerity struggles.

In chapter 6, Michael Byrne reflects on crisis and austerity in a reflexive inquiry into tenant self-organization with the Dublin Tenants Association (DTA), which he cofounded with colleagues in 2015. He describes the rise of the PRS in the context of diminishing mortgage availability, insecure employment and the eradication of social-housing funding and provision. The unregulated and deeply dysfunctional nature of the PRS, he contends, has created a perfect storm, with rents increasing by 40 percent nationally since 2011, a chronic supply shortage, frequent evictions and one-third of tenants residing in rent arrears. Situating the DTA and wider networks of housing activism in Dublin in dialogue with the *Plataforma de Afectados por la Hipoteca* ([PAH] or 'Mortgage Victims' Platform') housing movement in Spain, he examines the challenge of inventing organizational forms in housing activism that *produce* tenants as a community and as a political subject, thus aiming to counteract the individualizing and profoundly precarious nature of PRS tenancies.

In chapter 7, Living Rent (LR) members, Emma Saunders, Kate Samuels and Dave Statham, describe the movement's practice in Scotland, drawing extensively on interviews with fellow LR members. A dearth of social housing, the impossibility of homeownership and an ingrained resistance to progressive redistributive regulation, they argue, has left tenants with a housing market characterized by spiralling rent levels, tenancy insecurity and the growth of a usurious PRS. They survey the development of the organization from its origins in the Edinburgh Private Tenants Action Group (EPTAG) to the present day, paying particular attention to tensions between formal claims to the state for tenant recognition and the development of grassroots direct action. They document significant recent successes as well as their limits— including forcing the Scottish government to introduce rent controls in the recent Private Housing (Tenancies) Bill 2016, albeit in limited form—while reflecting on the emergent practices and possibilities of LR and PRS housing activism.

In chapter 8, Paul Watt surveys a sample of contemporary housing struggles in London, with a particular focus on the struggles of tenants and residents against displacement from their homes and communities as a result of galloping rent rises, evictions and housing benefit cuts. In the early 2000s, he argues, issues in council housing tenure dominated London's housing activism, but in the last five years, there has been an explosion of housing-based campaigns encompassing a wide diversity of tenures (private tenants, council tenants, cooperative tenants and leaseholders) and a similarly diverse range of practices. Discussing political occupations of empty properties, anti-privatization and anti-eviction campaigns, 'resistance by design' (the critical dissection of planning documents) and legal challenges to regeneration, he

xxxivIntroduction

shows how a multiplicity of struggles across diverse tenures address significant demographic changes in tenure across London.

In chapter 9, the first intervention in Part 3, Hamish Kallin and Tom Slater
discuss struggles for rent control against the deliberate production of ignorance through the concept of 'agnotology'. They argue that housing activism
in Britain must reinvent itself to respond to a raft of politicians, economists,
landlord-lobbyists, journalists, lawyers and conservative think-tank researchers who deploy stigmatizing images of social housing and free-market rheto-
ric to divert attention away from the political-economic relations responsible
for the exorbitant cost of housing. For them, ignorance of the achievements
of the 1915 rent strikes is typical of concerted attempts to quash resistance
to extreme housing injustice and must therefore be resisted by counternarra-
tives which simultaneously stress the brutal inequities of the current housing
market and the real achievements of tenant organization.

In chapter 10, Rory Hearne, Cian O'Callaghan, Rob Kitchin and Cesare
Di Feliciantonio discuss the 'relational articulation' of housing crisis and
activism in postcrash Ireland, paying acute attention to the specific local
conditions of capital accumulation and governmental intervention that generate particular forms of housing activism. They trace the evolution of housing activism in Dublin in response to specific cycles of structural crises in
Ireland's housing model over the course of the Celtic Tiger property bubble,
both in the crash and postcrash era. They provide an overview of new housing
campaign groups in Dublin—including nongovernmental organizations, trade
unions, tenant groups, direct-action housing groups, anti-eviction groups,
older 'social housing' community groups and Left political parties—analyzing the merits of these diverse forms of activism in relation to conjunctural
phases of contemporary economic and governmental reality.

In chapter 11, Sarah Glynn makes a case for municipal public housing
in a contemporary context where that project has been much denigrated
(see Kallin and Slater, this volume) and where the political, economic and
institutional context differs significantly from the period of the postwar
public housing boom. Elaborating a link between the 1915 rent strikes and
the contemporary era, she argues that a claim for public housing should be
a minimum demand for contemporary housing movements as part of a new
approach to housing policy that aims to minimize the exploitation of housing
as a vehicle for speculation and exchange, focusing instead on the use value
of housing as a home (a central plank of a decent, affordable quality of life
for everyone). She also advances proposals for avoiding a repeat of previous
problems with public housing—such as overcentralization, bureaucracy and
tenant marginalization—through the auspices of local control and tenant-
management schemes.

In chapter 12, Tim Joubert and Stuart Hodkinson argue for what they term 'the housing commons', seeking different forms of housing activism that can be politically articulated within what Dyer-Witheford (2006) has called the 'circulation of the common': the production and extension of collective-sharing processes beyond market exchange. Questioning the contemporary viability of the rent-strike tactic, as well as claims for public housing, in the context of four decades of housing-privatization policies, ongoing transformations from the welfare to the workfare state and the growing global financialization of housing provision, they argue that the rent-strike tactic may have been neutered as an effective response to the housing question today. Proposing a subtle dialectic between defensive and offensive housing struggles, they problematize forms of housing activism that merely rest on defending the status quo or demanding the state intervene, without forsaking such forms of struggle as an important defensive strategy. Instead, they suggest that housing movements radically repurpose housing activism as a form of resistance that can generate its own alternatives based on forms of commonwealth and collective power.

Overall, this book's objective, summarized in the Afterword, is to explore the continuing significance of the 1915 rent strikes for today, teasing out the continuities between then and now, while being attentive to what has changed in the interim period. Rethinking the rent strikes in relation to the contemporary housing crisis and the multiple and varied organizational responses to it, we believe, can contribute significantly to addressing the current housing question, providing an urgent and meaningful reference point for contemporary housing struggles.

NOTES

1. This book was initially intended as a close cross-sectional study of tenant and resident movements in Britain, but was later extended to include Ireland. Broadly similar geographically and culturally, Ireland has both interesting similarities and notable differences in housing policy and practise in comparison to Britain that seemed worthy of further comparative exploration.

2. A *factor* is an agent who manages land or property for its owner or holder.

3. https://remembermarybarbour.wordpress.com/

4. The 'golden era' of state-Keynesianism in the UK, we should recall, was propped up by colonial and imperial exploitation and a pronounced sexual division of labour that consigned women to the domestic sphere, dependent on the male-headed 'family wage'.

5. I will address the question of HA marketization, and what that means for housing activism, in more detail in the Afterword.

6. Intermediate housing is homes for sale and rent provided at a cost above social rent but below market levels, subject to the criteria laid out in national affordable housing definitions.

REFERENCES

Aalbers, Manual B., and Brett Christophers. 2014. "Centring Housing in Political Economy." *Housing, Theory and Society* 31(4): 373–94.

Beauregard, Robert A. 1994. "Capital Switching and the Built Environment: United States, 1970–89." *Environment and Planning A* 26(5): 715–732.

Beswick, Joe, Georgi Alexandri, Michael Byrne, Sònia Vives-Miró, Desiree Fields, Stuart Hodkinson and Michael Janoschka. 2016. "Speculating on London's Housing Future: The Rise of Global Corporate Landlords in 'Post-Crisis' Urban Landscapes." *City* 20(2): 321–41.

Bradley, Quintin. 2014. *The Tenants' Movement: Resident Involvement, Community Action and the Contentious Politics of Housing.* London: Routledge.

Bunge, William. 1977. "The Point of Reproduction: A Second Front." *Antipode* 9(2): 60–76.

Burness, Catriona. 2015. "Remembering Mary Barbour." *Scottish Labour History Review* 50: 81–96.

Byrne, Michael, and Michelle Norris. 2017. "Procyclical Social Housing and the Crisis of Irish Housing Policy: Marketization, Social Housing, and the Property Boom and Bust." *Housing Policy Debate* 28(1): 1–14.

Castells, Manuel. 1983. *The City and the Grassroots: A Cross-Cultural Theory of Urban Social Movements.* Berkeley: University of California Press.

Christophers, Brett. 2011. "Revisiting the Urbanization of Capital." *Annals of the Association of American Geographers* 101(6): 1347–64.

Damer, Seán. 1980. "State, Class and Housing: Glasgow 1885–1919." In *Housing, Social Policy and the State*, edited by Joseph Melling, 73–112. London: Croom Helm.

———. 1990. *Glasgow: Going for a Song.* London: Lawrence and Wishart.

———. 1997. "Striking out on Red Clyde" in *Built to Last? Reflections on British Housing Policy*, edited by John Goodwin and Carol Grant, 35–40. London: ROOF Magazine.

———. 2000a. "'The Clyde Rent War!' The Clydebank Rent Strike of the 1920s." In *Class Struggle and Social Welfare*, edited by Michael Lavalette and Gerry Mooney, 71–95. London: Routledge.

Dyer-Witheford, Nick. 2006. "The Circulation of the Common." Paper presented to the Conference on Immaterial Labour, Multitudes, and New Social Subjects: Class Composition in Cognitive Capitalism, 29–30 April 2006, King's College, University of Cambridge. http://www.fims.uwo.ca/people/faculty/dyerwitheford/Commons2006.pdf.

Engels, Frederick. 1942 [1872]. *The Housing Question.* London: Lawrence and Wishart.

Englander, David. 1981. "Landlord and Tenant in Urban Scotland: The Background to the Clyde Rent Strikes." *Journal of Scottish Labour History Society* 15: 4–14.

———. 1983. *Landlord and Tenant in the Urban Britain: 1838–1918*. New York: Oxford University Press.

Fields, Desiree. 2015. "Contesting the Financialization of Urban Space: Community Organizations and the Struggle to Preserve Affordable Rental Housing in New York City." *Journal of Urban Affairs* 37(2): 144–65.

———. 2017. "Urban Struggles with Financialization." *Geography Compass*. Doi: http://onlinelibrary.wiley.com/doi/10.1111/gec3.12334/full.

Fields, Desiree, and Sabina Uffer. 2016. "The Financialization of Rental Housing: A Comparative Analysis of New York City and Berlin." *Urban Studies* 53(7): 1486–1502.

Foster, John. 1990. "Strike Action and Working-Class Politics on Clydeside, 1914–1919." *International Review of Social History* 35(1): 33–70.

Glasgow City Council. 2017. Glasgow's Housing Strategy 2017–2022. http://www.glasgow.gov.uk/councillorsandcommittees/viewDoc.asp?c=P62AFQDND N0GZLT10G.

Ginsburg, Norman. 1979. *Class, Capital and Social Policy*. Basingstoke: Macmillan.

———. 2005. "The Privatization of Council Housing." *Critical Social Policy* 25(1): 115–35.

Glynn, Sarah. 2009. *Where the Other Half Lives: Lower Income Housing in a Neoliberal World*. London: Pluto Press.

Gotham, Kevin F. 2009. "Creating Liquidity out of Spatial Fixity: The Secondary Circuit of Capital and the Subprime Mortgage Crisis." *International Journal of Urban and Regional Research* 33(2): 355–71.

Gray, Neil. 2017. "Beyond the Right to the City: Territorial Autogestion and the Take over the City Movement in 1970s Italy." *Antipode* 50(2): 319–39.

Grayson, John. 1996. *Opening the Window: Revealing the Hidden History of Tenants Organisations*, edited by Maggie Walker. Manchester: TPAS and Northern College.

Harvey, David. 1985. *The Urbanization of Capital: Studies in the Theory and History of Capitalist Urbanization*. Baltimore: John Hopkins University.

———. 2012. *Rebel Cities: From the Right to the City to the Urban Revolution*. London: Verso.

Hodkinson, Stuart, and Glyn Robbins, G. 2013. "The Return of Class War Conservatism? Housing Under the UK Coalition Government". *Critical Social Policy* 33(1): 57–77.

Horsey, Miles. 1990. *Tenements & Towers: Glasgow Working-Class Housing 1890–1990*. Edinburgh: Royal Commission on the Ancient and Historical Monuments of Scotland.

Hudson, Michael. 2006a. "Real Estate, Technology and the Rentier Economy: Pricing in Excess of Value, Producing Income without Work." Speech delivered at the 'Economics of Abundance' conference, Kings College, London, July 3.

———. 2006b. "The New Road to Serfdom: An Illustrated Guide to the Coming Real Estate Collapse." *Harper's Magazine*, May, 39–46.

———. 2010. "From Marx to Goldman Sachs: The Fictions of Fictitious Capital, and the Financialization of Industry." *Critique* 38(3): 419–44.

Jameson, Frederic. 1991. *Postmodernism or the Cultural Logic of Late Capitalism.* London: Verso.

Jones, Rupert. 2016. "Average Rents in UK Fall for the First Time in More Than Seven Years." *The Guardian*, June 6. https://www.theguardian.com/money/2017/jun/06/uk-rents-fall-london-brexit

Johnstone, Charles. 1992. *The Tenants' Movement and Housing Struggles in Glasgow, 1945–1990.* PhD diss., University of Glasgow.

———. 2000. "Housing and Class Struggles in Post-war Glasgow." In *Class Struggle and Social Welfare*, edited by Michael Lavalette and Gerry Mooney, 139–54. London: Routledge.

Lees, Loretta. 2008. "Gentrification and Social Mixing: Towards an Inclusive Urban Renaissance?" *Urban Studies* 45(12): 2449–70.

Lefebvre, Henri. 2003 [1970]. *The Urban Revolution.* Minneapolis: University of Minnesota Press.

Madden, David, and Peter Marcuse. 2016. *In Defense of Housing.* London: Verso.

McCabe, Conor. 2011. *Sins of the Father: The Decisions that Shaped the Irish Economy.* Dublin: History Press Ireland.

Melling, Joseph. 1983. *Rent Strikes: People's Struggle for Housing in West Scotland 1890–1916.* Polygon: Edinburgh.

Mooney, Gerry, and Lynne Poole. 2005. "Marginalized Voices: Resisting the Privatization of Council Housing in Glasgow." *Local Economy* 20(1): 27–39.

Moorhouse, Bert, Mary Wilson and Chris Chamberlain. 1972. "Rent Strikes—Direct Action and the Working-Class." *Socialist Register* 9(9): 133–56.

Murie, Alan. 2015. "The Right to Buy: History and Prospect." *History and Policy*, 11 November. http://www.historyandpolicy.org/policy-papers/papers/the-right-to-buy-history-and-prospect

National Housing Federation. 2017. "How Many Homes Did Housing Associations Build in Quarter Three 2016/2017?" London: National Housing Federation. http://s3-eu-west-1.amazonaws.com/pub.housing.org.uk/Supply_briefing_note_201718_Q1.pdf

O'Callaghan, Cian, Mark Boyle and Rob Kitchin. 2014. "Post-Politics, Crisis, and Ireland's 'Ghost Estates.'" *Political Geography* 42: 121–33.

Orr, Lesley. 2015. "'Shall We Not Speak for Ourselves?' Helen Crawfurd, War Resistance and the Women's Peace Crusade, 1916–1918." *Scottish Labour History Review* 50: 97–115.

Osborne, Hilary. 2015. "Tenants in England Spend Half Their Pay on Rent." *The Guardian, July 16.* https://www.theguardian.com/money/2015/jul/16/tenants-in-england-spend-half-their-pay-on-rent

Petrie, Ann. 2008. *The 1915 Rent Strikes: An East Coast Perspective.* Dundee: Abertay Historical Society.

Robbins, Glyn. 2002. "Taking Stock—Regeneration Programmes and Social Housing." *Local Economy* 17(4): 266–72.

———. 2017. *There's No Place: The American Housing Crisis and What It Means for the UK*. London: Red Roof.

Robertson, Mary. 2015. "Re-asking the Housing Question." *Salvage* 1:161–172.

Smyth, James. 1992. "Rent, Peace, Votes: Working Class Women and Political Activity in the First World War." In *Out of Bounds: Women in Scottish Society 1800–1945*, edited by Esther Breitenbach and Eleanor Gordon, 174–96. Edinburgh: Edinburgh University Press.

Stafford, David C. 1976. "The Final Economic Demise of the Private Landlord?" *Social and Economic Administration* 10: 3–14.

Sklair, Leslie. 1975. "The Struggle against the Housing Finance Act." *Socialist Register* 12(12): 250–92.

Swenarton, Mark. 1981. "An 'Insurance against Revolution'—Ideological Objectives of the Provision and Design of Public Housing in Britain after the First World War." *Historical Research* 54(129): 86–101.

Vercellone, Carlo. 2010. "The Crisis of the Law of Value and the Becoming-Rent of Profit." In *Crisis in the Global Economy: Financial Markets, Social Struggles, and New Political Scenarios*, edited by Andrea Fumagalli and Sandro Mezzadra, 85–118. London: Semiotext(e) and the MIT Press.

Watt, Paul. 2009a. "Housing Stock Transfers, Regeneration and State-led Gentrification in London." *Urban Policy and Research* 27: 229–42.

Weber, Rachel. 2002. "Extracting Value from the City: Neoliberalism and Urban Redevelopment." *Antipode* 34(3): 519–40.

Part I

HISTORY AGAINST THE GRAIN

Chapter 1

'A Wondrous Spectacle'

Protest, Class and Femininity in the 1915 Rent Strikes

Pam Currie

The 1915 rent strikes were a central event in a turbulent period in Glasgow's history. This period saw Edwardian suffrage, militancy and emergent trade unionism, subsequently developing into 'Red Clydeside'—a city in revolt against the suffering of World War One and against bosses, landlords and the state. Such imagery has a powerful resonance to this day in the labour movement, no more so than in the stories of the rent strikes and of 'Mrs Barbour's army' of working-class women and children who stood up to the greed of the landlords, defied the factors and forced the government to implement rent controls. The nature and extent of women's activism during this period of rent strikes, suffrage, industrial organizing and the Women's Peace Crusade (WPC) has been documented in a number of accounts (Melling 1983; Liddington 1989), but there has been less exploration of the overlaps and inter-connections between these movements or indeed of the period after the war (though see Hughes and Wright, this volume).

Events such as the rent strikes, which drew significant numbers of working-class women into political activism, are often presented as a tem-porary outburst of anger over distinct and localized issues (McLean 1983; Castells 1983), in contrast to men's coherent, sustained organization through rank-and-file trade unionism in Glasgow's engineering industries. Smyth (1992, 187) acknowledges the overlap in women's wartime campaigns but argues that 'a direct line of continuity between the prewar militant suffrage campaign and the militancy of the rent strikes . . . cannot be substantiated', and that the connection is limited to just one woman, the formidable Helen Crawford, Women's Social and Political Union (WSPU) member and future Communist Party stalwart. In this chapter, I seek to challenge this assertion, arguing that the discourses, imagery and methods of the rent strikes allow us to see them not as an isolated outburst but as part of a wider continuum of women's political activism and radical social change in this period. The discourses and imagery created by and about the women involved are of particular interest, 'staking a claim' to identities through simple physical presence, acts of 'militancy' and new forms of gendered discourse (Stainton Rogers 2003).

In placing the rent strikes within a continuum of women's activism from approximately 1906 to 1918, and indeed with relevance beyond this to the modern day, it is important to acknowledge that 'class' and 'gender' were far from straightforward concepts. As Hannam and Hunt (2002) argue, the positions adopted by women activists questioned the use of sex and class as unproblematic, unified and opposed categories. From the start, for many Glasgow activists, issues such as rent controls were not just an end in themselves but also a critical component of the radical social change they sought—a struggle in which class and gender clearly intersected. This interaction was clear in the socialist movement in Glasgow, broadly divided between the 'ethical' Christian socialism of the Independent Labour Party (ILP) and the smaller, more explicitly Marxist groups such as the Social Democratic Federation (SDF). In the prewar period, this struggle 'with and against men at one and the same time' was expressed in activist meetings in the form of the 'Woman Question', the nature of women's oppression in a class-based society (Smyth 2000, 156). This was extensively discussed in the ILP, which appears to have had some success in orienting towards women, particularly in the cooperative movement (Gordon 1991). Many of the leaders of the rent strikes were ILP members, and the ILP enjoyed particularly close relations to the WSPU in the prewar years, with WSPU activists regularly contributing to the ILP newspaper *Forward* (King 1978).

SUFFRAGE IN GLASGOW: SETTING THE SCENE FOR WARTIME ACTIVITY

What was the nature of the suffrage campaign in Glasgow in the prewar years and to what extent did it shape women's activity in the rent strikes? Was it inherently middle class or did activists seek to engage broader support in working-class districts? Did the demand for the vote disappear in wartime activism, subsumed into more immediate struggles around housing and consumption, or can a meaningful connection be drawn between the two? The role of the ILP is critical here. The ILP enjoyed close links with the WSPU from the latter's establishment on Clydeside in 1906 (Leneman 1991), and this link helps to frame the nature of the WSPU in Glasgow and subsequent influences during the rent strikes. Young (1985, 104) claims that the suffrage movement was inherently middle class, relying on high-profile 'militancy' in the form of window-smashing and attacks on property and the public outrage that these generated. But such tactics came relatively late to Glasgow (Leneman 1991), and in the meantime, organizations such as the Women's Freedom League (formed in Glasgow in 1907) developed wider working-class support for suffrage and a more inclusive—yet still radical—campaign.

The militancy of the WSPU was significant not only in its impact upon society but also in transforming the lives of individual women. Joannou and Purvis (1998, 10) claim that the movement represented a 'deliberate and self-conscious attempt to break the traditional patriarchal mould of British politics and to discover new, radical and often collective ways of working', and in Glasgow this, together with the principle of women-organized and -led campaigns, can be seen to have laid out both a conceptual and a practical framework for the rent strikes. A report of the Women's Labour League conference held in the city early in 1914 argued that the movement had generated an understanding that women, 'like the men . . . must think and work *collectively*' (*Labour Women*, February 1914). Such sentiments prepared the ground for a wave of wartime activism, most notably the rent strikes. Echoing many of the contradictions of suffrage, they sought to 'legitimize' militancy—including physical resistance to the landlords and factors—through strategic appeals to natural justice and women's 'instinct' to protect her family and home. This militancy found expression for many working-class women on the housing question, an issue on which women's participation was not only sanctioned but also actively encouraged by a labour movement at times uneasy with suffrage (*Forward*, 26 June 1914). Housing was perceived to have the potential to unite the collective interests of (male) organized labour, acting as a material base from which working-class women, under the direction of male activists, might engage in collective action on a mass scale (*Forward*, 18 January 1915).

RENT STRIKES AND 'MILITANCY'

Women activists during this period negotiated the complexities of class and gender not only in theoretical and political discourse but also in their activism and lived experiences. Their 'presencing practices' alternately used and challenged gendered expectations and boundaries, ranging from meticulously planned 'militancy' to carefully choreographed 'spectacles' of protest in suffrage, imitated to varying degrees in subsequent movements. Although the rent strikes present a different context to the prewar suffrage campaign, the actions of the women in building political and physical resistance to the

factors demonstrates a conscious strategy of direct action and a vehement
resistance, which exceeded, at least on occasion, that sanctioned by suffrage leaders (*Govan Press*, 29 October 1915; *Forward*, 30 October 1915;
Crawfurd, n.d., 145). While this challenged expectations of 'respectable'
working-class women, it was situated in discourses of protection of the home
and family, creating a legitimacy which lessened the perceived breach of
gendered social norms (Robertson 1997).

Across all of the movements, from suffrage to the rent strikes and wartime
activity, women struggled to create political identities within competing
discourses of gender 'sameness' or 'difference' and of 'separate spheres'
(women's perceived role within society), specifically her domestic role
within the family. Activists alternately drew upon this role to engage women
as 'reformers' and struggled against its limitations, debating whether wom-
en's capacities were a natural given, which created inherent conservatism, or
whether women's consciousness was constructed and constrained by society.

Idealized assumptions around women's 'innate values' and of 'woman-as-
mother' informed not only the suffrage movement—and particularly what
women would *do* with the vote once enfranchised—but also recurred in the
rent strikes and beyond. The demand for sex equality appeared to many to
be integral to the vision of the socialist commonweal (*Forward*, January 12
1907), but it was tempered by a vision in which 'orderly and virtuous' homes
were to be built upon rigid gender roles and women's domestic labour (Wells
1907). This approach was not entirely shared by women on the Left. Writing
in *Forward* in 1912, one correspondent sought to downplay the argument
of biological 'difference' in favour of the commonalities of class. Presenting the interests of women and men as those of fundamental 'sameness',
she acknowledged differences of experience, arguing that enfranchisement
would turn attention to 'women's priorities'. Difference here, therefore, is
interpreted as a positive contribution to the movement and to a future society,
rather than an inevitable inequality.

In considering these contradictory discourses of gender and class, there are
useful contributions from later feminist writing on the politics of reproduction. Federici (1975) reframes women's unpaid domestic labour as a 'pillar'
of capitalism, central to the reproduction of male labour. In the context of the
rent strikes, the home was central both to the reproduction of labour for the
shipyards and wartime industries but also to the war effort, with frequent references to the sacrifices of soldier's wives and children (*Forward*, 4 December 1915). Dalla Costa and James (1972) argue that domestic responsibility
has been made a general material fact of women's role, regardless of her
class, but that it is the role specifically of the working class housewife, which
is central both to capitalist production and to the wider position of women in
society. All women are 'housewives'—in that all women share the burden of

domestic responsibility and the position of all women in society is shaped by this—and it is the isolation of women in unpaid domestic labour which forms the key element of their exploitation and the 'myth of female incapacity' that must be challenged collectively in the very material location in which this exploitation occurs (Dalla Costa and James 1972, 12).

For the rent strikers, concepts of class had a complex and potentially contradictory interaction with those of gender and 'womanliness'. Although reforms promised women's political equality and power, they were imbued also with ideas of morality and 'respectability'. Crawfurd disparaged middle-class 'charitable ladies' but saw the suffrage movement as an attempt to 'raise the moral, material and spiritual standards of the country' (Crawfurd, n.d., 70). A similar, quasi-religious discourse of 'decency' and 'crusades' is found in different forms in the housing and peace movements; in particular, it can be seen in concerns over the welfare of military dependents, left vulnerable by the absence of their wage earners. Describing the appalling condition of working-class tenements, Crawfurd (n.d., 141) wrote that many women would 'suffer ill health and die prematurely, or become sluts and drunken, broken-down derelicts, a plague to their families'. Failure in the domestic sphere, the disintegration of home and family in the face of poverty, was thus the worst failure imaginable—failure as a 'mother' and as a woman.

Activists such as Crawfurd fought for the emancipation of women, but they did so in a context which placed responsibility for the domestic sphere firmly on the wife and mother. The overcrowding and poor quality of the housing stock in the communities where the rent strikes took hold were a constant source of tension, and women faced 'a constant round of cooking, clean-ing and washing' to ward off dirt and disease, a routine reinforced by local sanitary inspectors who policed tenements for illicit overcrowding or neglect of shared facilities (Clark and Carnegie 2003, 14; Damer 2000b). The rent strikes provided a focus for resistance which was immediate and accessible. As Dalla Costa and James (1972, 20) argue, 'struggle demands time away from housework, and at the same time it offers an alternative identity to the woman who before found it only at the level of the domestic ghetto.' The forced proximity of the tenements reinforced opportunities for collec-tive action, facilitating contact between women and overcoming the isolation of the housewife to create a collective identity in struggle (12). Ross (1983) argues that the impetus for collective action came also from a vested interest in defending the reputation of their street and district, providing mutual aid and 'survival networks' at a time of crisis.

Robertson (1997) discusses the discourse of women's collective organiz-ing in the rent strikes in comparison to the Highland Clearances, an era which had a lasting impact on working-class consciousness and attitudes to land-lords. Disputing the 'dichotomy' of gendered protest in the Highlands, with women's resistance as a question of 'moral economy' and men's protests as emergent class consciousness, he argues that women acted with the support of their menfolk, absent at sea or seeking work, an imagery that resonates strongly with the 1915 rent strikes. With or without the support of their menfolk, women's wartime protests were perceived within class and gender norms, which contributed to the perceived 'legitimacy' of women's activism and the actions available to women in pursuit of their cause (*Forward*, 16 December 1911). The decision to withhold rent was presented by activists such as Sylvia Pankhurst, even in the prewar period, as a legitimate tool of political resistance in the hands of working-class women, comparable to male tax resistance in the 1830s, and while the tenant and householder were defined as male (*Forward*, 28 August 1915, 2 October 1915), the control of rent and wages was accepted as a woman's jurisdiction (*Forward*, 24 January 1914). Some women further justified activism as akin to a religious 'crusade' (Crawfurd, n.d., 87); appeals to a higher power were also made in frequent references to the laws of 'natural justice' (*Glasgow Herald*, 15 November 1915). As such, the women were able to legitimate their actions. P. J. Dollan commented that 'it is only by defying law and order that they are likely to compel the Government to prevent increases of rent' (*Forward*, 2 October 1915).

When the landlords attempted to exact revenge on their rebellious tenants by sending the factors to collect the rent or give notice of evictions, women's militancy moved beyond withholding rent and into physical struggle. There are numerous accounts in *Forward* and in the local press of sheriff officers coming under attack with flour and peasemeal, their notes being seized and being jostled or physically prevented from entering the close. One report in *Forward* on 30 October 1915 suggests that some Partick factors had refused to take rounds after one of their men was 'chased for his very life' by a 'crowd of angry women', escaping only by vaulting a high fence and crossing the railway line. Although this appears to have been an isolated incident, and the officer was unharmed other than 'the loss of all his writs and a new bowler hat', the apparent intent of physical harm against an individual represents a significant departure from previous suffrage militancy.

Crawfurd recalls other ways in which women adapted the bits and pieces of their daily lives as tools of resistance: ringing a bell in the close to sound the alarm when the factor or sheriff officer was spotted before picking up 'flour, if baking, wet clothes, if washing, and other missiles' to see off the threat (Crawfurd, n.d., 145). Their cause was serious, but there was also a strong element of humour and of the desire to humiliate, even emasculate, the factors rather than to cause deliberate physical harm. Such discourses find landlords positioned as weak, cowardly and emasculated, whereas the women are 'strong', 'fearless' and 'patriotic'—language which echoes around the 'war effort' with the landlords portrayed as the men who 'stayed at home' to benefit from the suffering of others (*Forward*, 7 October 1915). As with suffrage, women's activism in the rent strikes and other wartime struggles is contradictory; women are strong, defiant and militant and at the same time, strangely passive—war is something done unto them, and they are left vulnerable in the absence of their menfolk and must defend their 'femininity' and seek protection (*Govan Press*, 7 May 1915). While this to an extent was strategic and sought to engender public sympathy for their cause, the rent-strikers' strategies of defiance and resistance nonetheless evoked 'unfeminine' behaviours while still sustaining and reinforcing their dependence as wives and mothers and their domestic role.

War threatened established identities, and the impact of conscription, rent rises and food shortages combined to represent an assault on the 'family' and domestic sphere itself. The image of woman-as-mother underpins the discourse of war as an attack on womanhood, for the impact of war was above all an attack on her children—as with the home, inseparable from the interests of woman herself. War meant the loss of sons in the trenches, 'the destruction of a woman's creation and the wastage of many years' service on her part' (*Women's Dreadnought*, 10 June 1916). Notwithstanding the human tragedy of the slaughter of the First World War, this statement invests a woman's interests primarily, even exclusively, in the evolutionary urge to protect her young, a quasi-eugenic impetus to 'save' the race. Similar sentiments are found too around food prices and shortages, conditions which threatened 'slow starvation for the non-breadwinners' (*Votes for Women*, 5 February 1915). War shaped women's role within the domestic sphere, therefore, not only at the consumption end of the 'industrial screw' (Hannam and Hunt 2002, 141) but as women's contribution to the 'national effort' and as an expression of patriotism.

Within these contradictory positions, a campaign organized and led by working-class women experienced incredible success, culminating in the 1915 Rent Restriction Act. But in considering the interconnections and shared discourses of activism of the period, it is necessary not to stop with the celebrations in December 1915, but to look beyond this—in particular, to developments in 1916 and the subsequent success of the WPC—a campaign which drew heavily on the activist base and methods of the rent strikes, but over and above that, on the discourses and imagery of suffrage.

WARTIME ACTIVISM CONTINUES: 1916 AND BEYOND

Opportunities for women's political activism in the prewar period, for the majority of married, working-class women, had been limited, even when they

felt sympathy for the causes concerned. Before the rent strike, the Women's
Labour League Conference regretted this reticence: 'Many working women
... would rather spend their time in patching and polishing inside bad houses,
than come out to unite to demand good houses' (*Labour Women*, February
1914). War changed this, and over the next two years, working-class women
came out in their thousands to demand an end to rent increases and price rises
which forced many families into absolute poverty. New layers of women
were drawn into activism, and although war initially focused demands on
immediate concerns around rent and food, prewar issues such as suffrage did
not disappear completely and were to resurface in the months after the rent
strikes.

What, then, did the rent strikes represent? On one level, immediate consumption demands as an extension of women's 'duty' to protect her family
from the onslaught of war. They were also frequently presented as a woman's
contribution to the national war effort (*Forward*, 4 September 1915), her
side of the 'patriotic' contribution made by the men in the trenches—found,
for example, in the discourse of the landlords as 'Huns' and 'enemy agents'
(*Partick and Maryhill Press*, 14 May 1915). This creates a contradiction,
however, between images of the 'Prussians of Partick' (*Glasgow Herald*,
1 December 1916) and the internationalism espoused with the women and
children of Germany (*Women's Dreadnought*, 22 July 1916). Women's
patriotic duty to defend their homes, supporting the 'war effort' in resisting
the profiteers, stood uncomfortably alongside the threat war posed to their
children, and their subject position as mothers ultimately legitimizing their
opposition to war.

The rent strikes represented more than this, however. They were a powerful victory for working-class women, culminating in the 1915 Rent Restriction Act and the fixing of rents at prewar levels. It was a victory, moreover,
won with the support of male trade unionists and political activists but led
by the collective organization and resistance of working-class women. This
experience gave the women a voice and an impetus for further campaigns,
extending beyond the 'politics of the kitchen' to wider demands around suffrage and peace. The following summer saw 'Human Suffrage' protests and
the launch of the WPC in June 1916 (*Women's Dreadnought*, 17 June 1916).
Women such as Crawfurd and Margaret Nixon, active continuously since
their WSPU days, helped now to sustain and develop the women's movement
in this new direction. A United Suffragists (US) branch had been established
in Glasgow by Crawfurd during 1915 (*Votes for Women*, 6 August 1915),
and a rally in October 1915 attracted other suffrage veterans who dissented
from the Pankhursts' pro-war stance (*Votes for Women*, 28 October 1915)
and declared optimistically that 'the present moment offers many suffrage
opportunities [in Glasgow], where the recent Rent Strikes have brought home

to women the injustices they suffer' (*Votes for Women*, 5 November 1915). Crawfurd enjoyed a degree of success in linking consumption struggles to the wider 'woman question'; her friends Agnes Dollan and Jessie Ferguson, both rent strikers and housewives with no apparent prewar record of suffrage activity, followed her into the US, Ferguson becoming Secretary of the Glasgow Workers' Suffrage Federation (WSF) branch in 1916 and Dollan remaining active in the US for the duration of the war.

Although the ILP celebrated success in the rent strikes, its activists found less fertile ground on broader demands in the early years of the war, particularly when these conveyed an anti-war message. The ILP Conference report in 1915 reported the 'refusal of halls, the prohibition of open-air meetings and abuse, vilification, sneers and threats' (*Forward*, 10 April 1915). In Glasgow the *Govan Press* (6 August 1915), sympathetic to the cause of the rent strikes, attacked the ILP and other anti-war groups as 'a greater danger than the German spy'. The rent strikers' anxiety to present their actions as 'patriotic duty' and those of the landlords as treachery is thus understandable but also deeply gendered. To the press and mainstream opinion, to call for peace was unmasculine, attracting questions about the protagonists' motivations and credibility. On the Left as in the suffrage movement, this was a fault line, with the Glasgow radical John McLean among the voices opposing the war. By late 1916, however, the mood was shifting. Flushed by the success of the rent strikes, the women, united in a cohesive friendship network reinforced through shared experiences of activism, launched themselves into new campaigns, establishing the Food Protection Association (*Partick and Maryhill Press*, 20 October 1916), attempting to set up a union for Soldier's Dependants (*Women's Dreadnought*, 23 September 1916), and continuing to work for 'human suffrage' and equal pay (*Votes for Women*, March 1916). While initially presenting their actions as a necessity of the wartime situation, women's presencing practices also appear to change during this time, through individual gains in consciousness and confidence and through the collective momentum of their movements, particularly the victory of the rent strikes.

In this context, activists' energies turned to the war, which had overshadowed their lives and campaigns, with the formation of a WPC. The initial impetus for this campaign appears to have been a letter from S. Cahill of Lewisham to the *Labour Leader* (18 May 1916), which drew parallels to the demonstrations of German women for food and peace. Crawfurd responded indicating support for such protests in Glasgow where, she believed, 'there is a growing demand for Peace among the common people' (*Labour Leader*, 8 June 1916). The WPC was established in Glasgow in June 1916, characterizing war as an attack on women and an attack on the family—directly through the removal of husbands and sons and ideologically through an attack on women's role in the domestic sphere—at a time when rising food prices and rents were further threatening domestic security.

The forms of protest exhibited by the WPC drew heavily upon the methods and imagery of previous campaigns, both the rent strikes and suffrage. Open-air meetings were held on street corners and in back courts in areas which had been strongholds of the rent strike, often with leading rent strikers speaking (*Labour Leader*, 13 June 1918), such as Dollan, Crawfurd, Nixon, Ferguson and Mary Barbour. As with the rent strikes, local daytime, women-only meetings were favoured in working-class communities. Such an approach allowed working-class women to carve out a physical and psychological 'space' for women's organizing and activism without overtly challenging the contemporary assumption of domestic responsibility. Meetings held at 3 P.M. 'allowed' women to return home to prepare the evening meal (*Forward*, 16 February 1918). But there is an inherent tension here. As Federici (1984, 339) highlights, domestic labour and caring work are an ever-present factor for women, yet to challenge them we must disentangle our 'identification with housework' and seek to organize collectively with other women outside the home.

Although the WPC had a broader geographical spread than the rent strikes (*Labour Leader*, 23 August 1917), it existed first and foremost in spaces occupied by the same working-class housewives and created a space for women's activism distinct to the experience in England, where peace activists were dispersed and persecuted (*Labour Leader*, 22 August 1918). Liddington (1989, 110) attributes this difference to the 'neighbourhood culture' created by Glasgow women's wartime activism, suggesting that women such as Crawfurd and Dollan did succeed, to an extent, in using women's physical environment to create new and autonomous spaces in which their voices could be heard. One of the most striking aspects of the WPC is the vivid imagery created in its procession and demonstrations. Invoking the suffrage protests a decade before, this imagery is deeply gendered, as evidenced in a rare example of Dollan's writing, reporting on the 1918 May Day march in Glasgow, where she described a 'wondrous spectacle' in which 'the women [were] "pleasant and hopeful to behold" and the children an inspiration . . . which no kindly heart could reject' (*Labour Leader*, 9 May 1918). In creating this space and spectacle, women articulated their collective voice, their right to be heard, and in doing so, connected the wartime movements directly to the claim of suffrage. Dollan, speaking at a Peace Negotiations Committee Conference in Glasgow, was keen to stake women's claim for representation at peace talks, arguing that 'the full enfranchisement of their sex was necessary to secure permanent peace' (*Women's Dreadnought*, 17 March 1917).

Women's activism had turned full circle, drawing upon discourses of 'purity' and motherhood while praising the heroic strength of those who resisted injustices and the 'evils' of war. The issue of suffrage and the broader vision of women's emancipation had not disappeared with the outbreak of war but had instead diverged and regrouped under different banners, present through the wide range of issues addressed by activists during this period, drawing in working-class women and creating a space for women's political activism which did not exist in the prewar years.

THE RENT STRIKES AND THEIR RELEVANCE TO TWENTY-FIRST-CENTURY ACTIVISM

What lessons can activists today take from the experience of the rent strikes and the wider movement in which we have placed them? First and foremost, the rent strikes were a struggle for affordable, sustainable housing, prioritizing a 'domestic' concern—with far-reaching implications—and forcing a spotlight on the issue at a time of national and international crisis while carving out a space in public discourse for the concerns of working-class women. Within the wider question of housing activism, for many women activists the frustrations of combining activism with domestic life—in particular child-care—are as relevant now as they were a hundred years ago, and all too many female activists, given the recent history of the Left in Scotland and abroad, will nod at the idea of struggling 'with and against men' at one and the same time. The rent strikes drew working-class women into collective, organized resistance, drawing upon prewar suffrage campaigns and sustaining this into suffrage, food and peace protests during the war. In doing so, they challenged assumptions of women as conservative, inward-looking adjuncts of 'militant' male workers, but this challenge was often constrained and contradicted by the gendered discourses available to the activists and their supporters. Women's role, even in the most direct class struggle, was framed within the assumptions of family, caring and unpaid domestic labour.

This was challenged to an extent by the collective movements of women at the time, and from the 1970s onwards, has been comprehensively challenged by a half-century of feminist debate and critique. Activists in the twenty-first century work in a different context. Liberal feminism has delivered a raft of equalities legislation, giving (some) women access to education, careers and lives unimaginable to the rent strikers. Although the Left no longer positions women as inherently conservative creatures preoccupied by domestic concerns, caring and domestic labour still dominate the lives of most working-class women and acts as a real barrier to participation in activist movements. Moreover, how do we organize in contemporary conditions beset with the problems of the housing crisis, insecure work, the dismantling of the welfare state and the privatization of education? The rent strikes showed that it is possible to do things differently, creating a space for the voices, the activism, the needs of those who are marginalized not only in society but also, too often, in the socialist and labour movements, which profess to seek change. Central to the activism of these women was the creation of an activist identity, a self-belief. Local organizing made use of the spaces that women occupied in their day-to-day lives, creatively using space, resources and existing networks to push forward their demands.

Noteworthy too is the importance of the informal networks, the friendship networks that wove in and out of campaigns, sustaining activism, educating and enthusing. The rent strikers would no doubt have been committed proponents of the twenty-first-century social-media tools, which keep us connected and informed, but they would not have substituted 'clicktivism' for the graft of being out in the community, talking to working class people about the issues which concerned them, listening, organizing and resisting. The rent strikes are an example of a particular struggle of working-class women, but they offer a vision, a new and inclusive politics, as relevant today as a century ago.

REFERENCES

Primary Sources

Crawfurd, H. n.d. *Autobiography*.
Forward, 1907–1918.
Glasgow Herald, 1915–1916.
Govan Press, 1915.
Labour Leader, 1916–1918.
Labour Women, "Report of WLL Conference at Glasgow, January 26 1914." February 1914, 1(10).
Partick and Maryhill Press, 1915–1916.
Votes for Women, 1915.
Women's Dreadnought, 1916.

Secondary Sources

Castells, Manuel. 1983. *The City and the Grassroots: A Cross-Cultural Theory of Urban Social Movements*. Berkeley: University of California Press.
Clark, Helen, and Elizabeth Carnegie. 2003. *She Was Aye Workin'*. Oxford: White Cockade Publishing.
Damer, Seán. 2000b. "'Engineers of the Human Machine': The Social Practice of Council Housing Management in Glasgow, 1895–1939." *Urban Studies* 37(11): 2007–26.
Dalla Costa, Mariarosa, and James, Selma. 1972. *The Power of Women and the Subversion of the Community*. Bristol: Falling Wall Press.

Federici, Silvia. 1975. *Wages against Housework.* Bristol: Power of Women Collective and Falling Wall Press.

———. 1984. "Putting Feminism Back on Its Feet." *Social Text* 9/10: 338–46.

Gordon, Eleanor. 1991. *Women and the Labour Movement in Scotland, 1850–1914.* Oxford: Clarendon.

Hannam, June, and Karen Hunt. 2002. *Socialist Women: Britain: 1880s to 1920s.* London: Routledge.

Joannou, Maroula, and June Purvis. 1998. Introduction to *The Women's Suffrage Movement: New Feminist Perspectives*, edited by Maroula Joannou and June Purvis, 1–14. Manchester: Manchester University Press.

King, Elizabeth. 1978. *The Scottish Women's Suffrage Movement.* Glasgow: People's Palace.

Leneman, Leah. 1991. *A Guid Cause: The Women's Suffrage Movement in Scotland.* Aberdeen: Aberdeen University Press.

Liddington, Jill. 1989. *The Long Road to Greenham.* London: Virago.

McLean, Iain. 1983. *The Legend of Red Clydeside.* Edinburgh: John Donald.

Melling, Joseph. 1983. *Rent Strikes: People's Struggle for Housing in West Scotland 1890–1916.* Edinburgh: Polygon.

Robertson, Iain. 1997. "The Role of Women in Social Protest in the Highlands of Scotland, 1880–1939." *Journal of Historical Geography* 23(2): 187–200.

Ross, Ellen. 1983. "Survival Networks: Women's Neighbourhood Sharing in London before World War 1." *History Workshop Journal* 15(1): 4–28.

Smyth, James. 1992. "Rent, Peace, Votes: Working Class Women and Political Activity in the First World War." In *Out of Bounds: Women in Scottish Society 1800–1945*, edited by Esther Breitenbach and Eleanor Gordon, 174–96. Edinburgh: Edinburgh University Press.

———. 2000. *Labour in Glasgow 1896–1986: Socialism, Suffrage, Sectarianism.* East Linton: Tuckwell Press.

Stainton Rogers, Wendy. 2003. *Social Psychology: Experimental and Critical Approaches.* Maidenhead: Open University Press/McGraw-Hill Education.

Wells, Herbert G. 1907. *Will Socialism Destroy the Home?* London: ILP.

Young, James D. 1985. *Women and Popular Struggles.* Edinburgh: Mainstream Publishing.

Chapter 2

What Did the Rent Strikers Do Next?

Women and 'The Politics of the Kitchen' in Interwar Scotland

Annmarie Hughes and Valerie Wright

The rent strikes of 1915 were the most successful rent campaigns of the twentieth century, campaigns which involved women from all walks of life, those openly political and those for whom politics was an everyday struggle against poverty and exploitation. Elsewhere in this volume, Pam Currie considers how this struggle was waged by working-class women and men against landlords in the west of Scotland in the years leading up to 1915. In this chapter, we highlight the influence of the rent strikes on the subsequent politics of housing, which were central in interwar political discourse and which in turn would influence the formation of the welfare state after the Second World War (Thane 1990, 1991; Hughes 2010). This chapter explores the aftermath and influence of the rent strikes which acted as a lynchpin between community and formal political activity and also how it provided a framework for the strategies used by working-class women in the interwar years who continued to make the 'politics of the kitchen' central to their political agenda (Hughes 2010). As we show, this was very much influenced by the 'politics of everyday life' within which women operated and which proved central to their demands for improved housing in interwar Scotland (see also Hughes 2010, 181–98).

SETTING THE CONTEXT: RENT STRIKES AND GRASSROOTS ACTIVISM

The rent strikes were part of a series of broader social protests, which had marked Scotland in the years leading up to the First World War in the wake

of nearly eight years of on and off recession. The perceived inequality of sacrifice brought about by recession and wartime conditions exacerbated these
grievances. Food and fuel shortages gave rise to shop owners raising prices
of essential goods, and this was aggravated by rising inflation, which meant
real wages fell until at least 1917. At the same time, wealthier citizens had
more access to essential goods. Working-class women, as 'the exchequers of
the home'—those that budgeted for the family—became increasingly frus-
trated, and thus, politicized. They took direct action against food suppliers
as well as their landlords. Mr. Ewart, interviewed in the 1990s, recalled such
an episode in Partick during the First World War when he described an old
woman encouraging women to attack a cooperative lorry as it was heading to
the city's prosperous West End:

> And as she said: 'now's your chance. Here's the potatoes that you can't buy, but
> someone else can. They've got the money because you haven't, because you're
> not in the same class as them'. They attacked the lorry with knives and picked
> up their skirts and filled them with potatoes. Another driver actually tried to
> intervene to his physical detriment and the police were also attacked and some
> of the women ended up in court and prison. (Mr. Ewart, SOHCA/019/031/
> Glasgow)

The women involved in this incident were obviously anxious to feed their
families. As Ewart stated, 'They were trying to prove with their existence that
we had the right to be fed'. Such working-class women demanded justice and
fairness because while their men were away fighting, they were being forced
to sacrifice in ways that wealthier families were not. It is not surprising that
they took matters into their own hands. Similar protests around housing can
be placed in a broader context of working-class discontent, which was also
the case in the interwar years. Working-class women were involved in politics well before the rent strikes and they continued to be afterwards. Obviously it is difficult to find or reconstruct the narratives of unknown activists.
We may never know the point at which individual women were politicized or
if these individuals remained politically active beyond particular campaigns.
It is also challenging to trace the women who were involved in housing protests such as the rent strikes. Considerable attention has been given to figure-
heads such as Mary Barbour and to a lesser extent Helen Crawfurd (Burness
2015; Orr 2015). We also know a bit about what happened next for Agnes
Dollan and other prominent individuals involved in the rent strikes (Wright
2008; Hughes 2010). However, although it is difficult to determine whether
it was the same individuals involved, it is clear that women continued to
demand improved housing conditions as well as a better standard of living
for working-class people after the rent strikes.

The rent strikes involved grassroots movements of women who came together because of their shared anger at profiteering landlords and the cost of everyday essentials. They were not organized by a particular political party, and although many of the women involved in the strikes may have been members of the Scottish Co-operative Women's Guild (SCWG), the guild did not organize the strikes. Prominent activists, such as Barbour, were members of the guild, and it has been argued that this gave them the training they needed for public speaking, organizing campaigns, forming deputations and other political skills (Burness 2015). That may have been true, but not all strikers would have been members of an official political organization. Strikers were drawn from all walks of life; by November 1915 approximately 20,000 tenants were on strike (Melling 1983, 94). Political and militant in its own right, this was a protest organized by women for women with community being the most important motivation rather than party political aims. Women were resisting increased rents, they were protecting their neighbours, they wanted what was fair and they were confronting capitalist landlords who owned the properties in which they lived, thereby attacking capitalism itself, in an increasingly politicized 'domestic' sphere. Housing was a site of protest in the same way that the shipyards and munitions factories were in the much-discussed disputes of 'Red Clydeside' in the 1910s (McLean 1983; Foster 1990; Griffin 2015).

As the women involved in protests in tenement closes around the city became more organized, local groups were formed, and eventually many of these joined together under the umbrella of the Glasgow Women's Housing Association (GWHA) in 1914 (Melling 1980). The structure adopted mirrored that of the organizations aligned to the labour movement, broadly conceived, in an area that was largely dominated by skilled men who favoured 'respectable' conduct. The actions of the GWHA were therefore more formal and official than the direct action which had been previously favoured in neighbourhoods in the city. Notably, women as unskilled workers were more likely to have been involved in unofficial protests and strikes in the workplace too. This formalizing of housing protest gave a degree of 'respectability' and legitimacy to women's involvement in 'politics'. It was at this point that men of the labour or socialist movement, along with women's established organizations such as the SCWG, were able to become increasingly involved in trying to influence and shape the rent strikers' localized direct action into structured protest. The rent strikers, through organizations such as GWHA, increasingly adopted more formal forms of political activity using committees, deputations and meetings with Glasgow Corporation to press their demands.

This set the context for what would happen following the passing of the Rent Restrictions Act in November 1915. The male-dominated political parties involved in the latter stages of the rent strikes took credit for the act and capitalized on it for their own political ends throughout the interwar years. Within such accounts was a celebration of women's grassroots 'unorganized' protest, of women pelting bailiffs with flour, and so on, which inaccurately and effectively marginalized women from the serious business of negotiations and 'politics' in accounts of the strikes. The way in which the rent strikes became a victory for the labour movement, and not just the women who had started the protest in neighbourhoods in the city, has meant that the political work of women in housing in the 1920s and 1930s has continued to be marginalized by historians, politicians and even in the centenary celebrations of the rent strikes in 2015. The narratives of what the rent strikers did next is largely missing from such accounts and therefore is unknown to groups and individuals who have been involved in their own housing campaigns throughout the twentieth century and today. It is this absence that we wish to address, to provide an example of what can be achieved by the ongoing struggle for housing improvements.

THE ROLE OF WOMEN IN THE POLITICS OF HOUSING IN INTERWAR SCOTLAND: DIRECT ACTION OR COMMITTEE WORK?

Following the end of the First World War, women's position within the labour movement had arguably been negatively affected by their role in the 'dilution' of male-dominated occupations. Women's comparatively 'unskilled' and low-paid work in munitions factories and heavy engineering compounded by the adverse economic climate of the 1920s and 1930s meant that women workers were seen as a threat to the established trade unions and workers in relevant industries. As a result, it has been argued that women's political interests were sidelined as society was encouraged to return to traditional gender and class ideals. In other words, there was a backlash against women in the workplace and political sphere. Although this assumption has been challenged, especially in relation to women's involvement in politics, it remains the case that class identity remained a barrier to the cooperation of women of different backgrounds on social issues such as housing (Hughes 2010; Wright 2008).

For many women active in left-wing and socialist organizations, it has also been assumed that class identity was prioritized before that of gender. Ironically, however, it has also been suggested that women were confined to a female ghetto where they were given responsibility for campaigning on issues related to their domestic roles as mothers and wives, where they could only speak on issues such as health, education and crucially, housing (Scott 1998).

It is broadly true that women involved in left-wing politics often worked within their own women's organizations as part of the broader organization to which they were aligned. However, the assumption that women were limited to 'women's issues' by the men they worked with ignores women's power and agency in championing a politics of the kitchen, and their active choice to campaign on issues of relevance to them and other working-class women. It also fails to recognize the ways in which women of the Left in interwar Scotland were able to subvert and pragmatically challenge their roles as wives and mothers and instead use this to their advantage when demanding a more equal role in the movement of which they were a part. Therefore, by actively positioning themselves as 'respectable' working-class women, wives and mothers, and crucially workers in the home, the Scottish SCWG was able to discursively and practically extend its role in the co-operative movement rather than confining its members to their kitchens (Wright 2008; see also Federici 1984). Indeed, this was the basic premise of advocating a politics of the kitchen, taking the concerns of women who were housewives and mothers (and workers) and demanding their recognition in the political sphere (Hughes 2010). This included improvements in the workshop of the working-class woman, the home. In many respects this is similar to the 1970s Marxist-feminist demands that unpaid work in the home, what might be referred to as 'caring labour', be recognized as work. This is an argument which has remained influential in feminist discourse (Federici 1984; McLean 2015).

This was important in relation to housing, and standard-of-living issues such as the price of essential items including food and fuel. The politics of the kitchen was employed to create a space for women to participate in the political arena. More importantly the politics of the kitchen became essential to the agenda of the Independent Labour Party (ILP) and the Labour Party in Scotland in the 1920s. Indeed, women were responsible for placing welfare on the Labour Party's agenda (Hughes 2010). Housing was a major campaigning issue for both parties, and this issue remained firmly associated with women in this period. So although the ILP and Labour Party may have capitalized on the glory of the Rent Restrictions Act of 1915, it was the women in these political organizations that took the lead in, and responsibility for, campaigning against any amendments to this act. Also central to their ambitions were further material improvements to housing conditions for working-class families, as the ILP in particular were well aware. Following the partial enfranchisement of women in 1918 the ILP defined itself as the 'Real Women's Party', not only in Scotland but also across Britain (Hughes 2010, 39). Indeed, its journal, *Forward,* reported on 7 November 1922, that:

> The growing political power of women and their intense desire for better home conditions will be a great aid in effecting the peaceful revolution in municipal

administration. Women are practical and more concerned about securing a fuller life for their children. We are on the threshold of tremendous developments. Politics are being rapidly domesticated.

The politics of the kitchen was in turn based upon an informal politics of everyday life (Hughes 2010, 181–98), where direct action continued to act as a lynchpin between older ideas of the preindustrial moral economy of justice, fairness and equality and ideas of reciprocity which historians now link to the operation of the welfare state in Britain (Thompson 1971). However, as was the case with the rent strikes, direct action was increasingly substituted by more official campaigns through established political channels, with women's organizations forming deputations to the local authorities or secretary of state for Scotland. Meanwhile any further rent strikes of the interwar years were sanctioned by the Labour Party and trade unions and largely led by men. Arguably this 'institutionalization of domestic concerns' therefore 'displaced women's direct action' (Hughes 2010, 183). The undermining of spontaneous action may have been compensated for by increased coordination which encompassed more individuals, but it was not necessarily successful. In 1933 the Glasgow Council of Tenants Associations, representing around 30,000 tenants, requested a meeting with Glasgow City Council to forward demands for rent reductions, but irrespective of numbers, the meeting was refused (Hughes 2010, 183). When municipal authorities ignored the requests of such formal organizations, direct action was often an alternative response. In 1938, 600 women in Paisley marched on the county building to protest against rent increases, and they secured 'great concessions' from the council. There were similar actions in Glasgow, Aberdeen, Lanarkshire, Renfrewshire, Clydebank and Greenock (Hughes 2010, 184). Although such actions may have been supported by formal political groups such as the ILP, Labour or cooperative movements, it was not officially encouraged.

Nevertheless, women remained influential in formal organizational protests for improvements in housing and standards of living. The Rent Restriction Act of 1915 had embedded the ideal of state intervention in the housing market. Women's groups and organizations aligned to the socialist and labour movements used this legislation to demand not only fair rents, but also crucially increased municipal house building. In turn, the idea of council housing for all was central to ILP and Labour Party ideology and the politics of welfare in the interwar years, which in turn became the foundation of the postwar welfare state. Women were at the forefront of demands for low rent in decent council housing, which would free tenants from profiteering landlords. Therefore they demanded a state service for all which would replace the exploitative capitalist market place for the basic necessity of life, the right to a decent home. As working-class wives and mothers, whose role it was to ensure that their families could survive and thrive, the politics of housing was easily identifiable with their interests. This was their 'sphere', their 'workshop'.

As well as demanding municipal house building, funded by central government, working-class women had to protect the legislation that they had fought for in 1915. The First World War was barely over when landlords began challenging the Rent Restriction Act and putting pressure on the government to overturn it. Subsequent Acts in 1920 and 1923 ate away at the gains made in 1915 and caused sporadic rent strikes throughout the period. In protest against the recapitulation of the act, Clydebank tenants began a series of strikes from 1922 and the town was labelled the 'spiritual home of anarchy' by landlords (Hughes 2010; Damer 1982). Given Lloyd George's promise of 'Homes fit for Heroes' following the First World War, which was arguably a response to fears of more social discontent, it was no wonder that people remained angry about the conditions of overcrowding in many areas of Britain. Adding insult to injury, the Rent Restrictions Act ensured that rents could be increased if landlords carried out essential repairs. There was widespread protest when rents were increased where no repairs had been undertaken. In addition, in 1923 legislation to reduce rent controls in the private sector was proposed and was recognized by the working classes as a threat to the already limited gains made by the 1915 act.

In this political climate, landlords, including local municipal authorities, were able to victimize those involved in rent strikes through eviction, court actions and the denial of tenancies in newly built municipal housing by the use of black listing; this created widespread fear and prevented further action. Moreover, housing built after the First World War was not subject to the Rent Restrictions Act. This ensured that rents could be 'economic' in new municipal housing estates in Glasgow and elsewhere. In reality this meant that those who needed rehousing most urgently were priced out. As a result, only skilled men and their families, or more accurately the lower middle classes, could afford to live in such housing (Damer 1990). Even where housing estates were built for 'slum clearance'—the infamous 'rehousing' estates—the rents may have been low, but the housing was very poor quality with little or no public amenities (Damer 2000b). In private tenement flats, when a tenant with an agreed rent control vacated the property, rents could be increased.

A deep schism developed between the Labour Party, which advocated the parliamentary road to effecting change in housing policy, and the ILP, Communist Party and Scottish Labour Housing Association who all favoured direct action as seen in the rent strikes of 1915. The Labour Party at a UK level continued to support rent controls but did not support direct action with the trade union movement officially following suit. In 1923 the leadership of the Labour Party implied that as no official sanction had been given by organized labour for the withholding of rent, then the Communist Party must be behind the agitation. This approach to housing issues was very much driven by the male-dominated labour movement, which increasingly sidelined unorganized working-class women in political activity—those women who were members of affiliate women's organizations were influential as long as they followed these accepted strategies. By opposing direct action and the methods used by women in local communities at a grassroots level, and instead taking a parliamentary 'official' approach, concessions were allowed to be made to the 1915 act, which essentially resulted in rent increases.

In this context, women were expected to place their trust in the men leading the labour movement. Women's committees were replaced by tenants' associations, with men often taking leadership roles. Increasing unemployment in the late 1920s onwards also ensured that the issue of rents and housing more generally were sidelined in those organizations who continued to support direct action, being replaced by involvement in the protests of the National Unemployed Workers Movement and demonstrations and deputations against the Household Means Test. Notably, women were also involved in such action, too. With such issues competing for attention, women had to become increasingly strategic and pragmatic to ensure that housing remained on the agenda. Central to this objective was the continuing emphasis on the relevance of the politics of the kitchen to working-class interests. Housing was designated primarily as a 'women's issue', which gave women the opportunity to carve out a space to make their voices central to the politics surrounding the demands for improved municipal housing in the interwar years in Scotland and had profound implications for addressing inequality in society. Additionally, working-class women entered the world of formal politics in greater numbers after 1918, which was the logical extension of the formalization of previous direct action. Prominent rent strikers such as Mary Barbour, Agnes Dollan and Helen Crawfurd are most likely remembered because they stood as candidates in local and national elections and went on to hold prominent posts in the labour movement. Barbour became a city councillor where she continued to fight for improvements in working-class standards of living, including a scheme of home helps for postpartum mothers and free 'unadulterated' milk for all school children (Burness 2015). Dollan, a committed pacifist who cofounded the Women's Peace Crusade with Crawfurd, also retained her commitment to housing issues, health and the welfare of children in the remainder of her political career. Crawfurd went on to be a founding member of the Communist Party in Scotland (Orr 2015).

Although the paths of the women leaders of the rent strikes may have diverged, these women remained committed to political action and to establishing reforms which would form the foundations of the welfare state in which decent and affordable housing was a central tenet. While we can only speculate on the legacy of the rent strikes for the masses of women involved in communities and neighbourhoods throughout Glasgow and beyond in terms of their individual politics, it is clear that through membership of women's organizations working-class women remained politicized in the interwar years and took a prominent role in keeping welfare issues at the forefront of socialist politics in the city.

A PRAGMATIC APPROACH? WOMEN'S DEMANDS FOR IMPROVED HOUSING IN INTERWAR SCOTLAND

The need for improved housing was an issue prioritized by working-class women throughout Scotland. We consider the housing-related campaigns of the women of the SCWG in urban Scotland and Labour women in semi-rural coal mining. Each organization had to work within the ideological and discursive context available to it in interwar Scotland, and as a result, both pragmatically deployed a politics of the kitchen to stress the importance of their members' voices as women and mothers.

The SCWG was formed in 1890 in Kinning Park, Glasgow. By the 1920s it had branches throughout urban areas in Scotland, although its stronghold was in the west of Scotland. The guild was aimed at the wives of the 'better off' sections of the working class, and from its inception, the leadership was very much influenced by the ideologies of the cooperative movement, including thrift and self-improvement (Gordon 1991, 266). As was the case with other women's organizations affiliated to the broader labour movement, the guild's role within the Scottish cooperative movement was as the protectors of women and children (Callen 1952, 24–25). Members of the guild were successful in gaining representation on education, health and housing committees, all of which were associated with women's maternal caring roles. This could be viewed as a restricted sphere of influence, that women did not occupy equal roles but were given 'special' influence as mothers and wives (Scott 1998). However, the mobilization of a politics of the kitchen, which emphasized women's different needs, was both a pragmatic acceptance of the reality of their position as workers in the home, and a challenge to the conditions in which they toiled. Caring labour and domestic work and what would become known as the 'double burden' for those women working outside the home was the reality for working-class women. In this context a politics based on their lives was empowering, as the value of their work was central not supplementary to the work of men, nor was it inferior to the 'careers' sought by middle-class feminists (Federici 1984, 340). This strategy enabled the guild to prioritize the 'domestic' politics of housing and gave women an essential role in protecting the gains made in 1915 and demanding further improvements (Wright 2008). Crucially, such influence facilitated the guild in placing the everyday needs of their members on the agenda of the wider cooperative movement.

From its earliest days, the guild had prioritized improved housing for the working classes. Unsurprisingly many prominent members of the guild were also members of the ILP. From 1920, the guild demanded the continuation of rent restrictions and opposed the Rent Restriction Amendment Act, which would result in 'increased house rents' and 'would cause great hardship on a large number of the poorer and casual workers' (SCWG, 4 August 1920). The president, Mrs. MacDonald, also praised the 'vigorous protest being organized in certain districts against the increase in rents' including Clydebank (SCWG, 1 September 1920). The campaign resurfaced in the late 1920s with the government's attempts to decontrol rents. The guild, supporting the extension of the Rent Restrictions Act, took part in deputations to the secretary of state for Scotland in cooperation with the Scottish National Housing Association and Glasgow Women's Housing Association 'to state the case of the working women' (SCWG, 28 August 1929, 25 September 1929). The threat of eviction was a particular worry throughout the 1930s, and in 1932, the campaign was again reinvigorated with demands for an immediate return to prewar rents 'in view of grave unemployment and low wages prevalent among the working classes'. Alongside such formal protest, anti-eviction militancy was also a central part of the politics of everyday life in Scottish neighbourhoods (Hughes 2010, 181–98).

The guild also consistently called upon the government to assume responsibility for providing better housing and giving assistance to local authorities to enable them to build new houses and deal adequately with the slums. The central council welcomed the Wheatley Housing Act of 1924 and even Glasgow Corporation's later strategy of 'slum clearance' adopted in 1935. Although the latter resulted in the creation of poor quality housing estates with no amenities whose residents were quickly stigmatized (Damer 2000b), perhaps the pragmatic approach of the guild was to favour any construction over inaction. Anything would be an improvement on the exploitative, overcrowded and vermin-infested privately rented tenements. While at the forefront of demands for improved housing and 'reasonable rents', in many respects the guild was restricted by the use of accepted campaigning techniques such as deputations and petitions. It was unable to affect the changes in housing provision that were required by its working-class members and their families. However, the odds were stacked against such working-class women's organizations. Economic and political circumstances in the interwar years prevented sufficient municipal house building to solve the problems of overcrowding and poor quality housing. As early as 1919, the Scottish Office had found that 57,000 new houses were required in Glasgow (Butt 1978, 149;

Stenhouse 1931, 118). Despite the construction of significant numbers of council houses, it was found in 1935 that a staggering 100,000 houses were required to solve overcrowding in the city (Morgan 1989, 1260). Following the Second World War, it was estimated that around 60,000 houses were required to re-house people from the remaining tenement slums.

The situation was no better in coal-mining areas in Scotland. As Sprott (1996, 172) observes, 'although the evidence suggests that conditions improved over the years, this occurred so slowly that it made little difference to country dwellers'. Three-quarters of the houses inspected by the Scottish Housing Advisory Committee in 1937 were found to be 'unfit for human habitation' (*Scotsman*, 10 November 1937). In response, women living in such conditions actively campaigned for improvements and municipal house building, including Labour Party Women's Sections. Like the guild, Labour Party Women's Sections in rural areas in Scotland focused on politics which valued housewives as the 'Chancellors of the Exchequer of the Home', promoting housing as a 'women's issue' (Hughes 2013). Women's Sections in Hawick (formed in 1924) and Balerno and Currie in Midlothian (formed in 1929), raised extensive funding to support electoral campaigns of Labour candidates in rural areas. In addition to performing such 'domestic' organizing of the movement, the women also made their voices heard on issues of concern to their members such as 'housing education and co-operation' (Hawick Women's Section, 1924).

Women in rural and mining communities were underrepresented in political life; however, just as was the case in urban Scotland, some were able to penetrate local government and local public bodies and achieved prominence both in their communities and at a national level. For instance, Agnes Hardie Hughes, granddaughter of Keir Hardie, took a seat on Cumnock Town Council, Ayrshire in 1933. Mining villages have been identified with extreme patriarchy with men dominating the worlds of work and politics (Dennis et al. 1971; McIntyre 1980; Campbell 2000, 235). However, Hughes became convenor of the Public Health Committee in 1934, provost of the Town Council in 1935, and one of Scotland's earliest female magistrates. She was deeply committed to the provision of housing for working-class people, and in her role as Provost of Cumnock she challenged and defeated the landowner, Lord Bute of Cumnock, to ensure the removal of slum dwellings from his land and their replacement with low-rent partially furnished council housing. By 1945 three-quarters of Cumnock's population had been re-housed in council houses, many of them in highly sought after bungalows (*Scotsman*, 10 March 1936). Sarah Moore, described as 'probably the most outstanding personality in the district of West Calder', 'untiringly' fought for council houses for her constituents in the Lothians. She also 'brought into being the village of Moorelands, which was named after her at the desire of the inhabitants'.[1]

Arguably, women from rural and mining communities could be more successful than their urban counterparts in securing improved living conditions for their constituents.

CONCLUSION

We can learn a great deal from the strategies used in the rent strikes and from women's attempts to establish a sphere of influence in interwar politics. The first lesson is that direct action works but also that women must be central to 'official' formal political discussions. As highlighted here, socialist women successfully influenced the ILP and Labour party agenda by placing welfare at its core, including housing. They did so by utilizing a politics of the kitchen, which ensured that the interests of women as mothers, wives and crucially, workers in the home were recognized and central to the domesticization of left-wing politics, especially in the early 1920s. It has been argued that the use of maternalist arguments limited women to housing, education and health, but we have argued that these were among the core concerns of working-class women at this time and arose directly from the material conditions of their everyday lives (Federici 1984). Given the levels of overcrowding in Scottish towns and cities, most notably in Glasgow, the poor housing conditions in rural areas of Scotland, and the obvious poverty and inequality present in society, it is not surprising that women continued to demand improvements to their living conditions and in their working environment, for better education for their children and health care for their families. By politicizing the everyday, working-class women in the socialist left-wing movement in urban and rural Scotland were able to make their voices heard and achieve real material change in their living conditions.

In interwar Scotland, the workplace was not the only legitimate site of political protest around the reproduction of labour. Moreover, women continue to bear the burden of a higher share of 'caring work' whether this be housework, childcare or care for relatives, friends or neighbours, regardless of whether they work outside the home or not. The quality, cost and availability of housing and the politics of the kitchen therefore remain as relevant today as they did in 1915 and throughout the interwar years. Just as men joined the rent strikers and continued to support the politics of the kitchen in the years that followed, housing is also an issue for everyone today. The demand for affordable housing for all is as important as fair wages for all. The protest against exploitative landlords is as important as opposition to exploitative employers. Housing remains a crucial site of protest today.

So how do individuals make their voices heard and what can we learn from the rent strikers and the politics of the kitchen? It is simply not enough to ensure that housing is on the political agenda. Groups such as Living Rent (see this volume) are ensuring that the general public knows about people being exploited by private landlords, renting at exorbitant cost, living in poor quality social housing and those living in housing unfit for its purpose. But what will make the government take action? The history of the rent strikes and the politics of housing in the interwar years leave us with a legacy which demonstrates the importance of direct action at a grassroots level that speaks to a broad spectrum of those experiencing inequality and exploitation. This led to housing entering the political agenda and, over time, with the continued interwar campaigns for more and better housing, the politics of housing was embedded in the welfare demands that formed the basis of the welfare state after the Second World War. Perhaps, today, a politics of housing based on direct action as well as more traditional campaigns of petitions, letter writing and arguing for legislative change, is a way of saving what remains of that welfare state and opening up new political possibilities. Action for social change centred on housing has been successful in the past as illustrated by the Rent Strikes of 1915, and there is no good reason to think it cannot be successful again.

NOTE

1. See the website, 'Addiewell Heritage: Recording the History of a West Lothian Village'. http://www.addiewellheritage.org.uk/

REFERENCES

Primary Sources

Ewart, Mr. Scottish Oral History Centre Archive (SOHCA/019/031/Glasgow).
Forward, 7 November 1922.
Hawick Women's Section, 7 April and 23 September 1924.
SCWG, *Minute Books of the Central Council*, CWS1/39/1/8, 4 August 1920, 1 September 1920, 6 February 1924, 28 August 1929, 25 September 1929.
The Scotsman, 10 March 1936, p. 9, 10 November 1937, p. 7.

Secondary Sources

Burness, Catriona. 2015. "Remembering Mary Barbour." *Scottish Labour History Review* 50: 81–96.
Butt, John. 1978. "Working-Class Housing in Glasgow, 1900–1939." In *Essays in Scottish Labour History: A Tribute to W. H. Marwick*, edited by Ian MacDougall, 143–70. Edinburgh: John Donald.

Callen, Kate M. 1952. *History of the Scottish Co-operative Women's Guild: Diamond Jubilee 1892–1952*. Glasgow: Scottish Co-operative Women's Guild.

Campbell, Alan. 2000. *The Scottish Miners 1874–1939, Volume One*. Aldershot: Ashgate.

Damer, Seán. 1982. *Rent Strike! The Clydebank Rent Struggles of the 1920s*. Clydebank: People's History Pamphlet.

———. 1990. *Glasgow: Going for a Song*. London: Lawrence and Wishart.

———. 2000b. "'Engineers of the Human Machine': The Social Practice of Council Housing Management in Glasgow, 1895–1939." *Urban Studies* 37: 2007–26.

Dennis, Norman, Fernando Henriques and Clifford Slaughter. 1971. *Coal Is Our Life: An Analysis of a Yorkshire Mining Community*. London: Tavistock Publications.

Federici, Silvia. 1984. "Putting Feminism Back on Its Feet." *Social Text* 9(10): 338–46.

Foster, John. 1990. "Strike Action and Working-Class Politics on Clydeside, 1914–1919." *International Review of Social History* 35(1): 33–70.

Gordon, Eleanor. 1991. *Women and the Labour Movement in Scotland, 1850–1914*. Oxford: Clarendon Press.

Griffin, Paul. 2015. *The Spatial Politics of Red Clydeside: Historical Labour Geographies and Radical Connections*. PhD diss., University of Glasgow.

Hughes, Annmarie. 2010. *Gender and Political Identities in Scotland, 1919–1939*. Edinburgh: Edinburgh University Press.

———. 2013. "'A Clear Understanding of our Duty': Labour Women in Rural Scotland, 1919–1939." *Scottish Labour History Review* 48: 136–57.

McIntyre, Stuart. 1980. *Little Moscows: Communism and Working-Class Militancy in Interwar Britain*. London: Croom Helm.

McLean, Caitlin. 2015. "Beyond Care: Expanding the Feminist Debate on Universal Basic Income." WiSE Working Paper Series No.1, September. Basic Income Earth Network. http://basicincome.org/news/2015/11/caitlin-mclean-beyond-care-expanding-the-feminist-debate-on-universal-basic-income/

McLean, Iain. 1983. *The Legend of Red Clydeside*. Edinburgh: John Donald.

Melling, J. (Ed.). 1980. *Housing, Social Policy and the State*. London: Croom Helm.

Melling, Joseph. 1983. *Rent Strikes: People's Struggle for Housing in West Scotland 1890–1916*. Polygon: Edinburgh.

Morgan, Nicholas J. 1989. "'£8 Cottages for Glasgow Citizens': Innovations in Municipal Housebuilding in Glasgow in the Interwar years." *Scottish Housing in the Twentieth Century*, edited by Richard Rodger, 125–44. Leicester: Leicester University Press.

Orr, Lesley. 2015. "'Shall We Not Speak For Ourselves?' Helen Crawfurd, War Resistance and the Women's Peace Crusade, 1916–1918." *Scottish Labour History Review* 50: 97–115.

Scott, Gillian. 1998. *Feminism and the Politics of Working Women: The Women's Co-operative Guild, 1880s to the Second World War*. London: University College London Press.

Sprott, Gavin. 1996. "Lowland Country Life." In *Scotland in the Twentieth Century*, edited by Tam M. Devine and Richard J. Finlay, 170–88. Edinburgh: Edinburgh University Press.

Stenhouse, David. 1931. *Glasgow, Its Municipal Undertakings and Enterprises.* Glasgow: Corporation of Glasgow.

Thane, Pat. 1990. "The Women of the British Labour Party and Feminism, 1906–1945." In *British Feminism in the Twentieth Century*, edited by Harold L. Smith, 124–43. Aldershot: Elgar.

———. 1991. "Visions of Gender in the Making of the British Welfare State: The Case of Women in the British Labour Party and Social Policy, 1906–1945." In *Maternity and Gender Policies: Women and the Rise of the European States, 1880s–1950s*, edited by Bock, Gisela and Pat Thane, 93–118. London: Routledge.

Thompson, Edward P. 1971. "The Moral Economy of the English Crowd in the Eighteenth Century." *Past & Present* 50: 76–136.

Wright, Valerie. 2008. "Feminism and Women's Organizations in Interwar Scotland." PhD diss., University of Glasgow.

Chapter 3

'Oary' Dundee and Working-Class Self-Organization in the 1915 Rent Strike

Tony Cox

> We do not know whether we have corrupted the Clyde engineers or they us.
>
> —*Textile Workers' Guide* (1916)

While Glasgow has featured extensively in previous studies of the 1915 Rent Strike, Dundee has been largely neglected. This is, perhaps, not so surprising, because larger and more strategic industrial centres such as Glasgow, as with Liverpool and Manchester, bulked large in press coverage and government reports. Dundee was smaller with a class structure quite different from these larger cities with their more varied local economies and much greater concentrations of male skilled labour. For John Foster (1976, 26), in his classic study of the labour aristocracy, '[t]he really intense struggles were restricted to those areas where skilled workers formed a big section of the workforce and where the introduction of semi-skilled labour posed the biggest challenge'. The Dundee workforce was made up of predominantly semi- and unskilled labour, with only a small labour aristocracy. According to Foster's view, the militancy and organization demonstrated by events in the city should never have happened. The fact that Dundee actually emerged as a major 'storm centre' of the 1915 Rent Strike represents a conundrum that this chapter seeks to answer.

A more recent study by Ann Petrie (2008) has investigated the Dundee Rent Strike within the context of a timely and invaluable wider analysis of the wartime movement on the east coast of Scotland. Petrie contends that 'one of the most striking and significant features of the rent unrest was the high level of co-operation between various sections of the working classes and the

labour movement more generally' (Petrie 2008, 95), and she views the movement as having been 'carefully managed by the local Trades Council and left
radical and socialist political parties', a position shared by J. K. Young in a
wide-ranging and accomplished doctoral study of housing in Dundee (Young
1991, 376–78). This chapter assesses these claims by investigating the extent
of 'official' labour movement influence on events in Dundee and the way in
which the city's highly distinctive class structure and working-class culture
contributed towards a movement that seemed at its height to be moving
towards open confrontation with the British state.

SOCIAL AND HOUSING CONDITIONS IN JUTEOPOLIS

By the beginning of the twentieth century, Dundee was home to the largest
concentration of female industrial labour anywhere in the British Isles, a
legacy of the bitter struggle, spanning the decades from the 1820s to 1850s,
between artisan labour and the town's increasingly powerful linen manufacturers. Defeat for the weavers and hecklers[1] of Dundee led to their removal
and replacement with cheaper, unorganized and younger female workers
from Angus, the Scottish Highlands and Ulster, laying the basis for the
emergence of a distinctive method of labour control that, founded on almost
untrammelled levels of managerial and supervisory power, amounted to a
form of 'paternal despotism' (Cox 2013, 4–7). However, during the last two
decades of the nineteenth century, paternal despotism would face increased
challenges as managerial and elite perceptions regarding mill girl docility collapsed in the face of regular outbreaks of, sometimes industry wide, 'wildcat
strikes' and often raucous street protests, part of an emerging and distinctive
oary[2] culture of resistance, which itself represented the recurrence and pro-
gression of much longer-lived local traditions of workplace and community
mobilization and resistance and their melding with the cultural traditions of
the incoming migrant streams (Cox 2013, 82–88).

Up until the mid-nineteenth century, Dundee was known as Linenopolis,
reflecting the long-established importance of flax to the local economy,
stretching back to the medieval period. The development of the Crimean
War in the early 1850s, however, meant that the linen manufacturers were
denied access to their usual sources of Russian flax. Dundee thus turned
to Bengal jute, beginning a century-long imperial nexus, which underwent
a fundamental shift following the establishment of a massive jute industry
along the banks of the Hooghly River in West Bengal and its increasing challenge to Dundee in the export markets for cheap sacking during the 1870s
and 1880s. The response of the 'home industry' to mounting Indian competition—moving into more specialized product markets—led to a remaking of

the imperial nexus, with the largely illusory threat of 'cheap Indian labour competition' used as a justification for wage cuts, the increasing recruitment of *halflin*[3] labour and the bolstering of 'paternal despotism' (Cox 2013, 26–39).

By 1911, 66 percent of Dundee's occupied population was engaged in manufacturing, with the figure for the flax and jute industries at 48 percent, comprising around 40,000 workers, of which two-thirds were women (Jackson 1979, 98), while no less than one in eight were halflin workers of both sexes (Cox 2013, 68). As a result, Dundee became known as a 'she town' where many unskilled, and some skilled, adult male jute workers were periodically forced into becoming 'kettle boilers',[4] while shopkeepers within the city's mill districts were routinely forced to close their premises during the unpaid July summer holiday, or the 'Dundee fortnight', as it was locally known, because of a lack of paying customers. It can be surmised that there was barely a family in Dundee that was not in some way connected, either directly or indirectly, to jute.

Industrial production was clustered around the burns[5] that had encouraged the establishment of water-powered mills more than 100 years previously. These areas were linked by sometimes unbroken stretches of low-cost tenement housing in highly distinctive neighbourhoods and districts, such as Hawkhill, Coldside and the Hilltown. Although these districts offered accommodation of a sometimes highly rudimentary nature, they also provided important networks of support, including access to credit and information on job opportunities and wage rates, an essential requirement for long-term survival in the unforgiving labour market created by the imperial nexus and jute dependency.

The Dundee property market, as in Edinburgh and Glasgow, provided a modest but regular income for local investors, made up predominantly of shopkeepers and small businessmen, which, in effect, amounted to a middle-class form of social insurance (McCrone 1992, 183–84). The interests of these property owners were looked after by the Dundee Landlords' and House Factors' Association (LHFA). Despite its title, most of the members of the LHFA were actually factors,[6] tasked with letting and managing the properties of their landlord clients. The factors had extensive powers over the lives of ordinary Dundonians, particularly through the 'recommendations' that were required before a prospective client could rent a decent tenement flat, thus underlining the wider role of paternal despotism as a form of labour control and surveillance.

The amassing of local political power and influence had always been a prime objective of the LHFA from its establishment in 1882, when it had intervened on a whole number of issues that included preventing long-settled Irish immigrants and native unemployed workers from receiving poor relief and thus adding to the local rates. Their influence reached right into the heart of the city's council chambers. Many councillors had extensive property interests, including those who were also LHFA members, such as Charles Stewart, who, on becoming convenor of the Housing and Property Committee, gained extensive influence over decisions on unsanitary properties, lodgings and new buildings (Young 1991, 275–83).

While the LHFA proved to be quite effective in protecting the rights and interests of Dundee's propertied classes, it oversaw a housing market that seemed to be caught in an ever-deepening crisis. Although the 1890s had witnessed a slowing down in population growth, the city's housing situation actually worsened during this time because the tenements built earlier started to deteriorate. The council did close the worst of the slums, but this housing was only slowly replaced, leading to ever-worsening overcrowding.

By 1905, there was a habitation rate of 498 persons per acre in the most congested districts, but overcrowding was aggravated as a result of the city's high percentage of one- and two-room accommodations. No less than 49.2 percent of tenants lived more than two persons to a room, compared with 47.8 percent in Glasgow, 37.7 percent in Aberdeen and 32.7 percent in Edinburgh (Dundee Social Union 1905, vi–vii). Indeed, the figures for overcrowding in Dundee were actually more comparable to Calcutta, where it was thought that 'more than half the inhabitants have less than half a room per head, and 90 percent have three quarters of a room or less' (Gait 1984, 400). In effect, the establishment and remaking of the imperial nexus of jute had sowed the seeds for the emergence of social and housing conditions in Dundee that were more redolent of the so-called 'Orient'.

CLASS STRUGGLE AND SOCIALIST POLITICS IN JUTEOPOLIS

Between 1910 and 1914, a wave of industrial militancy enveloped many British cities in response to increased 'speed ups' and wage cuts and Dundee was no exception. During the course of the national carters' strike in 1911, the 'city fathers' became so alarmed by mounting tension on the streets that they requested the help of the military: three hundred troops from the first battalion of the Black Watch and two hundred extra policemen were despatched, but shortly thereafter on 24 December, 1911, negotiations ended the strike. This, however, provided only a brief respite before the resumption of strike action in early 1912 at the massive Camperdown jute works in Lochee. The action was marked by levels of industrial violence not witnessed since the Chartist period, and so alarmed the mill managers that they armed their foremen with automatic pistols (Cox 2013, 100).

It was also during the 1912 strike that a teenage Mary Brooksbank encountered the enigmatic 'lassie wi' the green felt hat', who had suddenly emerged as a leading street and mill-gate organizer. Brooksbank was spellbound by this mysterious mill girl's defiance and her formidable gift of persuasion; 'She blew her whistle and gathered the mill girls around her, and, with a half loaf of bread round her neck, marched the strikers around the rest of the mills seeking other support. Their united determination won them a rise of 15 percent' (Brooksbank 1971, 20).

Brooksbank's brief description is all we know of 'the lassie wi the green felt hat', who disappeared as suddenly as she had emerged, back into the protective anonymity of the mass, typifying the lengths worker militants had to go to in order to protect themselves from the very real prospect of being blacklisted. The fact that rent-striking mill girls faced the same threat perhaps explains why none emerged as public representatives of the local movement, especially so when we consider that more 'organized' labour aristocrats, such as engineers and railwaymen, with union cards that offered some protection, came very much to the fore.

The 1912 strike, which ended in a definitive defeat for the jute barons,[7] also coincided with a developing housing conflict over the introduction of new national legislation aimed at bolstering tenant rights, which, in characteristic fashion, was seized upon by the LHFA as a justification for raising rents by 10 percent over and above the 25 percent rise that was supposed to cover the costs of implementing the new legislation. The response provoked by the landlords' actions led to the return of armed troops to Dundee and to the convening of an 'indignation meeting', attended by more than two thousand tenants and labour activists in January 1912 and organized jointly by the Scottish Prohibition Party (SPP), British Socialist Party (BSP) and Dundee Trades Council (DTC) (Petrie 2008, 46–47).

Further meetings took place over the following weeks, but the developing rent strike was thrown into disarray when landlords began approaching tenants to agree to new rents at a lower compromise level. By the middle of February, the movement was beginning to fizzle out as more tenants struck individual deals with their landlords, before the strike was effectively ended on 27 February when the city council approved a rent increase of 29.75 percent, rather than the 35 percent demanded by the landlords. While the 1912 Rent Strike was only partially successful, it gave many socialist activists and tenants an indication of what could be achieved with determination and organization (Petrie 2008, 47–49).

The central role played by the SPP and BSP in the 1912 Rent Strike underlines the diversity and depth of Dundee's working-class political culture at this time. Despite disdain from local political classes, and particularly the growing labour variant, the SPP became a serious contender with the

Labour Party for mass working-class support. Its long, steady rise from the first years of the twentieth century was, in no small measure, as a result of the charismatic leadership of Edwin 'Neddy' Scrymgeour, who pioneered a highly distinctive and local form of socialist millenarianism that grew out of the mid-nineteenth-century wave of Christian revivalism and in response to a developing liberal hegemony in working-class politics that accompanied the marginalization of Chartist radicalism.

Neddy Scrymgeour and the SPP succeeded in winning the ear of oary Dundee because, in sharp contrast to the BSP and their reverence for a highly dogmatic form of 'scientific socialism', they worked with and not against the grain of popular tradition and culture. Indeed, the SPP contained within itself some remarkable similarities to an older form of Christian millenarianism that had shaped local radical politics during the late eighteenth century (Cox 2013, 92–97).

The appeal of millenarianism during the early years of the twentieth century was, like its previous manifestations, rooted less in religious enthusiasm and more in material distress, feelings of insecurity and of a dread regarding future prospects, or lack of them. For many, caught within the increasingly comfortless folds of jute dependency, it must have seemed that the Apocalypse had arrived, or at the very least that it was on its way, which allows us to re-interrogate Eleanor Gordon's (and others) notion of the so-called fatalism of the mill girls (Gordon 1991, 210). If fatalism it was, then it was a radical fatalism psychologically connected to the material reality created by increasing jute dependency, the remaking of the imperial nexus and paternal despotism, all of which brought in their train inherent job insecurity, underemployment and awful housing conditions.

WAR, WORKERS' MILITANCY AND RENT STRIKES

In February 1915, the Fourth Battalion of the Black Watch, known as 'Dundee's Ain', was cheered enthusiastically by huge crowds as it made its way from Dudhope Barracks, overlooking the city centre, to West Station to board the trains that would take them on the first leg of their long journey to Flanders. Many of these recruits were jute workers who had enthusiastically rallied to the flag a few months before, while some of the companies were proudly led by the newly commissioned heirs of the city's textile dynasties, such as George Cox and his brother William. By May 1915, at the same time as Dundee's Ain nervously waited to be 'blooded' at Aubers Ridge, Juteopolis was booming as a result of a government order for four million sandbags, but the jute trade unions were struggling to keep track of spreading strikes as workers demanded wage increases to counteract rising prices and rents.

Mounting tensions were also evident on Clydeside, with the eruption of a major engineering strike in February 1915, which was followed by the sudden emergence of a rent-strike movement in Govan that rapidly assumed Glasgow-wide proportions. The government was keeping a close watch on these events, but its attention was also increasingly focused on Flanders. The war was not going to plan and heavy military losses in early 1915 led to rising anxiety in government, which culminated in the formation of a Coalition Cabinet, with the inclusion of Labour Members of Parliament (MP) such as Arthur Henderson and George Barnes, the Lochee-born MP for Glasgow Blackfriars.

One of the first acts of the new cabinet was the rushed introduction in July 1915 of the Munitions of War Act, which made it a penal offence for workers to leave employment or to take a new job without their employer's consent. The new act not only laid bare the class nature of the state and the collaboration of the right wing of the Labour Party but it also broke down political barriers on the left and led to increased unity between revolutionary and reformist socialists (Stewart 1967, 53–54).

By the second half of 1915, Glasgow's rent agitation had mushroomed in scale and was now accompanied by spreading strikes over the Munitions Act, rising prices and 'dilution'[8] under the leadership of the newly formed but 'unofficial' Clyde Workers Committee. While the linking up of rent agitators and worker militants on Clydeside was beginning to worry the authorities, the rent issue was also starting to re-exert itself in Dundee.

In July 1915, following complaints from trade union members faced with demands for increased rents, Dundee Trades Council (DTC) sent a resolution to the city council 'urging them to approach parliament' to take action on the issue. The Lord Provost's curt response, that 'it was ridiculous to suggest that rents were being unduly raised', was supported by 'all the property owning Councillors' (*Forward*, 23 October 1915, quoted in Petrie 2008, 50–51), effectively putting the city council on a collision course with many tenants already struggling as a result of growing financial pressures. Indeed, even John Sime, the secretary of the Jute and Flax Workers Union (JFWU), who also faced eviction, informed the Hunter Committee of Enquiry, in November 1915, that '[m]y wife tells me she spends all my wages on food to keep the house going' (HMG 1915, 61). If a relatively well-paid union official such as Sime, earning the same wage he had received as a mill foreman, was suffering financially, the situation facing many of his much lower-paid union members was increasingly desperate. Although their wages had increased by around 20 percent during the course of 1915, the cost of provisions and fuel had risen an estimated 42 percent (HMG 1915, 61). And because they rarely earned what might be described as a 'family wage', households headed by unskilled male jute workers, which were also more likely to contain halflins, were in particularly bad straits.

One-third of all households in Juteopolis were also female headed, by widows, women separated from former partners and young single working women, often part of a larger shared household with close friends and siblings, including halflins. In effect, the two most militant sections of Dundee's jute workforce, comprising halflin and adolescent workers, were being invited to resist, while being encouraged and supported by older workers who were often more reluctant to openly face down authority.

In August 1915, and blissfully unaware of the gathering storm that was about to hit them, the LHFA gave official notice of a 15 percent rent increase from November 11. In early September, as thousands of factors' notices were being delivered throughout the city, a self-styled 'Tenant' writing in the correspondence columns of the *Courier* denounced the landlords as 'unpatriotic' for attempting to raise rents, before asking pointedly, 'Glasgow tenants are up in arms. . . . Are the Dundee tenants to knuckle under?' (*Courier and Argus*, 25 September 1915). The answer to this question became increasingly clear through the autumn of 1915, with reports of 'numerous street corner and work gate meetings' taking place throughout the city on a daily basis (Petrie 2008, 55). Faced with a growing movement from below, which was out of their direct control, the DTC attempted to bring 'organisation' into the spreading dispute through the establishment, in September 1915, of a Joint Committee, made up of leading activists drawn from DTC and the Dundee Labour Representation Committee (LRC) (Petrie 2008, 52).

While the newly established DTC/LRC Joint Committee convened to discuss the finer points of organization, tenants across Dundee were already girding their loins for battle. On 16 October, the *Peoples Journal* informed readers that 'excitement . . . is increasing with the issue of the [rent] missives, and in many "lands" the housewives are organizing stairhead opposition to the landlords and the rent gatherers.' A few days later, following the issuing of 'quit notices' by many landlords, tenants 'retorted by fixing placards in their windows' intimating 'to house hunters that they need not expect to be allowed to "see the house"' (*Peoples Journal*, 23 October 1915). The increasing determination and unity demonstrated by tenants not only underlined their seriousness, but it also undermined LHFA unity because growing numbers of factors attempted to negotiate lesser rent increases with their tenants.

The Dundee rent agitation was unfolding against the background of increasingly disquieting news from Flanders. In February 1915, the Fourth Battalion had embarked for France with a complement of 900 men, but by September, and despite the arrival of replacements, it was reduced to about 420, following bloody engagements at Neuve Chapelle, Aubers Ridge and Festubert. And over the course of three days, between September 25 and 27, Dundee's Ain were effectively wiped out when a further 230 men were killed or wounded at the Battle of Loos. This included all but one of the battalion's officers, who were easily identified by German snipers because of the gleaming red hackles on their bonnets.

As news of the carnage at Loos became known, widespread stupefaction quickly turned into a rising sense of anger. Mary Brooksbank (1971, 6), who was later jailed for forty days for her part in a local anti-war demonstration at the first Armistice Day celebrations, vividly recalled this many years later, when she wrote that the 'Cameronians, the Black Watch, and the Royal Scots claimed their recruits from Craigie mill, and as the casualty list grew, our Patriotism evaporated.' Anti-war activists, including Scrymgeour, now came into their own, and to the increasing attention of the authorities, for their denunciations of both the mounting slaughter and the actions of the city's landlords who were intent on increasing the rents of families with soldiers at the front.

The unprecedented slaughter of Dundee's Ain in 1915 contributed greatly towards the city's total wartime losses of around 4,123, representing an attrition rate of 1:48, compared with Glasgow's rate of 1:57. Indeed, Dundee earned the unenviable distinction of having the highest proportion of deaths of any large town or city in Scotland, which itself suffered a greater proportion of fatalities (26.4 percent, compared with a British army average of 11.8 percent) than all but two countries involved in the conflict, comprising Turkey and Serbia (Cox 2013, 221, 224). The extent of this legalized massacre also lent the Dundee Rent Strike a ferocity that completely wrong-footed the authorities at a local and national level and also contributed towards the further postwar radicalization of the city's working class.

In Glasgow, the Association of House Factors and Property Agents (AHFPA) had attempted to boost their ailing image by agreeing that servicemen's dependents would not have their rents raised (McLean 1999, 21). In Dundee, however, the LHFA had no such qualms. At the end of November 1915, Sheriff Baillie Barnes ordered a soldier's wife to remove herself and her three children from their tenement within a week after she had fallen two weeks in arrears with her rent. Mrs. McAdam, who had repeatedly tried to pay her rent at the old rate, protested strongly at the decision, remarking, '[w]hen your man's away they fling you onto the street.' (*People's Journal*, 27 November 1915)

In early October 1915, a letter to the local press, under the nom de plume 'Strafe der Landlords', had suggested that tenants should publicly unmask the 'landlord Huns', who were often also shopkeepers with businesses in the mill districts (*Dundee Advertiser*, 9 October 1915). This suggestion was enthusiastically taken up by tenant activists, who compiled a 'no payment' blacklist of local shopkeepers with rented property, while 'blackleg tenants' who accepted the houses of rent strikers were to be shunned (*Forward*, 23 and 27 October 1915, cited in Petrie 2008, 54). The halflin militants of Dundee also came to the fore by looking out for the approach of bailiffs and factors and by parading the streets with placards while singing the strike song, 'Are we downhearted?', which had been a popular ditty during the 1911 carters stoppage. On that occasion, local carters had received an outpouring of support and solidarity from oary Dundee, and in 1915 they reciprocated in kind by refusing to uplift goods from properties where tenants were on strike.

Throughout October, with notices defying the factors suddenly appearing in windows throughout the city, it was further reported that ad hoc yet 'highly organised' tenant groups were 'combining to refuse to pay the increase', while declaring their 'determination to oppose removal' (*Forward*, 18 October 1915, quoted in Petrie 2008, 55). Official concern regarding unfolding events in Dundee also mounted, to the extent that the Prime Minister, Lloyd George, was being briefed on the local protests (*Dundee Advertiser*, 25 October 1915).

The difficulties that labour activists were experiencing in bringing the gathering rent strike under control led to the calling of a citywide 'indignation meeting' on 11 October, which was swelled to such an extent by a 'considerable number of women' that an overflow meeting had to be held. The anger of many of the women in the audience startled the organizers, but, in sharp contrast to the approach of Glasgow's labour activists, the LRC avoided establishing a Dundee tenants' organization. Instead, a limited local strike within engineering and shipbuilding was proposed to force government to intervene on the rent issue, which underlined both the seriousness of the developing situation in Dundee, and the fear of local labour leaders that they could not properly control the jute workers.

With many jute workers—including a fair proportion with relations at the front—becoming increasingly militant, many labour leaders baulked at involving them in the proposed industrial action, which would have been akin to holding a tiger by the tail. It therefore made perfect strategic sense—from the point of view of the DTC/LRC—to concentrate strike action in shipbuilding and engineering, a strategy that would avoid the mass of the city's lower-paid jute workers suffering from loss of wages, while still allowing them to participate through street protests and the withholding of rents. In the event of evictions of any serious scale, however, it is unlikely that the labour leaders would have been able to prevent strike action from engulfing the jute industry.

As the 11 November deadline for the signing of the new rent agreements approached, the attempt to bring strikers before the courts was deplored by the local press, which commented, 'no matter what economics may have to say in such cases, merely to proceed with them is to play with fire' (*Peoples Journal*, 27 November 1915). In the event, the deadline came and went without the expected scenes of conflict. Very little flitting[9] was reported; the possibility of trouble seemed to stay the hand of those who may otherwise have been tempted to rent a striker's house. In the end, tenants and landlords alike waited to see how the national government would respond to the mounting crisis (Young 1991, 381–82).

Although the situation on Clydeside and Dundee was a particular cause of official concern in Scotland, rent strikes were also worrying the authorities in Aberdeen, Kircaldy and Leith on the east coast; Mid-Lanark, Clydebank, Greenock, Cambuslang and Hamilton on the west coast; and Annan and Gretna in the south. There were increasing fears within government circles that these disputes, if not brought to a speedy resolution, could threaten war production, and by linking up with the English rent strikes, become transformed into a unified and Britain-wide challenge to government authority.

The government was, though, becoming increasingly aware of the potential consequences of continued inaction, and on 17 November, the Scottish Secretary, MacKinnon Wood, delivered a memo to the Cabinet advocating a bill limiting working-class rentals to prewar levels. The reasons he gave for proposing this abrupt about-turn in government policy and classical political economy were compelling: 'The agitation is growing, and I think it is necessary that a prompt decision should be taken by the Government, otherwise there are signs that demands for interference will become more clamant and will expand in scope and character' (Quoted in McLean 1999, 23).

That these fears had some substance was demonstrated by the swelling rent agitation; in Glasgow, it was reported that fifteen thousand tenants had refused to pay increased rents by the end of October, and by mid-November this figure had increased to twenty thousand, including five Labour councillors (*Forward*, 30 October and 13 November 2015, cited in McLean 1999, 22). Wood's rising anxiety was shared by George, who had been keeping a close watch on the unfolding rent strike, and who, as we have already seen, was particularly concerned by events in Glasgow and Dundee. The scope of organization and reach of the rent strikes was worrying and seemed set to assume revolutionary proportions if the root cause for their emergence was not quickly removed. It was no surprise, then, that Wood's memo was accepted without demur by the Coalition Cabinet, and in the week before Christmas 1915, the government rushed a bill through parliament that restricted British rents to prewar levels (Milton 1973, 103–104).

CONCLUSION

The co-option of the Labour Party into the wartime coalition government was a defining event in British class relations, sparking a reaction of such fury from many labour activists that it temporarily 'fractured the trade union movement as an effective instrument of control' (Foster 1976, 25). In response, a new unofficial movement quickly emerged in many of Britain's major industrial areas, comprising rank-and-file workers' committees, alongside many rejuvenated and radicalized trades councils. It was these organizational groupings that, in most cities and towns, provided the leadership for the 1915 Rent Strike; a two-tier mass movement of trade union and socialist activists alongside ad hoc tenant groups, many of which were formed, as in Glasgow, under the influence of labour activists. The coming together of these separate but linked organizational strands gave the events of 1915 its militant, even revolutionary, character.

For John Foster, the eruption of the 1915 Rent Strike in Glasgow underlined the importance of the emergent 'unofficial' trade union movement: 'At last a situation had arisen in which the progressive, unifying class forces so long imprisoned inside the trade union movement could now be released' (Foster 1976, 25). There is some substance in Foster's argument, but questions remain regarding the extent of trade union influence on the 1915 rent-strike movement in Dundee. Although the DTC/LRC Joint Committee and socialist groupings did play an important part in presenting tenant demands to the authorities and in mobilizing local labour movement support, they did not, as claimed by Petrie, orchestrate or control the Dundee rent-strike movement (Petrie 2008, 52). Instead, it was organized on a street-by-street basis, through word of mouth, by informal groups comprising extended families, neighbours, friends and workmates. Indeed, the greatest achievement of the DTC/LRC Joint Committee may well have been their willingness *not* to impose their forms of organization and leadership on the oary rent-strike movement. This interpretation also challenges Young's (1991, 383) suggestion that:

> The unusual structure of household income which existed in Dundee, with its reliance on paid female labour, may in some ways have contributed to the lack of a local network of resistance. With the women tied to a long working day, and yet still responsible for family welfare, there would have been little time or energy left to devote to fighting the factors or marching to the city chambers.

In Glasgow, citywide coordination through the medium of a central tenants' organization was an essential prerequisite for the success of the rent strike, but Dundee was a much smaller and more compact city. Word of any evictions would have quickly spread, drawing large crowds from the immediate neighbourhood and from wider afield—and would almost certainly have led to the development of strikes within many jute mills. Although there was no formal organization in Dundee, aside from that provided by the DTC/LRC, working-class self-organization was very evident, as both Petrie and Young themselves acknowledge when they point to the 'stairhead meetings' that were reportedly taking place all across the city at the height of the rent strike in September and October 1915 (Young 1991, 383; Petrie 2008, 55).

These stairhead and close meetings quickly transformed themselves into neighbourhood networks of resistance during the rent strikes and were much more important to spreading and sustaining the movement than the DTC/ LRC Joint Committee. Indeed, Young herself states that it was the 'possibility of trouble, or tenant solidarity that put people off trying to rent a striker's house', and not the demands of the DTC/LRC for government regulation of housing policy (Young 1991, 383). It is also worth bearing in mind that 'long working hours' and responsibilities for 'family welfare' had failed to curb the militancy of married women jute workers in the prewar years and would prove just as ineffectual in curbing their rising militancy in the period up to and beyond the end of the war.

For both Young and Petrie, the absence of evidence for women jute workers emerging as public leaders and activists of the Dundee Rent Strike functions as evidence for their absence from *any* meaningful involvement in the local movement as a whole. However, perhaps, the real reason for their lack of presence in the correspondence columns of the local press and on the rostrums of public indignation meetings was more prosaic. As we have already seen, the blacklist was an ever-present threat for workers and rent strikers who dared to question or challenge the mill managers and factors, as is demonstrated in the case of Mary Brooksbank. She had started work in a jute mill at the age of eleven and became very familiar with the blacklist as well as various police cells as a result of her activities as a teenage worker militant and budding anti-war activist during the First World War. Her continued reluctance to bend the knee led to frequent sackings and long periods on the dole, forcing her to eke out a living picking raspberries, working in canning factories and at the sack sewing—pittance paying occupations reserved for the most desperate and wretched within Dundee's narrow labour market. For those many workers, militant or otherwise, who were not prepared to take the 'rauchle road'[10] trod by Brooksbank, but who were, compelled to challenge authority, the only alternative, as with 'the lassie wi' the green felt hat', was to keep their identities as secret as possible.

There were some jute workers, however, who were far from reticent about openly advertising their defiance. Halflin and young adult jute workers of both sexes participated in the events of 1915, not simply as raucous street mobs, but as major actors in their own right. Although their wages were low, many had a level of independence and confidence, which, when combined with youthful high spirits, ensured that they were often to the fore in work disputes. They were frequent instigators of wildcat strikes, which, as in 1895, could assume industrywide proportions that were often supported by older workers, not least because many families of the working poor depended on the wages earned by

Tony Cox

them. They were no marginal elements in a struggle that had little bearing on their lives, but an important, indeed leading, fraction of oary Dundee.

The 1915 Rent Strike graphically underlined the manner in which combined and uneven development led to a collision between two very different forms of class resistance and organization: on the one hand, oary community and neighbourhood mobilization; and on the other, the institutionalized and bureaucratic form of class organization increasingly practised by socialist parties and trade unions. The future may have seemed to belong to the latter movement, but the 1915 Rent Strike underlined the vibrant power of oary Dundee, and how, under certain conditions, the support networks and forms of community mobilization associated with it could develop into a potentially revolutionary force.

The interwar period would witness its continuing power and relevance, as revolutionary socialism and trade union organization sank deeper roots, impacting upon and merging with the oary tradition and enabling Dundee to vie with Glasgow to become recognized as *the* Red centre of Scottish and British socialism. The closely packed tenement districts of Juteopolis would survive into the period after the Second World War, before being largely obliterated by the first wave of urban 'regeneration', which, though badly needed, contributed to the breaking up and dispersal of the close-knit communities and dense support networks that had long sustained the oary culture of resistance. Despite its apparent peculiarity, there is much that the new housing movements can learn from oary Dundee, not least by underlining and confirming the thesis of many contributors in this volume, that modern movements resisting the neoliberal 'race to the bottom' can only be really powerful engines of radical political change when they are organized by and on behalf of those with most to gain from that change.

NOTES

1. Hecklers 'dressed' flax by using a comblike implement called a *heckle*. Although they were largely swept away by mechanization, the Dundee hecklers made their way into the English language, the term *heckling* being directly derived from their reputation for political disputation.

2. *Oary* is the distinctive Dundee rendering of the Scots word *orra* and is commonly used to describe the working-class Scots dialect of Dundee. It has multiple meanings, the most common being 'of persons or things spare, unoccupied; also meaning extra, odd or superfluous' (Robinson 1985, 455). I have employed the term to describe the distinctive working-class culture that emerged in Dundee during the nineteenth century.

3. Doric rendering of 'half timer', which referred to workers younger than age fourteen who mixed paid employment with schoolwork.

4. 'Kettle boiler' described a male worker who was often, but not always, married, and who stayed home to keep house while his partner or wife worked.

5. A *burn* is a small stream or river in Scots.

6. A *factor* is an agent who manages land or property for its owner or holder.

7. The employers fully accepted the JFWU demands for fixing an average rate of wages in preparing and spinning and the establishment of a labour disputes committee.

8. *Dilution* referred to the practice of replacing skilled with unskilled, particularly female, labour.

9. Scots and northern English term for moving house.

10. A phrase taken from the poem, 'Nae Regrets'. See Mary Brooksbank, 2009. *Sidlaw Breezes*. Dundee: David Winter & Son Ltd., 40. *Rauchle* in Scots refers to something ramshackle or dilapidated.

REFERENCES

Primary Sources

Dundee Advertiser, 9 October 1915, 25 October 1915.
Dundee Courier and Argus, 25 September 1915.
Peoples Journal, 16 October 1915, 23 October 1915, 27 November 1915.
Textile Workers' Guide (no. 2), April 1916.

Secondary Sources

Brooksbank, Mary. 2009. *Sidlaw Breezes*. Dundee: David Winter & Son Ltd.
———. 2017. *No Sae Lang Syne*. Dundee: Dundee Printers Ltd.
Cox, Anthony. 2013. *Empire, Industry and Class: The Imperial Nexus of Jute, 1840–1940*. Abingdon: Routledge.
Dundee Social Union. 1905. *Report on Housing and Industrial Conditions in Dundee*. Dundee.
Foster, John. 1976. "British Imperialism and the Labour aristocracy." In *1926: The General Strike*, edited by Jeffrey Skelley, 3–58. Southampton: Lawrence and Wishart.
Gait, Edward A. 1984. *Imperial Gazetteer of India: Bengal, Vol. I*. New Delhi: Usha.
Gordon, Eleanor. 1991. *Women and the Labour Movement in Scotland, 1850–1914*. Oxford: Oxford University Press.
HMG. 1915. "Report of the Committee to Enquire into the Circumstances Connected with the Alleged Recent Increases in the Rental of Small Dwelling houses in Industrial Districts in Scotland." Edinburgh: His Majesty's Stationary Office.
Jackson, J. M. 1979. "Economic Life: A General Survey." In *Third Statistical Account of Scotland: The City of Dundee*, edited by J. M. Jackson, 97–104. Arbroath: The Herald Press.

McCrone, David. 1992. "Towards a Principled Society: Scottish Elites in the Twentieth Century." In *People and Society in Scotland, Vol. III*, edited by Anthony Dickson and James H. Treble, 174–200. Edinburgh: John Donald.

McLean, Iain. 1999. *The Legend of Red Clydeside*. Edinburgh: John Donald.

Milton, Nan. 1973. *John MacLean*. London: Pluto.

Petrie, Ann. 2008. *The 1915 Rent Strikes: An East Coast Perspective*. Dundee: Abertay Historical Press.

Robinson, Mairi, 1985. *The Concise Scots Dictionary*. Exeter: Chambers.

Stewart, Bob. 1967. *Breaking the Fetters*. London: Lawrence and Wishart.

Young, Jean K. 1991. "From 'Laissez-Faire' to 'Homes fit for Heroes': Housing in Dundee, 1868–1919." PhD diss., University of St. Andrews.

Chapter 4

Spatial Composition and the Urbanization of Capital

The 1915 Glasgow Rent Strikes and the Housing Question Reconsidered

Neil Gray

Rent Strikes are a valuable subject for studying class experience and direct action by the working class. Their distinctive character and the alliance of interest forged in the communities indicate a neglected area of labour history. . . . Equally important perhaps as the point of production, is the point of habitation with its own forms of communication and expression, its own peculiarities, values and experience.

—Joseph Melling (1979, 43)

A narrow focus on the point of production in the workplace within the Left has tended to obscure what the geographer William Bunge (1977) refers to as *the second front*: 'the point of reproduction'. For Bunge, the actual geography of the working class lies overwhelmingly at the point of social reproduction, in areas such as housing, welfare, transport, schooling, care and amenities. Yet this sphere has received far too little attention in studies of class relations. As noted in the Introduction, such neglect is evidenced by the paucity of material covering community struggles over housing and consumption, which have typically been undertaken by tenants and residents without funding or institutional support from trade unions or other Left organizations (Moorhouse et al. 1972; Sklair 1975; Bradley 2014). As Grayson observes, such organizations have historically focused on predominantly male wage-labour relations in the workplace at the expense of typically women-led community and tenant organizations (Grayson 1996, 6). Notwithstanding the necessity of ongoing struggles in the workplace, here I share Bunge's (1977,

61) contention that a 'dual concentration' is required at both the point of production and the point of reproduction.

Addressing the neglect of the second front in relation to both the 1915
Rent Strikes and the contemporary housing situation, I re-examine Engels'
The Housing Question (1942 [1872]), an influential discussion on housing
within the Marxist milieu and beyond. Engels saw the politics of housing as
a 'secondary contradiction' behind the 'primary contradiction' of the wage-
labour relation, and this prognosis has been a central, if subliminal, influence
on how the Left more broadly addresses, or fails to address, the housing question. My contention here is that Engels' thesis had validity in the 1870s, and
arguably much of the twentieth century, when considered in relation to the
emergence of a powerful workers' movement within industry and manufacturing. But in a period in Britain and Ireland marked by industrial decomposition,[1]
a resurgent rentier economy (Hudson 2010; Harvey 2012; Robertson 2015) and
the increasing centrality of housing to respective national political economies
and the structures of capitalism, the housing question must be reconsidered.

Reappraising Engels' *The Housing Question* within the specific historical
context in which it was written, I mobilize the method of 'class composition'—
the most distinctive concept to arise from Italian Autonomist Marxism (AM) in
1960s and 1970s Italy (Cleaver 1979; Wright 2002)—to consider how housing
politics must be rethought within specific determinate historical-geographical
and socioeconomic relations. Class composition refers to the dialectical relation between technical and political composition. 'Technical composition'
relates to organized capitalist production, including the division of labour,
technological deployment, social planning, supervision and discipline. 'Political composition' refers to the degree to which workers make collective political subjectivity and self-organization a basis for counterpower (Cleaver 1979;
Wright 2002; Negri 2005; Midnight Notes 2002). Here, I develop the method
of class composition through the concept of 'spatial composition'. By spatial
composition I mean a study of the relation between the technical and political
composition of capital, as outlined previously, with an explicit focus on the
organization and contestation of socio-spatial relations. The aim of this chapter
is to provide a substantive theoretical and material rationale for engaging with
the housing question as a central, rather than secondary, arena of anti-capitalist
organization by illustrating the continuity of the housing problem, and tenants'
organizational attempts to overcome it, over a century of housing struggles.

THE URBANIZATION OF CAPITAL

Central to my deployment of spatial composition analysis is the work of
the Marxist urban theorist, Henri Lefebvre. Lefebvre's thesis in *The Urban*

Revolution (2003 [1970])—that urbanization was gradually superseding indus-trialization as a motor of capital accumulation in many Western economies from the late 1960s—becomes more relevant with each passing year. His 'capital switching' thesis provides a vital means for understanding the production of space as a general *tendency* with profound political implica-tions, much as Marx understood industrial *production in general* as the dialectical foundation for workers' organization in the nineteenth century. Lefebvre's then-speculative thesis has since been refined and mobilized by numerous critical urban geographers (Harvey 1982, 1985; Beauregard 1994; Gotham 2009; Aalbers and Christophers 2014) and defined as a switch of capital 'from the world of productive capital to the world of financialized, surplus-capital-swollen real estate' (Christophers 2011, 1361). But if capital-switching interpretations have been extremely useful in shifting attention to the urban question, in merely describing the relations between capital, governance and urbanism, they have tended to elide the situated, subversive aspects of Lefebvre's work along with his wider critique of political economy (Charnock 2010; Gray 2017). Reconsidering Lefebvre's urbanization thesis here through the radical theory and praxis of AM offers a more agency-oriented approach to the housing question, which is inextricably linked to the urban question.

Analysing the 1915 Rent Strikes through a spatial composition analysis, I aim to situate them within wider concerns over urbanization, social repro-duction and consumption—concerns which have often been obscured by a theoretical separation of productive and reproductive spheres. In this way, the rent strikes can be understood as part of a broader class contest characterized by what Melling (1983, 114) terms 'a mass concern with the facts of everyday life'. This position diverges from a certain reading of the rent strikes exem-plified by the influential urban sociologist, Manuel Castells, who follows Engels' position to the letter by characterizing the rent strikes as a 'secondary contradiction' behind the 'primary contradiction' of labour struggles in the workplace (Castells 1983, 36). In doing so, Castells restates Engels' convinc-ing polemic in *The Housing Question*: there can be no solution to the housing problem as long as the capitalist mode of production remains intact.

Engels' thesis has the great merit of viewing housing within a wider set of capitalist class relations, foregrounding the control and ownership of housing within a wider property regime. But this position has tended to undervalue the ongoing relevance and significance of housing struggles, with the leading role of women in the sphere of social reproductive struggles typi-cally relegated behind a 'forward march of labour' (Smyth 1992), a march that no longer holds the same strategic political capacity in deindustrialized Britain and never did in nonindustrialized Ireland (McCabe 2011). In a con-text where urbanization is a central pillar of capital accumulation in most of

Western Europe, where housing is one of the main drivers of British and Irish capitalism and where a usurious rentier economy, against predictions of its demise, has returned with a vengeance, housing struggles can no longer be seen as secondary concerns—if they ever could—but must be seen as central contradictions in themselves. In an ideal scenario, struggles at both the point of production and the point of reproduction should be combined, but history shows that the point of reproduction is typically relegated behind the point of production (Bunge 1977; Damer 2000a; Grayson 1996; Moorhouse et al. 1972). In this context, as Bryant (1982) asks: should tenant and resident organizations succumb to political paralysis without support from the labour movement and trade unions? Should activity on the housing question be seen as doomed to failure without such support? Re-examining Engels' original theses, I reaffirm housing as a central node of organizing against the relations of capital by way of a reconsideration of the 1915 Rent Strikes.

HOUSING STRUGGLE: A SECONDARY CONTRADICTION?

Most commentators agree that collective consumption and social reproduction were key concerns in the 1915 Rent Strikes (Damer 1980, 2000b; Melling 1983; Castells 1983; Smyth 1992). Yet for Castells, the rent strikes were not a struggle against capital and the capitalist class, but a more limited struggle against the banks, the rentier class, petty speculators, investors, landlords and bondholders. He reinforces this point by noting Melling's (1983) observation that industrial employers on Clydeside actively supported demands for rent control and state subsidized housing as a means to retain and enhance worker productivity in the factories.[2] Fearing unrest in the workplace and the difficulties of attracting skilled workers because of high rents, the employers themselves engaged in the construction of housing for workers while supporting housing reform as a means of 'ensuring social peace and creating channels for the integration of the militant working class' (Castells 1983, 35). This position accords with accounts of the financing of public housing after the First World War, which, to quote a parliamentary secretary was designed as an 'insurance against Bolshevism and revolution' by way of deflecting housing discontent and absorbing the labour of five million military-trained demobilized workers, in case they put that training to revolutionary use (Swenarton 1981, 94).

Castells is careful to acknowledge that such correctives to overly romanticized and one-sided accounts of the rent strikes should not negate their achievements: the high level of social consciousness and organization reached; the capacity of the working class to impose its own conditions on the processes of consumption and the social wage; and the general weakening of the capitalist class vis-à-vis the labour movement overall. In many ways, he argues, the 1915 rent strikers confirmed Engels' conclusion in *The Housing Question*: capitalism cannot be trusted to resolve the housing crisis. Yet, ultimately Castells contends that the rent strikes may only have 'instigated social reform within capitalism, while simultaneously integrating the political representatives of labour within the historical framework of liberal democracy' (1983, 36). Such a reading of the rent strikes follows another formulation in *The Housing Question*:

> As long as the capitalist mode of production continues to exist, it is folly to hope for an isolated solution of the housing question or of any other social question affecting the fate of the workers. The solution lies in the abolition of the capitalist mode of production and the appropriation of all means of life and labour by the working class itself. (1942 [1872], 77)

The importance of this statement has hardly diminished. Yet the capitalist mode of production in Britain and Ireland has changed markedly since Engels' time, and its potential supersession, as Marx and Engels foresaw it, has been thwarted, in Britain and much of Western Europe at least, by the decomposition of once powerful workers' movements. Any significant challenge to capitalism in this context will now require quite different means than those that could reasonably be forecasted in the nineteenth century. Re-examining *The Housing Question* through the autonomous Marxist method of 'the tendency'—in the context of the historical period within which it was written—the traction of Engels' analyses for the contemporary housing question is questioned here in light of significant transformations in class composition in Britain and Ireland. 'Tendency' here refers to an immanent method, devised by Marx and mobilized by AM, of grasping significant structural and institutional changes in modes of production and reproduction and the new forms of class composition and political organization that shape or respond to such transformations.

THE HOUSING QUESTION RECONSIDERED

With the recent 'proliferation of forms of rent' across the entire economic spectrum (Vercellone 2010, 85), *The Housing Question* has been revisited by numerous urbanists, geographers and housing scholars (Harvey 2012; Hodkinson 2012a; Slater 2013; Robertson 2015). As Harvey (2012) has shown, the 2007–2008 'sub-prime' housing crisis in the United States and Europe was no mere exception, but only one instance of a series of financial crises with origins in urban speculation since the 1970s. Yet, with the exception of critical urban geographers such as Harvey, the urban roots of financial crises have historically remained largely unexamined in both mainstream and Marxist political economy, with urban investment treated as secondary to other matters in the national economy, and urban struggles routinely dismissed as partial and reformist rather than systemic movements against capitalist relations:

> the structure of thinking within Marxism is distressingly similar to that within bourgeois economics. The urbanists are viewed as specialists, while the truly significant core of macroeconomic Marxist theorizing lies elsewhere. (Harvey 2012, 35)

With gentrification becoming a 'global urban strategy' (Smith 2002), and with housing centred in many national political economies (Aalbers and Christophers 2014)—with obvious detrimental effects—the urban question is now more mainstream. Yet, the political implications arising from the production of space *in general* (Lefebvre 1991, 2003 [1970]) have still to be properly grasped, and this requires a critical engagement with canonical Marxist texts. Harvey cites no particular examples, but probably the major reference point within Marxism is Engels' *The Housing Question*, a book compiled retrospectively from three pamphlets written in 1872 for *Der Volksstaat*, the central organ of the German Social Democratic Workers' Party. This intervention into contemporary debates around housing comprises a polemic primarily critiquing conservative calls for homeownership for the working classes within the German social democratic movement, bourgeois philanthropic views of socialism and the housing question and the German social democratic supporters of the French anarchist, Pierre-Joseph Proudhon. In particular it attacks Proudhon's defence of homeownership and his notions of exchangeable 'labour time' and 'eternal justice',[3] which Marx convincingly dismantled in *The Poverty of Philosophy* (1847).

Inverting the sequence of the book, I begin here with Part Two before discussing part One, the two most substantial sections. In *How the Bourgeoisie Solves the Housing Question*, Engels berates a certain Dr. Sax for adopting liberal, moral and legal phrases to resolve the housing question and for naively imagining that the bourgeoisie of the time could be persuaded to help raise the 'so-called property-less class' to the level of 'the propertied classes' (Engels 1942 [1872], 45). Notably, and perhaps counterintuitively for many who carelessly equate Marxism with statism, this involves an attack on Sax's moralistic and idealistic recourse to the (Prussian) state, which for Engels is 'nothing but the organized collective power of the possessing classes, the landowners and the capitalists as against the exploited classes, the peasants and the workers' (Engels 1942 [1872], 71). Such forms of bourgeois social-ism, Engels argues, desire to preserve the *basis* of all evils in society while wanting to abolish the evils themselves. Yet, he contends:

> it is an unavoidable preliminary condition of the capitalist mode of production that a really, and not a so-called property-less class, should exist, a class which has nothing to sell but its labour power and which is therefore compelled to sell its labour power to the industrial capitalists. (45)

Without explaining the housing crisis from existing conditions in their total-ity, he asserts that bourgeois socialism:

> has no other resource but to deliver moral sermons to the capitalists, moral sermons whose emotional effects immediately evaporate under the influence of private interests, and if necessary, of competition. (47)

In reality, Engels continues in some of his most famous passages, the bour-geoisie has only one method of solving the housing question, a method that continually reproduces the problem anew: 'This method is called Hauss-mann' (74). He refers here to Baron von Haussmann's notorious large-scale slum demolition and renewal programmes in Second Empire Paris, a model whereby the housing question is not resolved but rather '*shifted elsewhere!*' (77). This model was reproduced in numerous European cities afterwards, including Glasgow, where seventy thousand residents of the Old Town were made homeless in the late nineteenth century through the auspices of the Glasgow Improvement Scheme (1866–1901) and associated railway clear-ances, only to generate and exacerbate appalling slum housing conditions in Cowcaddens district and the city's East End (Edwards 1999). In a current context marked by widespread 'neo-Haussmannization' (Merrifield 2014), Engels' analysis here remains highly prescient.

However, in Part One, *How Proudhon Solves the Housing Question*, Engels' assertions are bound by historical contingency. Rightly lambasting Proudhon and his German followers for analyzing housing as only one frag-mented aspect of capitalist expropriation, he argues that housing is in fact only one of the numerous lesser 'secondary evils' resulting from the primary 'pivot' of exploitation in the reigning mode of production (22). For real social change to occur, he contends, the housing question must confront the labour question:

> it is not the solution of the housing question which simultaneously solves the social question, but only by the solution of the social question, that is, by the abolition of the capitalist mode of production, is the solution of the housing question made possible. (29)

56   *Neil Gray*

In a contemporary context where housing is routinely separated off into a specialist domain by policy makers, economists, planners, architects and academics (Madden and Marcuse 2016), this position has the great merit of examining housing within a totality of socially mediated relations, while placing the question of control of housing production frontally. This standpoint is more necessary than ever in the current conjuncture, yet Engels' emphasis on the centrality of concentrated mass industrial wage labour for social transformation—'accumulation and concentration of capital on the one hand and of the proletariat on the other' (Engels 1942 [1872], 79)—is historically and geographically conjunctural. At a time when the strategic capacity of an emerging industrial working class was a central political concern for the labour movement in Europe, Engels' position was timely and prescient. But those who follow his line of argument in the present era should be wary of extrapolating his political conclusions from a particular historical period that is markedly different from the current context in Britain and Ireland today. Even at the time, Marx was rethinking his position around the centrality of industry in relation to the revolt of the Paris Commune in 1870, which was not dependent on industry or manufacturing, but rather united the spheres of production and consumption (Ross 2015, 91–116). In the current conjuncture in Western Europe, where urbanization has become a central pillar of capital accumulation, drastically altering the relations between production and social reproduction, the housing question must be reconsidered as a matter of urgency. Through the AM theory and praxis of class recomposition and the tendency,[4] I aim to invert Engels' own historical-materialist critique back onto him, opening up the 1915 Rent Strikes, and the housing question more generally, to substantive reinterpretation.

THE HOUSING QUESTION RECOMPOSED: THE METHOD OF THE TENDENCY

The historical-geographical context for Engels' critique in *The Housing Question* was delineated in the preface to the second German edition in 1877, where he outlines Germany's conditions of small-scale rural and domestic industry. The 'tendency' of German large-scale production until the revolutions of 1866 and 1870, in contrast to England and France, was production for an internal market; nowhere else in Western Europe, except notably in Ireland,[5] was rural domestic industry so prominent, and nowhere else were wages so low (1942 [1872], 14). Herein, Engels contends, lies the so-called 'blessing' of house and land ownership for workers that Dr. Mulberger espouses under the influence of Proudhon's idealized conception of individual handicraft industry (Engels 1942 [1872]). Workers cannot earn enough from their small-scale agriculture, Engels argues, so must accept paltry piecework in small-scale domestic industry, and because they cannot earn enough money from combining both agricultural and industrial work, they are chained to their house and garden. Where large-scale industry *did* develop in Germany, it was precisely because of the low wages and living conditions of its workers that it gained a place in the world market. By 1877, Engels observes, the relative worker affluence that had once resulted from the combination of agriculture and industry—and the ownership of home, garden and field—had become a hindrance to the entire German working class and the basis of their 'intellectual and political nullity' (Engels 1942 [1872], 12).

For Engels, then, it was 'petty-bourgeois utopia' to offer the workers their own dwelling; in reality this would only chain them in semi-feudal fashion to their individual domestic production and their own particular capitalist (17). Moreover, domestic production was already being violently done away with by the inexorable development of industry, incorporating the transformation of rural domestic workers into industrial domestic workers; the eradication of rural workers' domestic isolation as they were dragged into the 'social whirlpool'; and the extension of the industrial revolution over rural areas. This would lead, Engels contended, to the transformation of a rural conservative class of the population into a 'revolutionary hotbed' and the expropriation of machinery by the peasants, leading ultimately to peasant insurrection (17–18). Some of the most lyrical and potent passages in Marx's *The Communist Manifesto* (1848), of course, are dedicated precisely to this position, recognizing the significance of bourgeois industrial revolutions for shattering the fetters of landed interests and clarifying class antagonisms between the bourgeoisie and the proletariat.

This conception of political struggle, based on the tendential development and primary contradiction and pivot of wage labour, was the basis of much Marxist theorizing in Western Europe in the late nineteenth and early twentieth centuries, and for good reason, as evidenced by the scale and intensity of industrial conflict in that period. Marx's method of the tendency, as Hardt and Negri (2006) demonstrate, provides a crucial framework for understanding such shifts in the 'technical composition' of capital and their significance for 'political recomposition'. As social reality changes, they contend, so must our praxis: 'the method and the substance, the form and the content must correspond' (140). The method of the tendency requires careful study of contemporary conditions and a speculative turn of mind. Indeed, when Marx conceived of the industrial proletariat as a coming revolutionary subject in the mid-nineteenth century, industrial labour constituted only a small proportion of the major European economies. Yet Marx recognized a tendency that would become increasingly hegemonic, providing the material basis of future struggles. In this sense, the method of the tendency can be conceived not as a determining, or teleological, schema but instead as an 'adventure of reason' concerned with understanding mass subjective necessity within a determinate historical epoch (Negri 2005, 27).

What is required, Sergio Bologna (2007 [1977]) argues, are self-reflexive movements which are the antagonistic social expression of general tendencies in the new class composition, and his immanent dialectical conception of class composition holds vital political implications. For example, in his historical studies of the self-managed workers and factory council movements of the 1920s in Germany and Italy, he surmised that these workers' positive attitudes towards technology and their willingness to self-manage the production process arose because of their position as highly skilled 'professional' workers (Bologna 1992). Yet the arrival of Fordist mass production decomposed these cultures of self-management just as they were being affirmed in the shape of soviets and workers' councils. For Bologna, the automobile industry under Fordism was of fundamental historical importance politically because of its role in the tendential development of assembly-line work and the mass worker. Organizing around the newly developed category of the 'mass worker', workers in Italy's 'Hot Autumn' collectively mobilized against the division of labour in the factories, bargained for the abolition of wage differences and hierarchical job classifications and rejected piecework and productivity-linked bonuses. In doing so, they generated probably the most militant, long-lasting workers' struggles of the postwar era (see Cleaver 1979; Wright 2002).

Crucially, the 'mass worker' was not a ready-made term handed to AM, but instead a strategic neologism designed to conceptualize the recomposition of working-class unity in and against tendential changes to the technical composition of capital (Negri 2005). Although the introduction of the mass worker contributed to the decomposition of the skilled worker in industry, when AM politically recomposed the same subject, the mass worker became the basis for a broad socialization and generalization of antagonistic tendencies within and against mass industry. Yet, just as mass Fordist production deposed the professional worker in the early decades of the twentieth century, so the mass worker was deposed by disinvestment and decomposition in industry, as well as capital switching into the built environment, thus engendering new waves of 'territorial community activism' across urban Italy (Bologna 2007 [1977]; see also, Gray 2018). The context has been less explosive in Britain and Ireland than in Italy's 'Hot Autumn', but the method of the tendency and considerations of class recomposition can still be very useful in reconsidering historical and contemporary modes of political struggle.

We can easily see how a tendential conception of class recomposition could be applied to Engels' analyses in *The Housing Question*, but the tendency he envisaged—from rural domestic workers, to mass industrial work, to the workers' expropriation of the industrial mode of production, to prole-tarian insurrection—did not ultimately transpire. The hegemony of industry and manufacturing that provided a basis for such generalized insurrection has long been displaced in much of Western Europe by deindustrializa-tion, casualization, urbanization, financialization and the service industries, alongside offshoring and the geographical dispersal and fragmentation of industrial production across the global north and south. These amount to very deliberate strategies by capital and the state to decompose the collective power of the mass-workers' movements in Western Europe, which reached their zenith in the late 1960s and early 1970s. At the same time, usurping previous predictions of the 'euthanasia of the rentier', the resurgence of the rentier economy and debt has been exponential since the 1970s (Harvey 2012; Hudson 2010; Turner 2008; Vercellone 2010), generating new contra-dictions in class relations. In this context, it is salient to consider now how much the concerns of the rent strikers remain the concerns of the present, while the context of heavy industry and the related concerns of industrial workers on 'Red Clydeside' bears little relation to contemporary reality in most of Western Europe.

SPATIAL COMPOSITION AND THE 1915 RENT STRIKES

The 1915 Rent Strikes in Glasgow were played out in an exceptional con-text of labour unrest during an intense period of wartime production (see Introduction). The issue of 'dilution' (the use of labour-saving technology and deskilling through the introduction of unskilled male and female work-ers in the workplace) was a central flashpoint (Damer 1980; Melling 1983; Foster 1990; Griffin 2015). Dilution, which can be seen as the decomposi-tion of a unified workforce, threatened craft hierarchies and wage levels and was undoubtedly sectional in that it set trade against trade, skilled against unskilled and male against female (Mclean 1983; Damer 1990; Smyth 1992). Yet the dilution issue also helped generate a highly volatile political context that threatened capital and state management of both the workplace and the domestic sphere, contributing significantly to wider unrest around the rent issue. Dilution contributed to decomposition in the workplace from the point of view of skilled craft workers, but it was also a locus of political recomposi-tion between the spheres of production and social reproduction.

Because many men were abroad at war, women experienced collective organized direct action in the unionized production process, often for the first time, and this experience was 'readily transferred' back to generate political unrest in the community and reproductive sphere (Foster 1990, 41). Such unrest is captured in official government reports of the time, which indicate deep concern over increased industrial conflict and the potential stoppage of wartime production via militant organization and workers' solidarity over substandard housing conditions (Castells 1983; Foster 1990; Glynn 2009). The threat of a general strike notice by the Govan Trades Council over increased rents, involving up to thirty thousand workers (Foster 1990), was undoubtedly one major reason why legislation over rent restrictions was hastily enacted. This fact is central to Castells' (1983) claim that the rent strikes were only a secondary contradiction and that the real reason the rent strikes succeeded was because of a militant munitions labour force.

Yet there was no *necessary* relation between industrial threat and rent concessions. The labour threat was strategically vital to the rent strikes—and there are important lessons there about combining workplace and social reproductive struggles, which have routinely been overlooked or merely given tokenistic attention by the labour movement and trade unions (Damer 2000a; Grayson 1996; Moorhouse et al. 1972)—but the organized housing struggle was *indispensable* to housing reform: there would have been no rent restrictions without the rent strikes and no public housing without the rent restrictions (Damer 1980). Stressing the allegedly indispensable role of organized labour for social reproductive struggles—though an ideal scenario—has the potential to leave tenants politically paralyzed and yearning for a workers' presence that historically was only ever occasional because the conventional workplace was always prioritized. This presence, of course, is now largely spectral in the deindustrialized context of Britain and Ireland. It is also worth noting that the areas hit hardest by escalating rent levels in the period of the Glasgow Rent Strike were Partick and Govan, where wages were highest because of the shipbuilding and wartime munitions industries and where landlords thus attempted to squeeze higher rents from tenants (Damer 1980; Melling 1983; Castells 1983). With housing and the workplace closely imbricated, these areas were the central hotspots of the rent strikes. Yet, such proximity and interconnectivity between workplace and home no longer holds true (see Joubert and Hodkinson, this volume). Contemporary housing struggles must start from where they are with what they have in a thoroughly mobile and precarious present.

Significantly, it was women who led the rent strikes, and women who forced the housing issue on the ground, even if strong support from other organizations was crucial (Damer 1980, 1990; Melling 1983; Smyth 1992). Yet when such activity is framed as secondary, its innovation and achievement is undermined, as is the wider basis for political struggle in the sphere of social reproduction. In wartime, even more so than usual, the defence of the home against landlordism and the task of domestic reproduction fell on women. The vast majority of rent strikers were working-class 'housewives', whose actions were based on their everyday experience of tenement life

(Smyth 1992; Hughes and Wright, this volume; Currie, this volume), with rent agitation providing 'a potent source of radicalization amongst working-class women' (Englander 1983, 303). The tenement[6] construction of much of Glasgow meant that any defence of the home was 'almost bound to become a collective act': each flat was part of a communal stairwell, or 'close', with the sharing of communal features, such as wash houses and toilets, making collective contact and communication a regular occurrence (Smyth 1992, 180). Much of the organization for the rent strikes was undertaken in 'close committees'—'two women for each close' (Melling 1983, 67)—and 'kitchen meetings', with homes secured by women-led mass pickets and the forcible expulsion of factors[7] where necessary (Smyth 1992, 180).

The 'politics of the kitchen' that emerged through the rent strikes broke down the traditional separation between public and private spheres as well as other gendered distinctions (Hughes and Wright, this volume; Currie, this volume), presenting social reproductive struggles as part of a wider class struggle on both 'fronts'. The rent strikes united 'male with female, skilled with unskilled, and not least Catholic with Protestant' (McLean 1983, xx; Castells 1983; Damer 1980, 1990; Foster 1990; Smyth 1992), and the role of the Glasgow Women's Housing Association (GWHA), formed in 1914, was decisive in this regard (Damer 1980; Smyth 1992). They organized large-scale public meetings and demonstrations, many of which were aimed at obtaining solidarity from the industrial workplace. Yet the GWHA was 'an autonomous women's body both in leadership and membership', whose regular public meetings were held on weekday afternoons at 3 P.M., indicating that day-to-day organization was geared towards the needs of housewives and the unemployed and not those in the paid workplace (Smyth 1992, 183). Ultimately, it was women-led struggle that 'forced the issue' in what some see as probably 'the most successful example of direct action ever undertaken by the Scottish working class' (Smyth 1992, 174; see also Damer 2000a), yet the relevance of this achievement for a challenge to *contemporary* class relations and the housing question is rarely examined in any depth.

Melling has suggested that women-led mass resistance to rent rises and landlordism possessed its own 'dynamic and significance', but that this was separate from 'the socialist critique of capitalism' (1983, 114). Castells largely follows this position, even while contrarily acknowledging the fact that the women-led rent strikes were 'decisive to the unification of work and residence, factories and housing, and created the conditions for a successful social struggle' (1983, 33). Damer (2000a), as I do, objects to the theoretical separation of housing and reproductive struggles from a direct challenge to capitalism, and in this respect it is also worth noting that Castells fails to acknowledge the centrality of gendered caring labour to the reproduction of male labour power (see Dalla Costa and James 1972; James 1975; Federici

1975, 2012). The separation of political and economic and productive and reproductive spheres is untenable, and even more so in the contemporary era when many more women routinely combine wage labour with domestic and social reproductive work in what feminists call 'double-work'.

Castells has argued that the rent strikes did not challenge the dominant faction of the capitalist class, but Damer, in my view, more persuasively argues that the rent strikes must be theorized as a critique of a pervasive social totality of capitalist relations 'in whatever form it appears' (2000a, 71). Tenants in the rent strikes, he continues, fought the dominant faction of capital in *their* lives—rentier landlords—from *where they could*: a seemingly circumscribed position in the sphere of social reproduction. It is for this reason that the rent strikes are so important for our present understanding, Smyth (1992) contends, precisely because of women's leading role, and precisely because it was in the domestic sphere that women faced capital in the form of the landlord, the factor and the sheriff officer. Thus, the rent strikes can productively be seen as a mass movement that helped prise open the social reproductive process as a central concern for everyday political struggle. This is not to deny the crucial ongoing importance of struggles in the production process. Yet, it must be stressed that wage gains in the workplace have always been recuperated at the level of consumption through inflationary pricing, and thus struggles across both the sphere of production and reproduction are vital for class contestation across the entire spectrum of social relations (see Bunge 1977).

Melling usefully observes how Independent Labour Party (ILP) leaders argued in 1915 that tenants must organize to refuse rental increases, just as industrial workers had organized to prevent wages being reduced, challenging contentions that no new theories of political struggle emerged in the rent strikes (Englander 1983, 299). He also notes how rent-racking, which the entire working class was subjected to, 'came to symbolize a whole range of attacks on living standards and values', with resistance to rent increases at the forefront of wider class resistance (Melling 1979, 43). In an era marked by the destructive play of capital in the built environment, where the proportion of the wage spent on rent has increased from 10 percent in the 1950s (Robbins 2017) to an average of 50 percent of take-home pay in England and upwards of 70 percent in London (Osborne 2015), housing must once again become a central node of generalized struggle against private property and contemporary capitalist relations.

CONCLUSION

The urbanization of capital, and the new spatial composition that has arisen from it, has shaped the conditions for political struggle in ways that necessitate a fundamental rethinking of the housing question in Britain, Ireland, Western Europe and North America. At the same time, a narrow focus on the productive sphere in the workplace historically has tended to elide the broader significance of struggles around housing and social reproduction (Bradley 2014; Damer 2000a; Grayson 1996; Johnstone 1992, 2000; Moorhouse et al. 1972; Sklair 1975). This was always untenable given that the sphere of social reproduction is where the working class—incorporating men, women, children, the elderly and the unemployed—lives most of its everyday life (Bunge 1977). It has become even more so now that housing has become so central to the national political economies of Western Europe. Re-examining Engels' influential theses in *The Housing Question*, I have argued that the 1915 Rent Strikes have more political relevance for the contemporary European and North American context than many accounts suggest, precisely because the housing question, and resistance to housing tyranny, have remained central to a continuum of political struggle in the sphere of social reproduction, while the specific context of heavy industry and its discontents on 'Red Clydeside' has largely been lost to the factory desert. Fundamental workplace contradictions have not disappeared, of course, and remain to be fought. But the massification and politicization of workers in central nodes of the British industrial and manufacturing economy has long been decomposed into a fragmented, casualized, precarious, service-based, low-paid workforce that does not at present hold the same strategic capacity to overthrow capitalism.

Questions remain about whether housing struggle represents a direct challenge to capitalism, but as Moorhouse et al. (1972) note, housing struggle forms a direct challenge to property ownership, and what could be more central to capitalism than property? Yet, here Engels reminds us of the radicalism required for the supersession of capitalism: the appropriation of the means of production and the expropriation of existing housing to overturn the myth of 'housing shortage' (1942 [1872], 36). As Madden and Marcuse (2016, 119) observe, what is required is a fundamental transformation of the political and economic structures of society, and this necessitates that the power-laden questions of production and ownership are addressed rather than waiting for private capital or relying on the 'myth of the benevolent state' to deliver a solution to the housing question. Both have shown repeatedly that it has never been in their interest to do so. In a current context where systemic transformation seems distant but more than ever necessary, we are left with attempting to achieve change that is accomplishable in this world, while revealing how changes within the present system are not enough: a nonreformist reformism that works between defensive and offensive strategies seeking to politicize, generalize and ultimately decommodify the housing question (see Madden and Marcuse 2016; Joubert and Hodkinson, this volume). With deindustrialization, housing financialization, hyper-commodification and a resurgent rentier economy, housing has never been more central to capital accumulation strategies. As such, housing contestation must also be central to anti-capitalist organizing strategies. As Bunge (1977) contends, a dual concentration at both the point of production and the point of reproduction is required. To paraphrase Marx, the social revolutions of the twenty-first century cannot take their poetry from the nineteenth century but only from the future.

NOTES

1. Notably, Ireland has *never* had a substantial industrial or manufacturing base.

2. A similar strategy by industrialists in 1870s Germany is noted by Engels in *The Housing Question* (1942 [1872], 56). Madden and Marcuse (2016) also show how housing construction was central to US wartime production in the twentieth century.

3. Proudhon's concept of 'labour time' was eviscerated by Marx for neglecting the crucial role of socially necessary labour time in the production of surplus value. It is hardly necessary to state Marx and Engels' objection to the idealist and a-historical concept of 'eternal justice'.

4. These terms are perhaps unfamiliar in the British and Irish context, but the Italian origins of the term *hegemony* in Antonio Gramsci's work have not prevented its widespread usage. Like hegemony, these terms have a level of abstraction that can be mobilized in vastly different historical-geographical contexts.

5. The profound ideology of homeownership produced in Ireland emerges from a similar material context of agriculture and small-scale industry, exacerbated by a desire to overcome forms of colonial enclosure and ownership.

6. A multi-occupancy building that is generally three to four storeys high with a shared stairwell.

7. In Scotland, where a property has more than one owner, as in tenements, and where there are parts of the property that have common ownership, owners may have to hire a property manager, otherwise known as a factor.

REFERENCES

Aalbers, Manual B., and Brett Christophers. 2014. "Centring Housing in Political Economy." *Housing, Theory and Society* 31(4): 373–94.

Beauregard, Robert A. 1994. "Capital Switching and the Built Environment: United States, 1970–89." *Environment and Planning A* 26(5): 715–32.

Bologna, Sergio. 1992. "The Theory and History of the Mass Worker in Italy: Part 2." *Common Sense* 12: 52–78.

———. 2007 [1977]. "The Tribe of Moles." In *Autonomia: Post-Political Writings*, edited by Sylvere Lotringer and Christian Marazzi, 36–61. Los Angeles: Semiotext(e).

Bradley, Quintin. 2014. *The Tenants' Movement: Resident Involvement, Community Action and the Contentious Politics of Housing.* London: Routledge.

Bryant, Richard. 1982. "Rent Strike in the Gorbals." *Community Development Journal* 17(1): 41–46.

Bunge, William. 1977. "The Point of Reproduction: A Second Front." *Antipode* 9(2): 60–76.

Castells, Manuel. 1983. *The City and the Grassroots: A Cross-Cultural Theory of Urban Social Movements.* Berkeley: University of California Press.

Charnock, Greig. 2010. "Challenging New State Spatialities: The Open Marxism of Henri Lefebvre." *Antipode* 42(5): 1279–303.

Christophers, Brett. 2011. "Revisiting the Urbanization of Capital." *Annals of the Association of American Geographers* 101(6): 1347–64.

Cleaver, Harry. 1979. *Reading Capital Politically.* Brighton: Harvester Press Limited.

Dalla Costa, Mariarosa, and Selma James. 1972. *The Power of Women and the Subversion of the Community.* Bristol: Falling Wall Press.

Damer, Seán. 1980. "State, Class and Housing: Glasgow 1885–1919." In *Housing, Social Policy and the State*, edited by Joseph Melling, 73–112. London: Croom Helm.

———. 1990. *Glasgow: Going for a Song.* London: Lawrence and Wishart.

———. 2000a. "'The Clyde Rent War!' The Clydebank Rent Strike of the 1920s." In *Class Struggle and Social Welfare*, edited by Michael Lavalette and Gerry Mooney, 71–95. London: Routledge.

———. 2000b. "'Engineers of the Human Machine': The Social Practice of Council Housing Management in Glasgow, 1895–1939." *Urban Studies* 37(11): 2007–26.

Edwards, Brian. 1999. "Glasgow Improvements, 1866–1901" In *The Forming of the City*, edited by Peter Reed, 84–103. Edinburgh: Edinburgh University Press.

Engels, Friedrich. 1942 [1872]. *The Housing Question.* London: Lawrence and Wishart.

Englander, David. 1983. *Landlord and Tenant in Urban Britain, 1838–1918.* Oxford: Oxford University Press.

Federici, Silvia. 1975. *Wages against Housework.* Bristol: Power of Women Collective and Falling Wall Press.

———. 2012. *Revolution at Point Zero: Housework, Reproduction, and Feminist Struggle.* New York: PM Press/Autonomedia/Common Notions.

Foster, John. 1990. "Strike Action and Working-Class Politics on Clydeside, 1914–1919." *International Review of Social History* 35(1): 33–70.

Glynn, Sarah. 2009. *Where the Other Half Lives: Lower Income Housing in a Neoliberal World.* London: Pluto Press.

Gotham, Kevin F. 2009. "Creating Liquidity out of Spatial Fixity: The Secondary Circuit of Capital and the Subprime Mortgage Crisis." *International Journal of Urban and Regional Research* 33(2): 355–71.

Gray, Neil. 2018. "Beyond the Right to the City: Territorial Autogestion and the Take over the City Movement in 1970s Italy." *Antipode* 50(2): 319–39.

Grayson, John. 1996. *Opening the Window: Revealing the Hidden History of Tenants Organizations*, edited by Maggie Walker. Manchester: TPAS and Northern College.

Griffin, Paul. 2015. *The Spatial Politics of Red Clydeside: Historical Labour Geographies and Radical Connections*. PhD diss., University of Glasgow.

Hardt, Michael, and Antonio Negri. 2006. *Multitude*. London: Penguin Books.

Harvey, David. 1982. *The Limits to Capital*. Oxford: Blackwell.

———. 1985. *The Urbanization of Capital: Studies in the Theory and History of Capitalist Urbanization*. Baltimore: John Hopkins University.

———. 2012. *Rebel Cities: From the Right to the City to the Urban Revolution*. London: Verso.

Hodkinson, Stuart. 2012a. "The Return of the Housing Question." *Ephemera: Theory and Politics in Organization* 12(4): 423–44.

Hudson, Michael. 2010. "From Marx to Goldman Sachs: The Fictions of Fictitious Capital, and the Financialization of Industry." *Critique* 38(3): 419–44.

James, Selma. 1975. *Sex, Race and Class*. https://libcom.org/files/sex-race-class-2012imp.pdf

Johnstone, Charles. 1992. *The Tenants' Movement and Housing Struggles in Glasgow, 1945–1990*. PhD diss., University of Glasgow.

———. 2000. "Housing and Class Struggles in Post-war Glasgow." In *Class Struggle and Social Welfare*, edited by Michael Lavalette and Gerry Mooney, 139–54. London: Routledge.

Lefebvre, Henri. 1991. *The Production of Space*. Oxford: Blackwell.

———. 2003 [1970]. *The Urban Revolution*. Minneapolis: University of Minnesota Press.

Madden, David, and Peter Marcuse. 2016. *In Defense of Housing*. London: Verso.

Marx, Karl. 1847. *The Poverty of Philosophy*. Marxists.org. https://www.marxists.org/archive/marx/works/1847/poverty-philosophy/

———. 1848. *The Communist Manifesto*. Marxists.org. https://www.marxists.org/archive/marx/works/1848/communist-manifesto/

McCabe, Conor. 2011. *Sins of the Father: The Decisions that Shaped the Irish Economy*. Dublin: History Press Ireland.

McLean, Iain. 1983. *The Legend of Red Clydeside*. Edinburgh: John Donald.

Melling, Joseph. 1979. "The Glasgow Rent Strike and Clydeside Labour—Some Problems of Interpretation." *Scottish Labour History Society Journal* 13: 39–44.

———. 1983. *Rent Strikes: People's Struggle for Housing in West Scotland 1890–1916*. Edinburgh: Polygon.

Merrifield, Andy. 2014. *The New Urban Question*. London: Pluto.

Midnight Notes. 1992. "Introduction to Zerowork 1." In *Midnight Oil: Work, Energy, War, 1973–1992*, 108–114. New York: Autonomedia.

Moorhouse, Bert, Mary Wilson and Chris Chamberlain. 1972. "Rent Strikes—Direct Action and the Working Class." *Socialist Register* 9(9): 133–56.

Negri, Antonio. 2005. *Books for Burning*. London: Verso.

Osborne, Hilary. 2015. "Tenants in England Spend Half their Pay on Rent." *The Guardian*, July 16. https://www.theguardian.com/money/2015/jul/16/tenants-in-england-spend-half-their-pay-on-rent

Robbins, Glyn. 2017. *There's No Place: The American Housing Crisis and What It Means for the UK*. London: Red Roof.

Robertson, Mary. 2015. "Re-asking the Housing Question." *Salvage* 1: 161–72.

Ross, Kristen. 2015. *Communal Luxury: The Political Imaginary of the Paris Commune*. London: Verso.

Sklair, Leslie. 1975. "The Struggle against the Housing Finance Act." *Socialist Register* 12(12): 250–92.

Slater, Tom. 2013. "Your Life Chances Affect Where You Live: A Critique of the 'Cottage Industry' of Neighbourhood Effects Research." *International Journal of Urban and Regional Research* 37(2): 367–87.

Smith, Neil. 2002. "New Globalism, New Localism: Gentrification as Global Urban Strategy." In *Spaces of Neoliberalism: Urban Restructuring in North America and Western Europe*, edited by Neil Brenner and Nik Theodore N, 80–103. London: Blackwell Publishing.

Smyth, James. 1992. "Rent, Peace, Votes: Working Class Women and Political Activity in the First World War." In *Out of Bounds: Women in Scottish Society 1800–1945*, edited by Esther Breitenbach and Eleanor Gordon, 174–96. Edinburgh: Edinburgh University Press.

Swenarton, Mark. 1981. "An 'Insurance against Revolution'—Ideological Objectives of the Provision and Design of Public Housing in Britain after the First World War." *Historical Research* 54(129): 86–101.

Turner, Graham. 2008. *The Credit Crunch: Housing Bubbles, Globalization and the Worldwide Economic Crisis*. London: Pluto Press.

Vercellone, Carlo. 2010. "The Crisis of the Law of Value and the Becoming-Rent of Profit." In *Crisis in the Global Economy: Financial Markets, Social Struggles, and New Political Scenarios*, edited by Andrea Fumagalli and Sandro Mezzadra, 85–118. London: Semiotext(e) and the MIT Press.

Wright, Steve. 2002. *Storming Heaven: Class Composition and Struggle in Italian Autonomist Marxism*. London: Pluto Press.

Part II

REPORTS FROM THE
HOUSING FRONTLINE

Chapter 5

Everyday Eviction in the Twenty-First Century

Vickie Cooper and Kirsteen Paton

I'm proud that we're the ones giving more than a million people the chance to have a house of their own. And if anyone wants to argue with us on that, I say bring it on. We're going to build the home owning democracy this Party has always stood for.

—George Osborne (2015)

We live in Britain, not a Third World country. The benefit cap introduced by the Tories is almost criminal. It's just not designed for families as large as ours. All I want for me and my family is a home.

—evicted tenants, Lee and Katrina (*The Mirror* 2015)

Evictions have become everyday occurrences in the United Kingdom. There have been a surfeit of news headlines outlining the extent and cruelty of eviction processes taking place across the country today. The severity of housing inequality exacerbated under the present climate of austerity and the direction of change in housing and welfare policies cannot be underestimated. In 2015, the Conservative government made a commitment to advance homeownership, in the same year in which evictions reached a record high, estimated at 115 a day (Ministry of Justice 2015). This chapter draws parallels between the scale of evictions pre-1915 and the present day, with a view to assessing the role that rent strikes might have as a contemporary strategy of resistance to housing inequality in the twenty-first century. We see this as a meaningful comparison given the main form of housing tenure in the early twentieth century was private renting, with no rent regulation. Now, we are seeing a return to this level of private renting, similarly underscored by a lack of rent regulation. Much like the events leading up to the 1915 Rent Strikes, there has been an unprecedented rise in evictions across the United Kingdom. Families and communities are being removed from their homes as a result of the growth in the private-rented sector (PRS), the subsequent lack of affordable accommodation and the failure of the state to intervene.

We begin this chapter by outlining the practices of what we call 'state-led eviction', which aims to politicize the role of the state in facilitating evictions today by looking at how they operate in the political economy. We define state-led eviction as the cumulative and negative impact of government cuts in social support for housing and the promotion of private housing market activities, which not only increase the eviction risk among low-income households, but also through various legal repossession frameworks, actively endorse it. We suggest that state-led eviction comprises two aspects. The first relates to transference of debt, achieved through recent welfare cuts, which directly affect housing benefit payments and ergo rent affordability. The second relates to transference of wealth to the private sector, which involves the state working in partnership with the private sector including enforcement businesses. This 'eviction industry' is far greater in scope than the activities of individual-profiteering landlords pre-1915. We outline how this eviction industry and the decomposition and diversification of housing tenure since the 1980s (alongside the decomposition of labour and class) present several challenges to the collectivization of a resistance movement to tackle housing inequality in the twenty-first century.

Given these changes, this chapter considers the ramifications for resisting evictions and for rent strikes in housing activism today. We consider some of the current experiences of housing activists in relation to housing inequalities, looking at some features of the counter-hegemonic response. By counter-hegemony we are referring to the various resistance movements and community-led organizations that strongly oppose the dominant political ideas and assumptions that shape our current housing political landscape. The present neoliberal hegemony expresses forms of rule which position housing as a private commodity and financial asset which, within the private market, can cater to the needs of middle- and working-class groups alike. As we will show in this chapter, communities are adversely affected by and oppose these neoliberal assumptions and values. Today's housing activist movements—compromising diverse classes and tenures—focus primarily on rent. Our discussion here draws from ongoing research with UK housing activists as well as policy and secondary data analysis of housing and welfare changes. We end the chapter by asking how we might build upon the rent strike strategy of 1915 and create an effective class platform for resistance.

STATE-LED EVICTIONS IN THE
TWENTY-FIRST CENTURY: RENT MATTERS

Many of the social, political and economic conditions that led to the 1915 Rent Strikes echo those of today: high levels of housing privatization, no rent control, lack of affordable housing and high demand. In 1912 in Glasgow, the population increased because of immigration (from Ireland and the highlands of Scotland) by approximately seventy thousand, yet only two thousand tenements were built to meet this demand for housing (Caird 2013). Consequent overcrowding was compounded by poor-quality conditions and increased costs of living. At this time more than 90 percent of UK housing was rented from private landlords (Spicker 1988) who found themselves in a situation where housing demand far exceeded supply. Given the lack of regulation, landlords had a rapacious response: increasing rents at little notice by as much as 23 percent (Spirit of Revolt 2015) and evicting anyone who fell into arrears because tenants could be summarily evicted and properties re-rented almost immediately. Landlords' quests for profit through rent ignited resistance among tenants which culminated in the 1915 Rent Strikes. This action subsequently led to the state intervening and mediating a housing provision to protect the tenant from the vagaries of the market. Regulative policies such as the 1915 Rent Restrictions Act followed, and then latterly, the creation of the welfare state and the provision of council housing, providing secure tenancies that protected tenants against rent exploitation for much of the second half of the twentieth century.

However, the provision of housing within the postwar welfare settlement was said to be its 'wobbly pillar' (Malpass 2003) because housing straddled both private and public realms; it was never fully one nor the other. As such, the pillar of housing security has been chipped away since its conception. Since the creation of the welfare settlement, the state has actively pursued housing privatization through a suite of polices and urban strategies such as the Right-to-Buy, Housing Stock Transfer, regeneration and gentrification. That said, even while this was being implemented, tenants were still protected from being evicted by state regulation that secured tenancies contractually and prevented displacement occurring through much of the twentieth century.

That protection was undermined following the financial crisis of 2007–2008 with the introduction of austerity measures and increased financialization of housing, leading to changes so significant that they are deemed to have constituted a global paradigm shift in housing by the UN rapporteur on housing at the time, Raquel Rolnik (2013). This means that, on the one hand, the state increasingly creates policies that support housing as a financial asset, giving precedence to the housing industry where housing policies such as Right-to-Buy and laxer mortgage borrowing regulations bring people ever closer to the vagaries of the housing market. On the other hand, the state is simultaneously withdrawing welfare support in housing, curtailing social housing building and forcing people to live in unaffordable and unregulated private-rented housing. Where social housing and welfare support once provided a buffer against housing poverty, they are now offered on an emergency only basis (Fitzpatrick and Pawson 2014) and the role of the PRS has never been so dominant since 1915. Today's housing problems are therefore not entirely new. Land and rent have always been key to the functioning of capitalism as expressed by David Harvey's (2007) long-standing position on second circuit capitalism and 'accumulation by dispossession' where the key mechanism of exploitation is through rent. This is demonstrated fundamentally through housing. Without sufficient regulation of the housing market, rent occupies a key source of value and profit and, by extension, exploitation. The disinvestment of social housing and withdrawal of housing support means that people become increasingly reliant on the PRS. This housing precarity is further compounded by austerity politics.

Since 2008, at the height of austerity, local authority expenditure has rapidly reduced as a result of fiscal discipline. The local state has progressively sold its land as an asset to generate revenue, cementing a shift from governance once characterized by managerialism to managerial entrepreneurialism. This entrepreneurial shift in governance has been evident since the 1980s with the introduction of large-scale regeneration initiatives which initiate gentrification such as harbour and dockside developments to more recent mega-sporting events. Indeed Watt (2013, 101–102) points out how the London Olympic Games exemplified the shift in state activities from social to financialized ventures in housing: 'simultaneously creating rent gaps and cutting out the last vestiges of Keynesian welfare state (KWS) public council housing and associated land ownership'. These urban developments also mark the removal of twentieth-century state protection and the creation of housing as a global financial product. This shift, we argue, manifests in forms of state-led evictions.

We see state-led evictions today as being borne of the recent changes made to welfare under the austerity measures implemented following the financial crash. We characterize this change as involving the redistribution of public debt from state level to individual level as a means by which to resolve the financial deficit. This transference of debt involves the reduction of welfare expenditure and support for social housing but sees the creation of personal debt, payday loans and borrowing arrears to meet growing costs, such as private rent rates. State-led evictions are also precipitated by actively blocking people's right to social housing and, instead, actively promoting the PRS as the dominant source of housing. This has led to a redistribution of wealth where public funds are now literally transferred over to the private-rented market. For example, it has been estimated that from 2012 to 2014, £35 billion of housing benefits, which are public funds, have been spent in the PRS, given to private landlords (Ramesh 2012). So in today's eviction climate, the rise in demand and rent rates in the PRS is not about state absence, but a different type of state activity in the service of private capital. This encompasses strategies around enforcement and dispossession, supported by the legal repossession framework and private business: a type of state intervention that makes capital accumulation in the PRS permissible.

In what follows, we lay out our understanding of the changing role of the state in evictions processes in our political economy reading of contemporary evictions. This is based on ongoing policy and secondary data analysis of housing and welfare reforms in addition to qualitative interviews with housing activists in London and Liverpool. There has been an inexorable rise in housing activism since 2014 (Duxbury and McCabe 2015). This has seen high-profile activities and protests such as *Focus E15 Mothers* in occupation of Carpenters Estate in London, *Love Activists* in the former Bank of England building in Liverpool and student rent strikes in response to growing housing inequalities. We draw from some activist experiences in the final part of the chapter to consider the main challenges they face given the nature of growing housing inequality and evictions today.

TRANSFERRING DEBT:
WELFARE CUTS AND HOUSING POLICY

Paradigmatic changes in housing are tantamount to a redistribution of wealth and debt (Rolnik 2013). This begins with a shift in how tenants become the recipients of welfare to recipients of debt. In 2012, the Liberal-Democrat Conservative Coalition government introduced a historical set of welfare reforms. One of the most controversial and pernicious changes was undoubtedly the so-called 'bedroom tax', the tax on housing benefit levied at social-housing tenants deemed to be 'under-occupying' their home with a 'spare' room. One year after its implementation in April 2014, research found that two-thirds of households in England affected by the bedroom tax had fallen into rent arrears, while one in seven families received eviction risk letters and faced losing their homes (National Housing Federation 2014). Around 6 percent of benefit claimants affected by the bedroom tax moved as a result (BBC 2014). As such, the backlash has been potent, and the bedroom tax has faced significant legal challenges (as we will discuss later in this chapter).

However, more pervasive changes were, in fact, introduced through the 'benefit cap' (or Universal Credit). The benefit cap limits the total weekly income an individual or family can receive in welfare payments, with an estimated 58,700 households experiencing a reduction in Housing Benefit (45 percent of people affected by the benefit cap live in London). When a household exceeds the set level, their benefit income is capped. This cap is administered primarily through housing benefit payments, therefore household rent. It is estimated that fifty thousand households have lost around £93 per week and 15 percent are losing around £150 per week (Shelter 2011). These households have to make up the subsequent shortfall they face in rent. Given that the cap is administered primarily through housing benefit payments, it would be more useful to reconsider the benefit cap as a 'rent cap' because it automatically reduces a person's rent income. In many ways the benefit cap is more insidious than the bedroom tax because it is more widespread, with no real possibility of recourse or appeal. Those in poverty and receiving welfare benefits face the greatest financial challenges in relation to rent and therefore face a greater risk of eviction. The inability of households receiving welfare benefits to pay their rent has seen hundreds of thousands of households fall into rent arrears. From 2007 to 2013, the number of households in rent arrears has increased by 130 percent (Money Advice Trust 2013), and these arrears have resulted in unprecedented levels of repossessions and evictions. This rent shortfall is even greater for PRS tenants exceeding the cap.

This transference of debt is not limited to the individual level welfare benefit cuts. It also occurs in how housing tenure is increasingly diversified and privatized. Given the growth of the PRS and shrinking of investment in social housing, the Coalition government introduced the Localism Act 2011, allowing local authorities to house the poorest households in the PRS, despite uneven rent inflation in this sector. So, we argue, this transference of debt equates to a transference of risk whereby individuals are put in precarious housing positions, facing greater danger of eviction and homelessness. For example, in 2013, 115,000 possession orders were granted to evict tenants in private-rented accommodation as a result of rent arrears. In England and Wales more than 43,000 households in rented housing were evicted by county court bailiffs in the twelve months to June, which is a 50 percent increase from the previous four years, and the highest level since records began in 2001 (Ministry of Justice 2015). This unprecedented rise in eviction is mirrored by rising rates in homelessness. From 2010 to 2016, rough sleeping has increased by 134 percent (Homeless Link 2017) and from 2008 to 2016, the number of families living in temporary accommodation has increased from 630 to 12,000 (House of Commons Library 2017).

These changes in welfare and housing tenure are therefore distinct but inter-related modes of transferring debt to individuals and redistributing wealth to the private sector, exposing the most vulnerable to a volatile housing market and the risk of eviction. And there is more of this to come as benefit expenditure per household dropped again more recently. In 2016 the Conservative government reduced the 'benefit cap' even further and expanded universal credit through the Welfare Reform and Work Bill. This is already having further implications on rent affordability, where it is forecasted that some 100,000 families in the United Kingdom will be gravely affected by these cuts (Butler 2016a). The ramifications of this worried many activists we spoke to who foresaw the imminent effects. One research participant, an independent housing consultant, stressed to us the seriousness of what was in store. 'You ain't seen nothing yet', they said in reference to the impending cuts: 'It sounds so incredulous that people don't recognize it. . . . there are 64,000 homeless families (officially), 93,000 homeless children. This is set to increase next year'. Altogether, these cuts mean that tenants have to make up an even greater shortfall in rent. They plunge many tenants into what we would call an 'eviction risk period', where they have to find new ways to meet these payments or face eviction. The eviction risk period is a critical time for people in terms of seeking protection and support against eviction. And it is anticipated that finding this support will also prove challenging because the housing and advocacy services set up to support vulnerable families are also facing massive cuts. Public sector grant money for charities has declined from £6 billion in 2006, to £2.2 billion in 2013 (Allcock Tyler 2016).

Although these austerity measures have reduced household income, thus increasing rent arrears and debt levels for poor income earners, the government's 2016 Housing and Planning Act actively curtails housing choice by further privatizing the housing sector. For example, the act replaces the obligation to build homes for social rent with a duty to build starter homes, extends the Right-to-Buy, compels local authorities to sell 'high value' housing and offers laxer planning permission. This act underlines the paradigm shift in housing from a socialized to financialized entity. The complexity of such changes denotes other critical dimensions of state-led evictions, which involve not only the transference of debt to the individual but also the transfer of wealth to the private sector. The retraction of social housing and expansion of the housing market shifts public money into private hands and so too does the state's partnership activities with private enforcement businesses who profiteer from rent and evictions.

EVICTION INDUSTRY

Private businesses have profited from rising tenant insecurity and displacement, a housing condition engineered and exacerbated by years of neoliberal housing and welfare policies. As rent arrears and the ultimate consequence of evictions increase, we are seeing a parallel expansion of the enforcement and bailiff businesses directly involved in the collection of debt and enforcement of evictions. These businesses include but are not limited to: credit-consumer agencies that lend to tenants who must make up their rent shortfall; bailiff companies that take back what is subsequently owed; and enforcement agencies that carry out evictions. This is tantamount to an 'eviction industry', which, we argue, comprises private businesses that profit from enforcing possession orders *and* the legislative framework that effectively protects and profits from these businesses.

For example, when landlords and housing authorities want to evict tenants, this is dealt with as a civil matter, where possession claims are ordinarily made to the county court. However, we have recently seen a rise in the number of High Court claims because evictions are carried out more efficiently by High-Court enforcement agencies. Paid on a results basis, these enforcement officers and bailiffs seek to profit from each possession order they receive. And business is booming. One of the largest High-Court enforcement and bailiff companies is *The Sheriffs Office Ltd.*, as seen on the BBC Television programme *The Sheriffs are Coming* (BBC 2016). A profitable and highly successful enforcement business, it was awarded *Enforcement Team of the Year* by the Chartered Institute of Credit Management in 2015, and further demonstrating the expansion of the industry, the Chief Executive of the Sheriffs Office (Ltd.) has stated, 'we launched a number of specialist services and entered new markets, all leading to growth in all sectors of our business' (Credit Strategy 2016). Indeed, profit growth among the largest debt recovery groups in the austerity period from 2010 to 2016 highlights an expanding economy that is attracting multinational investment. *Marston Group Limited*, one of the largest debt recovery companies, increased its annual profit by more than 100 percent,[1] and the acquisition of small debt collection and enforcement companies has increased in the austerity period (for instance, *Marston Group Limited* recently acquired *Rossendales Limited*). In 2015, the multinational investment firm *Outsourcing Inc.* acquired the debt recovery and enforcement company *JBW Group Limited* for £24 million and recently announced a 61 percent increase in profits. *Outsourcing Inc.* also has a large portfolio of international companies operating in the public sector.[2]

But this lucrative economy of debt recovery and enforcement of eviction does not lie outside the purview of the state. Although run by private companies, bailiffs and enforcement officers have a range of legal powers as court officials, which allow them to break entry into people's homes and remove them from the premises. These legal powers present some challenges to mobilizing resistance against rent arrears and eviction. People actively obstructing duties carried out by court officials can be prosecuted for contravening Section 10 of the Criminal Justice Act 1977. Given the range of powers and legal protection, bailiffs and enforcement companies are a key component in state-led eviction, where any challenge to that authority is met with the threat of prosecution. To put it differently, the eviction industry helps us to understand the might of the state in the displacement of tenants who fall into rent arrears and the hybrid use of civil and criminal legislation to forcibly remove them. The police also play a critical role; it is not uncommon for the police to be present during tenant evictions. Evictions are civil incidents, not criminal, and in principle, the role of the police in these matters is to 'maintain independence'. However, our research with activists who have been present at evictions reveals that the police do not maintain an independent position, and furthermore, have a symbolic effect surrounding public perceptions of eviction. A participant explains their experience of and issues with police presence during evictions:

> There's a wider problem around housing and the police. In the sense that these are civil matters so they shouldn't be involving the police. But when the police get involved, they take the side of the landlord and they see it as their role to intervene even when the eviction is not their role, it's a civil matter.[3]

The role of police during evictions further supports the notion of state-led eviction. As the preceding participant alludes to, police presence can lead tenants and communities to believe that the occupiers have committed a criminal offence, where none has occurred. Indeed, it exposes the failure of the police to act independently, where they side with the landlord and bailiffs carrying out the eviction. The expansion of enforcement and bailiff companies that are able to profit under the current legislative repossession framework is crucial for thinking about state-led eviction because the role of the state is not simply about withdrawing housing support but advancing the power and profitability of private businesses prospering from rent arrears and eviction. This power is further consolidated by the police through their role in the eviction process, including the 'symbolic effect' on tenants and communities. Altogether, the role of the state in evictions, especially the hybrid use of criminal and civil legislation, presents some challenges to the counter-hegemonic response and strategies for resisting housing inequality. While eviction is foremost a civil matter, any resistance or obstruction to the official authorities carrying out evictions can have punitive ramifications.

WHERE NEXT FOR ACTION? COUNTER-HEGEMONIC RESPONSE

Given the scale of housing inequalities leading to a growth in evictions and the structures endorsing them, we have also seen a correspondent growth in housing activism in the United Kingdom as a counter-hegemonic movement.

This movement comprises tenants' associations, unions, charities and community activist groups. These disparate groups collaborate on a range of resistance activities, such as lobbying campaigns against revenge evictions and welfare cuts, and more general awareness-raising actions. Responding to the rise in household rents and thus evictions, one of the most common activities has been eviction watches rather than rent strikes (Cooper and Paton 2015; *Liverpool Echo* 2014). These involve volunteers coming together collectively to block bailiffs sent to evict tenants. This is, understandably, a temporary measure and is carried out most commonly in cases where children or vulnerable tenants are involved. The primary aim is often to buy more time to ensure that alternative suitable accommodation is in place. In lieu of previous statutory protection, born out of the success of the 1915 Rent Strikes but since eroded, eviction watches are now the frontline in protecting people from evictions.

But housing campaigners' activities are not limited to eviction watches as a means of resistance. The main form of inequality commonly identified among activist groups is still rent, both social and private rent and problems around 'affordability'. As such, the most referenced resistance practice by campaigners and activists is the possibility of implementing national rent strikes to the same historical impact and effect as 1915. One GMB Union member we interviewed told us that their campaign group was researching rent strikes to assess how they could be used: 'The Glasgow Rent Strikes; that just seemed like the best fun in the world, pulling bailiffs pants down and ringing bells anytime anyone was going to be evicted'.

This renewed interest is warranted given the success of recently emerging rent strikes. In 2015, approximately eighty students in London withheld their rent because of high noise levels, unhygienic living conditions and general poor quality accommodation. Beginning with door-to-door campaigns in university halls of residence, students demonstrated and spoke out against high student rents and student housing conditions more generally. In response, the university threatened students by withholding their end-of-year results, thus, potentially preventing them from re-enrolling for the next academic year. However, the university later capitulated and awarded all students compensation to the sum of approximately one-term's rent. The success of this rent strike demonstrates how a common housing tenure, shared by tenants of a collective social group—students—helps to mobilize a resistance against the owners of that property. Although shared tenure and group membership helped the success of this strike, these conditions are not entirely reflective of the diversification of housing composition and precarious income earners in the United Kingdom today.

Given the activities of the state in relation to welfare cuts and the eviction industry, rent strikes are a potentially important tactic, *but* only one of many because housing is being attacked on diverse fronts. Indeed, rent strikes may not be the most viable option for benefit claimants, particularly for those in the PRS, whose rent is first and foremost paid by the government (see also Joubert and Hodkinson, this volume). This example raises questions around the possibility of rent strikes in the twenty-first-century housing landscape. The diversity is a consequence of neoliberal restructuring over the last three decades, which has fragmented housing tenure and simultaneously divided class struggle. Class decomposition and dispossession, poor quality of work and the 'low pay, no pay' churn (Shildrick et al. 2015) traps people on benefits, positioning them at the greatest risk of housing poverty. Today's landscape of classed housing poverty requires a diverse collective resistance. This is further required because of regional and national variation which poses certain challenges for effectively mobilizing a unified housing activist approach. For example, in Scotland, strong tenant campaigning put pressure on the Scottish government to assuage the hazardous effects of the bedroom tax. The 'bedroom tax' remains in place but the government foots the bill. Although this is a testimony and small victory for tenants' campaigning, it does not eradicate the national policy. Housing campaigners' activities in the north of England, still adversely impacted by the bedroom tax, focus on advocacy and appeals. And as the Housing and Planning Act (England and Wales) threatens the end of council housing, which has specific and acute effects in central London, campaigning has focused on resisting social cleansing and demanding access to housing.

The diversity of the counter-hegemonic movement and uneven experiences of housing inequality geographically and across tenures creates the risk of fighting on divided fronts. Without a doubt, this movement has helped to bring housing inequality into mainstream party politics. However, the complexity of housing inequality was a key question for the activists we spoke to. As one interviewee from the GMB Union observed:

> we argued like hell over what was a priority: so you have people like 'do we take the members who have been looking to buy their own home; those who want to own but can't afford it; what about council tenants facing evictions . . . ?' [sighs]. I think there's recognition [of the problem] across the housing network and the union movement about what the actual end goals are.

Given the diverse nature of housing inequalities and the increasing role of the state in facilitating these, a universal end goal in the movement is still incipient. The work of campaigners in protecting people facing eviction is strong, but the diverse make-up of the group in terms of class and tenure poses a challenge to collective organization that must be addressed.

CONCLUSION

The frontier of housing privatization and inequality has advanced, and it is therefore paramount that we conceptualize the entire ensemble of actions that comprise state-led evictions and the counter-hegemonic response to them. The state is active in these processes like never before, whether in supporting eviction enforcement and debt recovery activities or retracting housing-benefit payments. All of these state-led activities contribute to profit extraction and making evictions permissible. This has important ramifications for how we resist housing inequalities and how, or if, the strategy of rent strikes can be effectively utilized today. The success of the 1915 Rent Strikes resistance—where state intervention arrived in the form of rent regulation—relates to a previous emerging hegemonic project and period where the state was forced to intervene and act as an intermediary between tenant and market. The question then remains, where and how can such counter-hegemonic strategies leverage the most power, given the tenor of changes we have highlighted.

In this chapter through considering the political economy of evictions, we have demonstrated how state-led eviction facilitates the transference of debt, achieved through austerity measures which directly affect housing benefit payments and ergo rent affordability. These same measures facilitate the transfer of wealth from social housing to the private sector. Austerity exposes the most vulnerable to a volatile housing market, where they must make up the rent shortfall and thus, face the greatest risk of eviction. The state plays a key role in this, not only through welfare cuts and the transfer of wealth but also through shared private interests with enforcement businesses. This involves a hybrid use of civil and criminal legislation to forcibly remove tenants for profitable aims. These changes in housing policy and state-led activities raise key questions about avenues for housing activism, such as the benefits in supporting those tenants facing an 'eviction risk period' and the possibility of legal recourse in challenging enforcement measures or discriminatory practices, as highlighted by the recent Court of Appeal judgment on the bedroom tax (Butler 2016b).

Despite the diversification of housing inequality and the role of the state today in facilitating evictions compared to 1915, one thing still remains: rent matters. It is crucial and should be at the forefront of resistance in the same way it is at the forefront of exploitation. Moreover, just as the state is active in extracting profit from the most vulnerable in complex ways, so we require correspondingly diverse tactics. This is emphasized by Hodkinson and Lawrence (2011, n.p.) in their assessment of what is required to combat the housing crisis and neoliberalization:

> Genuine cross-tenure housing movement that mobilises at every point of housing precarity—overcrowding, homelessness, unaffordable rents and mortgages,

unfit conditions, ruthless private landlords, privatisation, housing and welfare benefit cuts, homeowners in mortgage arrears or facing repossession, etc.

Because rent matters, rent strikes matter, but when facing the new brutality and diversification of housing inequality in the twenty-first century, tenants and residents need to be armed and united with much more.

NOTES

1. This data is publicly available from *Companies House*, the national registrar of company data. https://beta.companieshouse.gov.uk.

2. Company information available online: http://www.outsourcing.co.jp/en/.

3. Generation Rent, http://www.generationrent.org.

REFERENCES

Allcock Tyler, Debra. 2016. "In Four Years There will be No Grants for Charities—It Will Destroy Communities." *The Guardian*, February 11. https://www.theguardian.com/voluntary-sector-network/2016/feb/11/grants-local-charities-campaign-appeal-government-cuts.

BBC. 2014. "Housing Benefits: Changes See 6% of Tenants Move." http://www.bbc.com/news/uk-26770727.

———. 2016. "The Sheriffs Are Coming." http://www.bbc.co.uk/programmes/b01q1j5d/episodes/guide.

Butler, Patrick. 2016a. "Benefit Cap Will Hit 116,000 of Poorest Families, Say Experts." *The Guardian*, Nov 1. https://www.theguardian.com/society/2016/nov/01/extended-benefit-cap-hit-116000-families-housing-experts.

———. 2016b. "Appeal Court Rules Bedroom Tax Discriminatory in Two Cases." *The Guardian*, January 27. http://www.theguardian.com/society/2016/jan/27/appeal-court-rules-bedroom-tax-discriminatory-in-two-cases.

Caird, Trish. 2013. "Mary Barbour and the Glasgow Rent Strike." *Counterfire*, March 8. http://www.counterfire.org/women-on-the-left/16331-mary-barbour-and-the-glasgow-rent-strike.

Cooper, Vickie, and Kirsteen Paton. 2015. "Tenants in Danger: The Rise of Eviction Watches." *Open Democracy*, April 17. https://www.opendemocracy.net/ourkingdom/kirsteen-paton-vickie-cooper/tenants-in-danger-rise-of-eviction-watches.

Credit Strategy. 2016. "High Court Enforcement Group Acquires Sheriffs Office." https://www.creditstrategy.co.uk/news/news/high-court-enforcement-group-acquires-sheriffs-office-339.

Duxbury, Nick, and Jess McCabe. 2015. "The Rise of the Housing Activist." *Inside Housing*, May 1. http://www.oceanmediagroup.co.uk/features/housingprotests/.

Fitzpatrick, Suzanne, and Hal Pawson. 2014. "Ending Security of Tenure for Social Renters: Transitioning to 'Ambulance Service' Social Housing?" *Housing Studies* 29(5): 597–615.

Harvey, David. 2007. *The Limits to Capital*, 3rd ed. Oxford: Blackwell.

Hodkinson, Stuart, and Beth Lawrence. 2011. "The Neoliberal Project, Privatization and the Housing Crisis." *Corporate Watch Magazine* 50, Autumn/Winter 2011.

Homeless Link. 2017. "Rough Sleeping—Our Analysis." http://www.homeless.org. uk/facts/homelessness-in-numbers/rough-sleeping/rough-sleeping-our-analysis.

House of Commons Library. 2017. "Households in Temporary Accommodation (England) House of Commons Briefing Paper." House of Commons Library, October 23. http://researchbriefings.parliament.uk/ResearchBriefing/Summary/SN02110.

Liverpool Echo. 2014. "Merseyside Family Saved from Christmas Eviction after Vigil Outside their Home." *Liverpool Echo*, December 16. http://www.liverpoolecho. co.uk/news/liverpool-news/vigil-outside-home-merseyside-family-8295650.

Malpass, Peter. 2003. "The Wobbly Pillar? Housing and the British Post-war Welfare State." *Journal of Social Policy* 32: 589–606.

Ministry of Justice. 2015. "Mortgage and Landlord Possession Statistics Quarterly, England and Wales April to June 2015." *Ministry of Justice*, August 13. https:// www.gov.uk/government/uploads/system/uploads/attachment_data/file/ 453265/ mortgage-landlord-possession-statistics-april-june-2015.pdf.

Money Advice Trust. 2013. "Rent Arrears the Fastest Growing UK Debt Problem." *Money Advice Trust*, October 16. http://www.moneyadvicetrust.org/media/news/ Pages/Rent-arrears-the-fastest-growing-UK-debt-problem.aspx.

National Housing Federation. 2014. "Stark Results in Bedroom Tax Report." http:// nationalhousingfederation.newsweaver.com/update/p4cckkn64wo?a=1&p=45004 585&t=22527345.

Osborne, George. 2015. "George Osborne's Speech in Full." Last modified, October 5. http://www.conservativehome.com/parliament/2015/10/george-osbornes-speech-in-full.html.

Ramesh, Randeep. 2012. "Extra 10,000 Working People a Month Reliant on Housing Benefit, says Report." *The Guardian*, October 22. http://www.theguardian.com/ society/2012/oct/22/working-people-housing-benefit-report.

Rolnik, Raquel. 2013. "Late-Neoliberalism: The Financialization of Homeownership and Housing Rights." *International Journal of Urban and Regional Research* 37(3):1058–66.

Shelter. 2011. "Welfare Reform Bill—House of Lords Report Stage Joint Briefing on Clause 94: The Overall Benefit Cap." *Shelter*, January 7. https://england.shelter. org.uk/__data/assets/pdf_file/0019/410590/Welfare_Reform_Bill_Clause_94_ briefing.pdf.

Shildrick, Tracy, Robert MacDonald, Colin Webster and Kayleigh Garthwaite. 2015. *The Low-Pay, No-Pay Cycle: Understanding Recurrent Poverty*. York: Joseph Rowntree Foundation.

Spicker, Paul. 1988. "Wrong foot forward." *Roof*. January–February: 42–43.

Spirit of Revolt. 2015. "Rent Strikes: 100 Years On." *Spirit of Revolt*, November 30. http://spiritofrevolt.info/rent-strikes-100-years-on-exhibition/.

The Mirror. 2015. "First victims of Tory Welfare Cap: Family of 9 Evicted from their Home by Bailiffs". February 16. http://www.mirror.co.uk/news/uk-news/ first-victims-tory-welfare-cap-5780398.

Watt, Paul. 2013. "'It's Not For Us': Regeneration, the 2012 Olympics and the Gentrification of East London." *City* 17(1): 99–118.

Chapter 6

Tenant Self-Organization after the Irish Crisis

The Dublin Tenants Association

Michael Byrne

The Irish financial crisis was particularly sharp and severe, driven by more than a decade of unprecedented house-price increases and cheap credit, which led to the collapse of the country's banking sector. In the aftermath of 2008, distressed mortgage debt and a 50 percent collapse in house prices were the main issues in public and policy debates. However, by 2014 these concerns were largely overtaken by a systemic housing crisis caused by extremely limited supply of new housing and the disappearance of investment in social housing. By 2014, house prices were rebounding rapidly and rent prices escalated, creating a crisis in the private-rental sector (PRS). The unaffordability of the PRS, shortage of supply and homelessness have dominated debates since then. Financial markets have reorganized themselves in response to mortgage market turmoil, while a growing number of households find themselves locked out of home ownership and relegated to the fate of lifelong renters. The combination of volatile changes in housing investment and demand, on the one hand, and a poorly regulated PRS, on the other, has left tenants scrambling to keep a roof over their heads.

A similar pattern can be observed across the world and in particular in those countries most affected by the credit bubbles of the late 1990s and the early 2000s (Fields 2015; Fields and Uffer 2016). In response, a new generation of tenant organizations have emerged aiming to challenge the exclusion of tenants from the right to housing and to politicize the rental sector. Spain, England, Scotland and Ireland have all seen the recent emergence of grassroots tenant organizations. Tenants have tended to lack high or even moderate levels of political organization and advocacy, and the rental sector itself can be seen as the 'poor cousin' of housing policy in Ireland and internationally.

The challenge faced by these organizations is to develop organizational forms and political practices which respond to the experiences of tenants but also politicize the antagonism between rental accommodation as a site of social reproduction and as an 'asset' subjected to financialized and speculative logics.

This chapter examines the experience of the Dublin Tenants Association (DTA). Like many of the new breed of tenant organizations across Europe, the DTA combines collective support around the everyday housing struggles of individuals with a wider repertoire of political activities. The organization focuses on tenant-led, collective responses to the individualized and individualizing nature of renting a home. Examining this experience is useful to reflect on the politics of tenant organizing as well as identifying the limitations and challenges of some current practices. The chapter begins by introducing the role of the PRS historically and in particular during and after the financial crisis. It then contextualizes tenant organizing by way of a comparison with the *Plataforma de Afectados por la Hipoteca* (PAH)—an inspiring housing movement responding to the mortgage arrears and eviction crisis in Spain—to tease out the specificities of tenant organizing. Finally, the chapter builds on this comparison to describe and analyse the politics of the DTA and the challenges the organization is currently confronting.

FINANCIALIZATION AND THE PRS

At the outset of the twentieth century, Dublin's housing system was characterized by the dominant role of the PRS in housing much of the working and middle class. Over the course of the century, however, and particularly in the postwar years, the PRS steadily declined. This occurred through massive government involvement in housing provision and in the mortgage market; by the 1950s and 1960s social housing output made up almost half of all new dwellings (Norris 2016). Direct government supports for the homeownership sector, as well as extensive tenant purchase schemes, also ensured the steady growth of owner occupancy throughout the twentieth century. The combination of these elements saw the PRS dwindle to slightly more than 10 percent of households by the year 2000 and homeownership rise to 80 percent. In the late 1990s and early 2000s declining public housing levels and pro–homeownership policies collided with a massive wave of credit. The financialization of housing and property (Kelly 2014; Downey 2014) was made possible by an expansion of foreign borrowings by Irish banks via the interbank lending market (O'Riain 2014). This was in turn driven by the wider process of financialization and in particular economic and monetary union in the Eurozone and the consequent deregulation of the financial system (Norris and Byrne 2015). The consequence of all this was that by 2008 house prices had tripled within ten years and Ireland was building houses twice as fast as any other European country, with the exception of Spain (Norris and Byrne 2015). The media narrative after the crash was that this credit bubble carried the Irish public towards universal homeownership as everyone took advantage of cheap credit and deteriorating credit standards to get on the 'property ladder'. In reality, once the bubble entered its most acute phase from 2002, the homeownership rate fell, from 80 percent in 2001 to around 70 percent today. Would-be homeowners were increasingly priced out of the market. In this context, the share of households in the PRS began to increase again for the first time in the history of the Irish state. Buy-to-let mortgages grew from 18 percent of outstanding mortgage loans to 27 percent between 2004 and 2008 (Norris and Coates 2014).

Thus, while the financialization of housing in Ireland has generally been considered as closely linked to homeownership, the PRS also played an important role. In the years since the crash of 2008, this has become all the more obvious. Output (new dwellings completed) in both private housing and social housing collapsed between 80 and 90 percent between 2010 and 2014, leading to an explosion of the rental sector and an acute shortage of supply (Lyons 2017). The rental sector has doubled in size within a decade and now makes up around one in five households and is even the majority tenure in a number of urban areas (Central Statistics Office 2017). Rents have sky-rocketed by 60 percent in Dublin since 2010 and are now 15 percent higher than at the peak of the boom (Lyons 2017). The consequence of this has been an explosion of rents and a homelessness crisis.

The intensity of the crisis in the PRS can be explained not just by the impact of the boom and bust on the rental sector but also by the weak regulation of the tenure. As in many European countries, rent controls were abolished in 1982 and the sector remained virtually unregulated for decades. In 2004, leg-islation was introduced in the form of the Residential Tenancies Act (RTA) which still regulates the sector today (Sirr 2014). The RTA established the rights and obligations of landlords and tenants, introduced some basic regula-tion with regard to security of tenure and rent reviews and provided for the establishment of the Private Residential Tenancies Board, later renamed the Residential Tenancies Board (RTB). The latter is tasked with a number of functions related to the regulation of the sector, in particular dealing with disputes between landlords and tenants. Where either party feels there has been a breach of the terms of the RTA, they may register a dispute with the RTB. This is similar to a court process but is less formal, expensive and time consuming and does not require legal representation.

From a tenant's perspective the key aspects of the RTA relate to security of tenure and rent reviews. The RTA established four-year tenancy cycles known as 'Part IV tenancies', but this period was subsequently extended to six years in 2016. During the first six months of a tenancy, the landlord may terminate the tenancy without providing any reason. After this six-month period, a tenancy can be terminated for any of the following reasons:

- Landlord wishes to sell the property.
- Landlord wants the property for family use.
- Landlord intends to substantially refurbish the property.
- Tenant fails to pay rent.
- Tenant engages in anti-social behaviour or causes damage beyond normal wear and tear.

With regard to rent reviews, the RTA stipulates that rent may only be reviewed once every year and that rent may only be increased in line with 'market rents'. 'Market rents' are defined as what a willing tenant would pay a willing landlord. This is essentially meaningless and has done nothing to keep rent increases in check. Following the election of a new government in early 2016, and in the context of growing media discussion and civil society pressure, the Minister for Housing developed a National Rental Strategy, eventually published in December 2016. From a tenant's point of view, the most significant aspect of legislative change was the introduction of rent regulation. This took the form of a 4 percent cap on rent increases in certain designated areas, known as 'rent pressure zones',[1] similar to recently introduced measures in Scotland (see Living Rent, this volume). These include all major urban areas and will likely be extended to include many more areas in future.

These changes, in particular in relation to rent regulation, represent a significant change for tenants and are a positive example of what can be achieved by civil society and social movements. Nevertheless, the crisis in the rental sector is far from being resolved. In particular, rent levels were already extremely high when the 4 percent rent cap was introduced and increases of that level still far outstrip wage increases. Moreover, any understanding of policy must be combined with a recognition of the informal practices that constitute the reality for most tenants. The number of situations in which landlords may terminate a tenancy are so broad that in practice they are used by landlords maliciously to terminate tenancies if and when they choose. The fact that landlords can do this undermines the effectiveness of the RTB because any tenant wishing to challenge their landlord may risk eviction. As such, few tenants register disputes with the RTB.[2] This has led to a culture of non-compliance among landlords and an enforcement vacuum.

HOUSING ACTIVISM IN DUBLIN

From 2014, the 'housing crisis' saw many new activist groups emerge, many of whom employed a combination of direct support to people experiencing housing issues as well as more traditional methods of campaigning, such as protest actions and occupations. In this regard, they reflect a wider turn to practices which have variously been dubbed 'direct action case work', 'collective case work' and 'social syndicalism'. The DTA was the first group to attempt to combine collective case work with a wider set of practices and tactics focused on the right to housing for tenants in the PRS. The DTA was set up in late 2014 and initially took the form of a discussion between a handful of activists. By early 2015 the participants were engaging in the study of the legislative and policy framework for the rental sector as well as developing a format for collective case work. The task of developing a format for collective case work involved two challenges; first, a form of support that would be useful to the individual but would be politicizing, and second, a format that would be feasible and sustainable given limited resources and which could potentially be easily reproduced by other groups. By the spring of 2015, DTA had initiated a pilot phase of collective case work and experimented with different models. This period involved a relatively high level of engagement and represented a steep learning curve, but it gave participants good insights into the reality of the sector, tenants' experiences and how the regulatory framework operated in practice.

Throughout 2015, the DTA solidified its approach and gained several new members, but remained a small organization. The year 2016 saw a move to broaden the activities of the association to include more public activities and campaigning. This involved a number of public talks and a campaign during the summer of 2016 titled #rentripoff (see figure 6.1). This was an online campaign which encouraged tenants to post photos of themselves holding placards in which they communicated the reality of living in the rental sector.

The campaign was successful, membership of DTA increased, and it also saw DTA emerge as a commentator on the PRS in the mainstream media. As mentioned previously, the government published a National Rental Strategy in late 2017. In the run-up to this the DTA organized a second online campaign with the theme of #rentcontrolsnow. This involved producing a policy document, which was submitted to the Minister for Housing, and an online campaign featuring infographics, memes and media advocacy. Following the introduction of partial rent controls under the National Rental Strategy, the DTA's focus in 2017 was on security of tenure, moving towards protest actions and direct action and building alliances with other activist groups. As with many housing activists across Europe, the DTA was strongly influenced by the Spanish PAH. The PAH is widely considered by housing activists across Europe as incorporating a number of novel political practices which hold great potential for housing activism. It has been effective in relation to short-term and small-scale goals and in changing the broader politics of housing in Spain (Colau and Alemany 2012). As such, the following section examines the politics of the PAH as a way of introducing the approach

Figure 6.1   #rentripoff Campaign. Mick Byrne.

adopted by the DTA but also discusses some of the key differences between organizing tenants and homeowners more widely.

THE PAH AND THE POLITICS OF HOMEOWNERSHIP, REPOSSESSION AND DEBT

The PAH was established in 2009 and 2010 and has gone on to become a nationwide movement (Colau and Alemany 2012). The organization arose in the context of a repossession epidemic, which hit Spain following the financial crisis of 2008. Since then, more than half a million households have been evicted as a result of mortgage arrears. From this situation of extreme social exclusion and apparent hopelessness, the PAH has created a series of powerful political practices (García-Lamarca 2017a). Central to its practice is the model of collective case work. Mortgage holders attend weekly meetings where they share their experience, describe the problems they face (from mortgage arrears to immanent eviction) and collectively develop a strategy for responding to these challenges (Di Feliciantonio 2016). The collective thus develops knowledge and experience, which are both practically useful and empowering. These practices are accompanied by direct actions focused on individual cases—for example, sit-ins and creative protests in bank offices to demand a meeting, as well as physically blocking evictions (Colau and Almeny 2012). However, the PAH also engages in campaigns focused on the wider legislative, economic and political structures and on the occupation of vacant buildings to be used as housing for families and households in need.

These practices begin with the emotional and affective level (often feelings of guilt, shame and failure), immediate material needs, the knowledge which is immediately required and so on. From there, it moves to collective actions which respond to immediate needs and from there on to structural analysis and action. This approach has made the analyses and practices of housing activists relevant and useful to thousands and thousands of people. Di Feliciantonio (2016) has drawn on the work of Gibson-Graham to theorize the politics of the PAH in terms of the 'politics of the subject' and the 'politics of collective action'. The politics of the subject relates to empowering or transforming subjectivities and everyday relations and practices in any form of political change. The politics of collective action refers to collective processes which seek to construct new social and economic realities in the 'here and now'.

The politics of the subject is most evident in the transformation of the mortgage holder's experience of the process of repossession and indebtedness (Garcia-Lamarca and Kaika 2016). In the process, the mortgage holder moves from being alone to being part of a collective but also changes their relationship with their home, with their debt and with their bank. Political subjectivization intervenes in the subjective relations which are bound up with and sustain a set of economic relations, thus contributing to a potential reshaping of mortgage holders' material conditions. From here, the mortgage holder can 'perceive him/herself as an actor who has the right to affordable housing and affirms it through collective action and engagement' (Di Feliciantonio 2016, 51). The politics of collective action builds on this process of subjective transformation and involves 'conscious and combined efforts to build a new kind of economic reality' (Gibson-Graham quoted in Di Feliciantonio 2016, 51), for example, the occupation of vacant housing. Given its success, it is perhaps no surprise that various forms of collective case work have become much more common within housing movements across Europe. The PAH, through their 'international commission', have played a key role in this themselves, for example, through their participation in the European Action Coalition for the Right to Housing and the City.

The discussion of the PAH provided is a useful starting point in understanding the politics of tenant organizing. At a subjective level, the position of the tenant is quite different to that of the homeowner, at least in societies in which homeownership is the norm. Homeownership is culturally framed as part of a person 'growing up' and becoming a full member of society. The experience of indebtedness and repossession can be understood as the total collapse of an individual's life project and future. In contrast, tenants for the most part are low-income households often in nontraditional family forms (such as sexual minorities, one-parent families, single adults or cohabitating younger people). Their sense of a 'life project' is usually not expressed through their home. Although for tenants eviction can be devastating, at an emotional and psychological level, many tenants *expect* to be evicted. There is also a significantly different form of antagonism at stake in these respective tenures. In particular, mortgage holders' chief antagonists are banks. Banks are, of course, very large and extremely wealthy businesses. Landlords, in contrast, are for the most part (in Ireland but also in many other countries including the United Kingdom) small-scale operators. Very low levels of professionalization in the rental sector can mean a tenant often has direct interpersonal contact with landlords and even friendly relations with them. The more personalized and unprofessional nature of landlordism makes for a different form of antagonism. Finally, homeownership and mortgage markets are highly cyclical, especially in the epoch of financialization. In the Spanish context (and indeed elsewhere), this resulted in a 'big bang' moment in which the housing and financial system simultaneously collapsed. Crises in the rental sector unfold more slowly, appearing as a series of individual housing crises which are geographically dispersed, apparently isolated and often remaining 'below the radar'.

Given all this, the DTA has sought to develop a politics which draws fundamentally on the PAH's attention to the individual, personal experience of housing inequality, exclusion and crisis and builds primarily through collective subjectivization and action to challenge structural economic and political dynamics. As Di Feliciantonio (2016, 52) contends, 'the action of the PAH is aimed at giving a concrete solution to the housing problems of the people involved, not at creating an oppositional dialectics with capitalist institutions'. Likewise, the DTA adopts a similar 'hands on', even pragmatic, ethos.

THE POLITICS AND PRACTICES OF THE DTA

We can now turn to the activities which define the DTA. These practices stem from a particular view of tenant organizing characterized by an emphasis on the material relations which constitute the rental sector, including the antagonism between a rental property as an 'asset' held by the landlord and as the home of the tenant (i.e., as a site of extracting value or as a site of social reproduction). The work of the DTA involves the development of practices that intervene at this level. This section develops these themes through three lenses: first, the transition from individual to collective experiences; second, the transformation of the subjective relationship to home/property; and third, some of the tensions and challenges that have emerged for the DTA.

From Individual to Collective Experiences

When tenants get in touch with the DTA because of a difficulty they are experiencing, the first thing they are told is that there are no individual solutions to the housing crisis and that only by working together can we overcome the problems we face. Although these are just words, they also reflect an ethos embedded in DTA practices. The most common issues are evictions, rent increases and standards and maintenance issues. For the tenant, the experience often begins with receiving a letter, e-mail or text message from a landlord. For the vast majority of tenants, this is the only point at which they are motivated to contact someone to ask for help, support or guidance. In responding to such situations, the aim of the DTA is both to support the tenant and to facilitate and encourage a shift towards a more collective experience of being a tenant.

When a tenant has an issue, they are linked in with two members of the DTA who are willing to provide support.[3] This means, first of all, providing information about tenants' rights in a given situation, the options open to tenants and the likely outcome of different courses of action. Once the tenant has decided on a course of action, the DTA can work with them in pursuing that. This might include the tenant attempting to negotiate with a landlord or the DTA negotiating with a landlord on a tenant's behalf. It may also include bringing a case against the landlord to the RTB. This involves preparing evidence and supporting the tenant during the RTB hearing. When DTA works with a tenant, a number of things happen which encourage a collective understanding and experience of being a tenant. First, working together on an individual's problem is already a material assertion of collective action by tenants. The DTA is always careful to emphasize that this is not about charity but about recognizing that collective action is the only way to resolve our own housing needs. Second, DTA members can empathize with tenants; usually there is at least one member who has gone through a similar experience. Third, the DTA encourages tenants to see the positive impact of their action for other tenants. In most cases, tenants are reluctant to challenge their landlord. In such instances, the DTA says that if tenants do not stand up to a given landlord, he or she will just do the same thing to the next tenant. This often motivates tenants and again creates a sense of being part of a shared social relationship. Finally, to get support, tenants must attend the DTA's weekly meeting.

Nevertheless, involving tenants in a sustained collective process has been challenging. Despite the DTA's attempts to emphasize that it is a collective political project, tenants tend to relate to DTA members simply as a source of useful information and support and are unlikely to get involved once their situation is resolved. Many tenants, for example, contact through social media and e-mail and providing advice in this format can feel very much like unpaid service provision from the point of view of a DTA member. Tenants that have joined the DTA and have become active organizers tend to be those that had preexisting experience of challenging their landlord (e.g., by bringing a case to the RTB) or very strong feelings about the lack of tenants' rights. In this sense, at times it can feel like DTA is more about providing a space for a cohort of particularly motivated tenants rather than an organizational form, which in itself produces a collective experience of being a tenant and catalyses an organized collective response.

Transforming Relationships

The subjective relationship between tenants in the PRS and their home is remarkable. In Ireland up to one-third of all social housing tenants are in rent arrears. Yet evictions are almost unheard of. Similarly, at the height of the crisis there were as many as 100,000 mortgage holders in serious arrears. And yet the number of evictions as a result of repossession remains extremely low. This is primarily because the legal rights of a homeowner are extremely well protected. In stark contrast, PRS tenants often receive a text message saying the landlord wants them out and within as little as twenty-eight days they may have to leave the property. Whereas the relatively small number of homeowners who have been repossessed has received massive media attention, the tidal wave of evictions in the rental sector is filed under 'business as usual'. At the heart of all this is how tenants relate to 'home' and 'property' and the wider culture around it. For the majority of tenants, the place they are renting is something that the landlord is allowing them access for the time being. The DTA has heard many accounts from tenants of how they have not unpacked all of their stuff even after a year in a new place; of how they do not decorate and furnish their place as they might like; or of how they do not feel it would make sense to plant vegetables in the garden because they may not be there to harvest them. But most importantly, tenants are disinclined to challenge a landlord when they are evicted. Indeed, they often do not consider it an eviction as such, but rather that their time in a given place has come to an end and it is time to move on.

This subjective relationship to home must of course be considered within the context of a policy regime which affords little security of tenure (see Living Rent, this volume, for a discussion of the implications of this for tenant organizing) and is ultimately based on the landlord's right to control his or her asset rather than on the tenant's right to a home. Nevertheless, transforming this subjective relationship is a crucial part of tenant organizing. The normalization of eviction and precarity within the sector can only be challenged when we ourselves come to experience these events as outrageous and unacceptable and come to believe that a home is something we have a right to fight for. Challenging this involves confronting a foundational component of Irish housing policy and the property industry: that those who do not own a property have no right to a home. To challenge this, the DTA engages in producing shared discourses that articulate another relationship towards rental property and the possibility of having a 'home' in the rental sector (i.e., the possibility of having a home while not owning a property). For example, in the #rentripoff campaign, the DTA asked tenants to share their experiences and their frustrations of the rental sector. As part of this, both members of the association and others shared their experiences of evictions, rent increases, poor standards and housing precarity. A second strategy is to highlight the absurdity of the current situation (see figure 6.2). For example, in articles and opinion pieces in the mainstream media, the DTA argue that a consumer has more rights when renting a car than when renting a home. Other interventions provide a public articulation of the impossibility of organizing a life given the

Figure 6.2   DTA Demonstration. DTA.

levels of precarity that are currently the norm and making comparisons with
rental sectors in other countries where tenants enjoy strong rights.

   To return to the conceptual categories mentioned previously, most of the
DTA's activities take place at the level of the politics of the subject. It is
about, to quote Di Feliciantonio once more, a tenant perceiving himself or
herself 'as an actor who has the right to affordable housing and affirms it
through collective action and engagement' (2016, 51). But this subjective
transformation is also a directly material and economic one because by transforming the relationship between a tenant and the property they make their
home in, we transform a fundamental relationship, which is at the heart of the
Irish housing market and indeed the wider Irish economy—the relationship
between property ownership and the right to a home. Intervening at this level
thus engages a crucial point of antagonism in terms of the conflict between
home as a site of social reproduction and property as an asset and a vehicle
for the accumulation of wealth. Politicizing this antagonism is thus central to
bringing about meaningful change of our housing system.

The Challenges of Housing Politics in the First Person

The practices and methodologies developed by the DTA have met with
mixed success. By developing an analysis and discourse around the rental
sector, which is based on conversations among tenants and on our experiences and frustrations, the DTA has been successful in communicating in a
way which resonates with tenants. The methodology for dealing with housing
issues and the in-depth knowledge that DTA members have gained means
that much of the organizations' activities are relevant and useful to tenants.
The 'case work' aspect of the DTA also makes it easy to communicate what
the DTA is about with tenants. Ultimately, this aspect of the DTA is about
tenants helping each other; people helping each other is something almost
everyone understands and values. Case work also makes possible everyday
contact with a wide variety of tenants. This allows the DTA to communicate
its events, activities and media work to tenants and, in particular through
the Facebook page, create a space for analysis and debate around issues that
effect tenants. Finally, the combination of practical activities and sharp analysis has allowed the DTA to become a contributor to debates within the media
and develop allies within the academy and policy making.

   Nevertheless, the core objective of the DTA has been to create a space
which makes possible processes of collective political subjectivization that are
grounded in and draw strength from the materiality of tenants' experiences,
creating genuine connections between tenants. This has proved extremely
difficult. The case work methodology in particular has not led to long-term
or even medium-term relationships with tenants. Those who come with

specific housing issues usually discontinue contact once they have received the information they require or their issue is resolved. Rarely has a tenant gone from approaching the DTA with a specific housing issue to participating in meetings. It is unclear why the case work methodology has run up against these difficulties, and the DTA has struggled to develop other mechanisms to overcome this challenge. In addition, this type of work, which involved relationship building and connecting at an affective level, can be time consuming and difficult to find motivation for, particularly for a volunteer organization.

These limitations can be further analysed by drawing out a tension between what we might call 'organizing tenants' and 'organizing *as* tenants'. The DTA aims to enact politics in the first person, to experiment with new forms of organizing at the level of political subjectivization (organizing as tenants). However, media work, online activism and case work are sometimes characterized by what we might call a more 'representational' politics more akin to 'organizing tenants'. In the latter form the DTA are 'experts' (experts in policy, experts in media work, experts in activism, experts in case work) who are 'helping' or 'representing' tenants. For example, although the DTA is a regular commentator on the rental sector, the media tends to frame DTA as an 'interest group' which is 'representing tenants'. Rather than speaking 'as tenants', DTA is invited into the media game which tends to focus on policy, market dynamics and so on. In terms of 'case work', both tenants who come to the DTA with specific housing issues and other groups with whom the organization works sometimes relate to the DTA as 'experts' who are providing a service for tenants. As noted, moving beyond this type of relationship towards tenants has proved challenging.

However, media work, case work and lobbying have all been quite successful and are activities that many DTA members are already quite skilled at, leading to more 'results'. The aspect of the DTA's work, which focused more specifically on political subjectivization and building a collective transformative process, has been slower, more difficult and has required much reflection and analysis. For any organization, reflection and analysis can easily lead to stagnation and can result in difficulties maintaining motivation. In short, organizing tenants is easier than organizing as tenants. It also leads to more immediate and tangible results, which facilitates expanding membership and maintaining momentum. This tension remains unresolved, but it is likely that both forms of politics will be required to bring about any meaningful change in the PRS.

CONCLUSION

The DTA can be considered to be in a phase of experimentation. Therefore, it would be too hasty to suggest that we can draw robust conclusions from the successes and challenges of the last two years. Nevertheless, it is clear that the objective of generating collective political subjectivization is indeed challenging in the context of the PRS, where tenants are perhaps more interested in short-term and individual housing solutions than collectively changing the structure and political economy of the housing system. Moreover, the antagonisms between rental property as a site of social reproduction and as a financialized or speculative asset is fundamental to the rental sector and is likely to grow in intensity given the increasingly volatile and privatized nature of housing systems. Tenant organizing is thus an extremely important form of political intervention and a possible site of widespread radicalization and political organizing.

With this in mind, the relationships between tenant organizations internationally is an important and hopeful sign. Such organizations have already developed relationships and exchanges of ideas and experiences and there are ongoing attempts to strengthen this. Part of this process must involve an honest reflection on what works and what does not in current forms of political practice. Importantly, tenant organizing must remain sensitive to the specific material and subjective dimensions of the rental sector. Understanding both the affective and material everyday level will be crucial in developing organizational and discursive forms of intervention which are useful for tenants, which resonate with tenants and which can facilitate the emergence of a collective process of contestation and transformation.

NOTES

1. There are a number of exemptions to this regulation. In particular, properties newly brought to market are exempt, allegedly to maintain supply.
2. One piece of data, which is not definitive but substantiates this, is that approximately the same number of disputes are lodged by landlords each year as by tenants, despite the fact that there are three times as many tenants as landlords and tenants' experience the vast majority of violations.
3. Initially just one person took on such cases, but this was changed as dealing with cases can be difficult and stressful.

REFERENCES

Central Statistics Office (CSO). 2017. CSO 2016 Profile 1: Housing in Ireland. Dublin: CSO.
Colau, Ada, and Adria Alemany. 2012. *Mortgaged Lives. From the Housing Bubble to the Right to Housing*. Barcelona: Cuadrilatero Libros.

Di Feliciantonio, Cesare. 2016. "Subjectification in Times of Indebtedness and Neo-liberal/Austerity Urbanism." *Antipode* 48(5): 1206–27.

Downey, Daithi. 2014. "The Financialization of Irish Homeownership and the Impact of the Global Financial Crisis." In *Neoliberal Urban Policy and the Transformation of the City*, edited by Andrew MacLaran and Sinead Kelly, 120–38. London: Palgrave Macmillan UK.

Fields, Desiree. 2015. "Contesting the Financialization of Urban Space: Community-Based Organizations and the Struggle to Preserve Affordable Rental Housing in New York City." *Journal of Urban Affairs* 37(2): 144–65.

Fields, Desiree, and Sabina Uffer. 2016. "The Financialization of Rental Housing: A Comparative Analysis of New York City and Berlin." *Urban Studies* 53(7): 1486–1502.

García-Lamarca, Melissa. 2017a. "From Occupying Plazas to Recuperating Housing: Insurgent Practices in Spain." *International Journal of Urban and Regional Research*. doi: 10.1111/1468–2427.12386.

García-Lamarca, Melissa, and Maria Kaika. 2016. "'Mortgaged lives': The Biopolitics of Debt and Housing Financialization." *Transactions of the Institute of British Geographers* 41(3): 313–27.

Kelly, Sinead. 2014. "Light-Touch Regulation: The Rise and Fall of the Irish Banking Sector." In *Neoliberal Urban Policy and the Transformation of the City*, edited by Andrew MacLaran and Sinead Kelly, 37–53. London: Palgrave Macmillan UK.

Lyons, Ronan. 2017. Irish Rental Report Q4 2016. Dublin: Daft.ie. https://www.daft.ie/report/ronan-lyons-2016q4-rental.

Norris, Michelle. 2016. *Property, Family and the Irish Welfare State*. London: Palgrave Macmillan.

Norris, Michelle, and Michael Byrne. 2015. "Asset Price Urbanism in the Irish and Spanish Housing Crises." *Built Environment* 41(2): 205–21.

Norris, Michelle, and Dermot Coates. 2014. "How Housing Killed the Celtic Tiger: Anatomy and Consequences of Ireland's Housing Boom and Bust." *Journal of Housing and the Built Environment* 29(2): 299–315.

Ó Riain, Seán. 2014. *The Rise and Fall of Ireland's Celtic Tiger: Liberalism, Boom and Bust*. Cambridge: Cambridge University Press.

Sirr, Lorcan. 2014. "An Ideology of Renting." In *Renting in Ireland*, edited by Lorcan Sirr, 1–19. Dublin: Institute of Public Administration.

Chapter 7

Rebuilding a Shattered Housing Movement

Living Rent and Contemporary Private Tenant Struggles in Scotland

Living Rent
(Emma Saunders, Kate Samuels and Dave Statham)

Living Rent is a Scottish organization of private tenants with branches in Edinburgh, Glasgow, Aberdeen and Stirling. We formed in 2014 to campaign around a consultation for the Scottish Government's Private Housing (Tenancies) (Scotland) Bill, introduced in 2015 and passed in March 2016, and we are now in the process of expanding into a national union of tenants. Here, we look back to our origins, reflect critically upon our tactics and campaigns and outline our ambitions and future directions. Three members of Living Rent produced this chapter based on extensive interviews with fellow Living Rent members between October 2015 and February 2016. The housing situation we describe is thus largely the one preceding March 2016, as we have yet to see the full impacts of the bill. Unless named, 'we' is used throughout to express the collective voice of our members, themselves both tenants and activists. The following sections reflect on the origins of Living Rent, its principles and aims, the situation for tenants in Scotland prior to the new bill, the tactics used and the victories won within this context. Lastly, we reflect on recent developments following the ratification of the bill in March 2016.

THE ORIGINS OF LIVING RENT

Living Rent began as a result of a campaign around a consultation organized by the Scottish Parliament in 2014 over the new Private Housing (Tenancies)

(Scotland) Bill. People from different backgrounds and groups came together to campaign: tenant activists from Edinburgh Private Tenants Action Group (EPTAG) joined student activists from the National Union of Scotland (NUS), alongside community organizers from ACORN Scotland. As relayed by Becka, a member of Living Rent, all recognized the need to channel the 'growing frustration with the state of housing in Scotland' into coordinated action on a national level. A brief history of the private-rented sector (PRS) in Scotland and of the creation of EPTAG highlights why this diverse group came to believe that fighting at this scale—national legislation—was needed to improve tenants' rights.

In Scotland, and more widely in the United Kingdom, the PRS has historically represented a small portion of postwar housing. Until 1993, PRS tenants represented 7 percent of the Scottish population (Scottish Government 2014a) with PRS residence typically seen as a temporary step before homeownership or social housing. Despite this 'temporary' status, between 1915 and 1989 the PRS was regulated through different forms of rent control: a direct legal result of the 1915 Rent Strikes. This situation—a regulated and small PRS—dramatically shifted after the introduction of short tenancy agreements in 1985, which generalized insecure six-month or one-year leases. Additionally, the revocation of rent controls in the 1988 Housing Act and the dismantling of social housing—notably through the Right-to-Buy scheme initiated from 1980; housing 'stock transfer' from Council Housing to Housing Associations (HAs); and the promotion of different policies to encourage private ownership such as HA tenure-mix and 'Buy-to-Let' mortgages (Bentley 2015)—helped exacerbate an explosive new context in the PRS, marked by a lack of regulation. In contrast to many European countries with a much larger PRS, the UK legal system features few protections for private tenants, even though the number of people living in the PRS has doubled. Indeed, 15 percent of the Scottish population now lives in the PRS, a situation disproportionally affecting young people (Berry and Berthier 2015, 5).

Rent levels have soared since 1989. The Office of National Statistics shows that the price of private rentals in Scotland increased by 7 percent between January 2011 and July 2015 (Berry and Berthier 2015, 8). Rent for a four-bedroom flat rose by more than 65 percent in Aberdeen between 2010 and 2014 (Scottish Government 2014b) and by the first quarter of 2015, Scottish private-sector rents stood at 'an all-time high' (Citylets 2015). Providing a broader UK perspective, Bentley (2015, 11) argues that 'rent now costs private sector tenants on average 40 percent of their household income', in contrast to owner-occupiers who spend 20 percent of their income on their mortgage. Between 1989 and 2014, escalating rents have contributed to the doubling of the housing benefit bill for PRS tenants, which is forecasted to reach 10 billion by 2018/19 (13). 'Spiraling rents', Bentley contends, 'have a self-reinforcing impact on the evolution of the housing market as increasing numbers of people get caught in a "rent trap" with nothing left to save towards a deposit on a home of their own' (2015, 12).

An increasing number of people now live in a situation for which there are few institutional regulations, while landlords' interests prevail in the contemporary housing landscape. Contesting this situation, activists angered by the soaring rent prices and the blatant abuses of landlords formed EPTAG[1] in Edinburgh in 2011. They directed their energy towards single-issue housing campaigns and towards supporting individual struggles fought by renters. EPTAG members believed the fight for decent housing could enable a form of grassroots politics centered on achieving tangible victories while feeding into an intensely political fight around social justice issues. Many perceived a widespread stagnation of Left activism and wished to sidestep party politics without sidestepping political activism. EPTAG fought and won small but tangible victories against criminal landlords and against the predatory fee-charging practices of letting agencies.

However, when EPTAG attempted to campaign against unacceptable aspects of current housing legislation such as illegal letting agency fees and evictions, these efforts often faltered for lack of minimum basic rights. As explained, the PRS sector was unregulated; there was no security of tenure, no rent regulation and no quality standards to abide by.[2] Tenants could not make demands or negotiate on many issues. An early EPTAG campaign targeted the 'no fault' grounds for eviction: a particularly nasty section of the law that entitled landlords to evict tenants at the end of a tenancy absent any 'fault' on the part of the tenant. This constituted a major hurdle to organizing; few people were willing to get involved when they knew that they could be easily evicted from their home while their landlord was excused from providing reasonable justification. Thus, EPTAG's campaign failed to get off the ground, undermined by the problem it aimed to resolve. The lesson was clear: tenant security is an essential precondition for successful organizing. To achieve it required change on a national level.[3] Against the background of an escalating housing crisis, just fighting for small gains seemed necessary but insufficient.

EPTAG activists increasingly realized that although single-issue based campaigns and direct action could achieve concrete victories ('single-issue campaigns could only get us so far') 'something much more coordinated' was needed (Susan). Members started to envisage a national movement for tenants capable of lobbying the government for change. But how such a movement would be organized lacked focus and coherence. The Scottish Independence Referendum, and shortly following this, the consultation on the Scottish Government's Private Housing (Tenancies) (Scotland) Bill in October 2014 provided the catalyst for our tenants' movement. The immediacy of the independence issue and its framing in terms of everyday concerns fueled a wave of democratic engagement and politicization. There was a sense that 'politics' could be grassroots, pragmatic and address everyday issues. As Becka recalls, '[t]he aftermath of the referendum campaign gave us the opportunity to meet enthusiastic campaigners who wanted to continue the momentum the referendum campaign had sparked politically in Scotland.'

One month after the referendum, the Scottish government launched a public consultation on new tenancy arrangements for the PRS, as part of the development of the Private Housing Bill. The Scottish government was proposing substantial changes to the existing tenancy type, and activists from various movements believed that this provided the ideal opportunity to represent tenants' issues nationally. Rather than each organization drafting an individual response, EPTAG members, National Union of Students (NUS) activists and ACORN organizers agreed to draft a coordinated response under a single Living Rent campaign. Taking advantage of the radical sentiment inspired by the referendum, Living Rent was conceived as one of the first steps towards once again being able to take collective action *as tenants*.

PRINCIPLES, AIMS AND TACTICS

As private tenants, we have limited power over our basic living conditions. As Susan joked, 'As it stands in the current law [before March 2016], you probably have more rights buying a sandwich than renting a home.' This lack of power is brought into stark relief when one considers the relationship between a tenant and their landlord. Of course, the *economic* and income disparity is glaring. But what's perhaps less obvious is the amount of *political* inequality. In the absence of any organized tenant opposition, the views of landlords and councils occupy the political stage when it comes to housing. Landlords organize into prominent and vocal bodies to represent their interests. Councils, pushed by cuts and competition, increasingly concentrate on the interests of investors and developers. By contrast, in 2014, no representative, independent organization with any political weight and campaigning goals existed exclusively for tenants in Scotland. Living Rent aimed to rectify this situation.

When Living Rent formed, it was a coalition of organizations. Since July 2016, we have formed as a union of tenants. As our current mission statement has it, we are 'a union for tenants in Scotland, fighting for tenants' rights and decent and affordable housing for all'. We fight for more power and rights for renters. Currently this goal boils down to three key aims: for the power imbalance between tenant and landlord to be redressed; for houses to be seen first and foremost as homes, not as investment opportunities; and for everyone in Scotland to have access to decent and affordable housing. These aims are underwritten by our core principles:

1. We are a democratic organization led by and for tenants.
2. We adopt a range of tactics to achieve our goals. Throughout our recent existence, we have continuously emphasized multiple approaches (direct action, campaigning and lobbying) at a range of scales: from the local to the national scale and targeting both private actors, such as letting agencies, and public authorities.
3. We are independent, unaffiliated to political parties and work with all who share our concerns and goals.

These principles reflect our belief that 'the only way those of us who rent will have any power is through collective action', and that collective action should be democratic (Becka). In many ways, we are no different from previous tenants and activists who have recognized the power of collective action and built powerful housing movements in the United Kingdom. Yet at the same time Living Rent has developed primarily as a PRS movement, deviating from more traditional public housing movements in the postwar era. Collective PRS activism is an emerging development, urgently borne from a dramatic historical shift from public to private housing in the United Kingdom since 1980 (see also Byrne on Ireland and Spain, this volume). Although we value the role of charities such as Shelter and Crisis, and of experts advocating in favour of housing issues, we believe it is essential that private tenants speak *for themselves* at all scales. We take a more aggressive stance than charities are willing or able to, challenging the received opinion that the current tenant-landlord relationship is a cooperative, equal or win-win situation. The issue is not just one of 'rights':

> Campaigners who tell tenants what their rights are miss the point that tenants *don't have* rights. For example, even when a tenant pays their rent on time, their landlord can evict them without reason at any time of the year. Even if what rights that do exist were actually enforced, the [tenant's] situation would still be terrible. Even if there were no illegal fees or deposits withheld, it would still be an exploitative relationship. (Marc)

Owing to its initial focus on influencing the development of a new tenancy type, Living Rent began as a heavily policy-orientated campaign. Much of the organization, groundwork and recruitment was carried out with a primary focus on getting the best deal we could out of the Scottish Private Housing Bill. However, our vision has always remained broader than this. As Marc explained, although that campaign was still active:

We always had an ambition to combine both policy and direct action. We wanted to be professional, lobby and also do direct action and be grassroots. [But] we have been heavier on one side with policy, because it would have been weird to do lots of direct action during a consultation. There will be a point where government says yes or no to our suggestions in this Bill and [then] we might need to take a more direct approach.[4]

In the next section, we examine more closely the campaign around the bill, before exploring how Living Rent is currently organizing following the bill's approval.

CAMPAIGNING AROUND THE PRIVATE HOUSING (TENANCIES) (SCOTLAND) BILL

The bill gave us the opportunity to draw attention to two core issues that had stymied previous attempts to organize: increased tenant security and rent controls. We believe that the two necessarily go hand in hand. Without direct intervention in the market to bring down extortionate rent levels, increased tenant security would just bind tenants into already unaffordable tenancies. With the introduction of rent controls, tenants would still have to appeal to authorities individually if they deemed that their rents had reached an 'unfair' level. Yet, tenants cannot fight in their own corner when they are under threat of eviction. The same goes for any further demands, at both the individual and collective level. Tenants will only be able to assert their rights when they can do so without fear of reprisal and eviction and have a secure claim to their home.

Security of Tenure and Rent Controls

Before the promulgation of the bill in March 2016 and reflecting the legacy of thirty years of retrenchment of private tenants' rights, most private tenants in Scotland faced a legal situation which provided them with little protection, no security of tenure and an absence of flexibility in an explosive housing market. The existence of the 'no-fault' ground for eviction and the system of rolling tenancies threatened any sense of security. In Scotland, most tenants in the private sector were offered short-assured tenancies instead of more secure ones, such as assured tenancies. These short (usually six-month) contracts provided the tenant minimum security and bargaining power because of the inclusion of the no-fault grounds; after the first six months, landlords could easily 'reclaim' their property under the no fault grounds for repossession. Following the expiration of a short-assured tenancy, the contract automatically switched to a rolling, month-by-month tenancy. This meant that tenants were often scared to ask for repairs or to complain about rent increases because the alternative could mean no housing at all. We would hear from tenants who were frightened to ask their landlord to carry out basic repair and maintenance work, or who felt the need to hide their beliefs or sexuality in the knowledge that the no-fault grounds effectively allowed the landlord to refuse a tenancy extension without justification. As EPTAG experienced, under such conditions, tenant organizing is heavily compromised.

Even tenants with a slightly more secure assured tenancy faced serious difficulties. The law legislated for mandatory grounds for eviction, which, if the grounds were proven, meant that a court was legally obliged to grant an eviction order, irrespective of the tenant's circumstances. Thus, tenants falling into rent arrears could easily be made homeless by the courts. If the landlord simply wished to renovate the property, this, too, was grounds for eviction without compensation. Challenging these conditions, we have argued that as an absolute minimum all grounds for eviction must be discretionary, meaning that courts would have the power to deny an eviction order in cases where this would lead to severe financial hardship, the worsening of a serious illness or the disruptive relocation of young children from their local schools. On the other hand, short-assured tenancies also locked tenants into a contract for six months; a tenant could not leave early without being penalized financially even if their circumstances changed drastically. We heard of people losing their job but being trapped into paying for flats they could no longer afford and of tenants being trapped living in abusive relationships because of their inability to leave the property. We argued that contracts should be flexible enough to allow for tenants, under a minimum notice period, to leave tenancies that could put them in severe financial hardship or dangerous situations.

As shown, the state of the current 'housing market' hammers home the aforementioned message that the fight for more secure housing does not make sense without a fight for affordable rents. Knowing that in a year's time you will have the right to stay in a home you can't afford is of little comfort. In the current situation, we believe that rent controls are a necessity, and this claim formed the second cornerstone of our campaign around the new bill. From October 2014, we fought hard on these two primary objectives. We fought against the no-fault grounds, advocating for the replacement of mandatory grounds for eviction with clearer discretionary grounds, and demanding the right for tenants to stay in their homes as long as they like, coupled with the ability to leave when they need to. We also raised the controversial issue of rent controls into public and political consciousness, perhaps for the first time in the United Kingdom since rent controls were substantially revoked in the Housing Act 1988.[5]

From Lobbying to Street Stalls

Much of our work surrounding the bill was shaped by the nature of the parliamentary process, both in terms of the kinds of demands that could be made (and listened to) and in terms of the activities best suited to the task of making them. We chose lobbying and campaigning as tactics, not as ends, because we felt they were the essential means of achieving our goals. We believe that at each stage the process was improved by the work we carried out alongside and in complement to it. We used a range of tactics—from coalition building to alternative knowledge production, from street stalls to twitter storm—to promote our two clear tenant demands: security (including flexibility for tenants) and affordability. With regard to the bill, we believed Members of Scottish Parliament (MSPs) and civil servants were the potential agents of immediate change. Thus, we directed much effort towards speaking directly with MSPs and civil servants and maintaining regular contact with them. Our political neutrality allowed us the freedom to be critical at every stage of the debate and to ensure that we could sustain widespread support from people of all political persuasions. We openly challenged parties where necessary and praised them when they listened. We cultivated a broad support base spread across the Scottish National Party (SNP), Labour, and the Greens, all of whom have been vocal in supporting Living Rent to varying degrees. We also reached party members at the branch level, mindful of the fact that, despite strict hierarchies, support at every level would ultimately work in our favour.

In addition to this, Living Rent volunteers put in an immense amount of work to run stalls, public meetings and door-knocking campaigns all over the country. We spoke at events addressing trades unions, student unions, party conferences, picket lines and charities. There, we received an overwhelmingly positive response; people were passionate about the housing question. In quantitative terms, this engagement with the public culminated in the second of our petitions receiving more than eight thousand signatures endorsing our demands for rent controls and increased security of tenure. Although acknowledging the limits of many petitions as a mode of political activism, in this case, our petition amounted to a massive proportion of the responses to the government's public consultation on the proposed bill and was essential to demonstrating the degree of public support for tenants' rights. Given the massive effort landlord lobbies put into answering the consultation as well, we believe this petitioning concretely influenced the outcome. Without it, only landlord and letting agencies' voices would have been heard.

Of similarly immeasurable worth was the amount of interest and support these activities generated for the campaign. A movement needs members, and although social media is crucial for recruitment and publicity, the campaign showed that offline activities engaged with more people. Segerberg and Bennett (2011) argue that online activism has a greater reach than offline activism, but we found that this only worked for us when the offline event took place first. For example, after doing a stall and sharing photos of this on social media, we would often get more petition sign ups online. As Phil claims, 'offline gathering was greater than clicktivism'. Our aim has always been to *persuade* and mobilize people around our core aims, and for that, face-to-face conversations are necessary. Often, by sharing a personal story of our renting experience, we were able to get people on our side. Across Scotland, branches in Edinburgh, Glasgow, Aberdeen, Dundee and Stirling organized numerous public stalls. As Marc recalls, 'we had to stop people and win the argument. There were lots of people who were not convinced at first, but after speaking for only five minutes they were!' It was a matter of resuscitating interest in an issue that had disappeared from public debate: tenants' rights. Our conversations were often initiated by simply asking people on the street: 'Is your rent too high?'; 'Would you like rent controls?'; 'What do you think about housing in Scotland?' People's responses, once prompted, were overwhelmingly similar: rents are too high, there are no rights and it's unfair. Following these three statements, signing the petition was almost inevitable. Rent controls and increased tenancy security, we found, were popular issues; it was only a matter of reintroducing them into the public conversation.

We enjoyed significant coverage in both the national and regional press. The landlord lobby always seemed to be ready with a misleading response to any development regarding the bill, and we worked hard to anticipate and publicly counter this. Coalition building with other organizations was also central. Major unions and a significant number of charities affiliated to the campaign.[6] Working with trades unions and other groups gave us access to substantial preexisting membership bases, as well as winning us political influence and perceived *respectability*. One now hears Unite, for example, talk about housing and rent controls as a major issue. Such a broad-based coalition was central to pushing rent controls higher up the political agenda and making politicians listen. Finally, we engaged in alternative knowledge production. Our blogs and public interventions countered the demonization of rent controls and security. We demonstrated, on the contrary, that these are legitimate, respectable and sensible policies. Our volunteers researched the different rent systems in France, Germany and the Netherlands. We worked with different groups, hosted speakers (including the Chief Economist of the Swedish Union of Tenants) and produced our own policy recommendation paper, which we distributed at our events.

Campaign Results

So much for the value of public outreach in building the campaign, what have we actually achieved in terms of the bill? We gained significant improvements in security of tenure and put the issue of rent controls back on the political agenda. The bill, as published on March 18, 2016, has scrapped the no-fault grounds for eviction; landlords now need to provide legally sound reasons to evict their tenants. Tenants can now demand repairs, claim back illegal fees and report malpractice without undue fear of repossession. In terms of flexibility of tenure, the position of Living Rent was that terminating fixed contracts would give tenants more security. The final bill reflects this position because the majority of political parties agreed about the danger of rigid tenancy contracts after discussing the issue with us. We believe such indefinite contracts, with a list of defined grounds for eviction, provides a more secure legal framework for private tenants.

Notwithstanding these gains, we regret that many of the grounds remain mandatory and ambiguous. Grounds for eviction mentions 'intention'—in the case of a landlord 'intending' to refurbish his or her property—which we believe is far too vague. Similarly, eviction on the grounds of rent arrears remains unacceptably easy. The high cost of renting in combination with ongoing wage stagnation makes the possibility of falling into arrears common for many private tenants. Punishing tenants with rapid eviction proceedings in the event of an inability to pay is an unjust response to a social problem that is structural and systemic. We advocated for a Hardship Defence mechanism to be put in place rather than mandatory eviction in the event of rent arrears. However, the bill as voted failed to introduce such a mechanism. Finally, there remain several clauses that could punish tenants for their landlord's mistakes; for example, the failure of a landlord to register with the local authority is grounds for tenant eviction. We thus continue to advocate for discretionary grounds for eviction to give tenants a chance to fight back against unfair decisions.

Regarding rent controls, the bill mentions a form of regulation of rent increases, and it includes provisions for rent controls in 'rent pressure areas'. The bill provides local authorities with the opportunity to apply to the government to implement rent controls in an area where it can be proven that rents are rising too quickly or are causing undue hardship at current levels. This would set a cap on the possible percentage increase in any rent in the area for up to five years following a formula involving the Consumer Price Index (accounting for inflation) + 1 + a positive number chosen by the central government. We have yet to see such measures implemented. However, here are some of our concerns. Quite what counts as a 'rent pressure area' is unclear, and the possibility remains open for a cap to be introduced without forcing any truly significant change in local rent levels. The cap also applies only to sitting tenants, meaning the temptation to hike up rents in between tenancies remains and cannot be punished. In areas of high turnover—which happen to be those most likely to qualify as pressure areas—such controls are unlikely to be effective. What's more, one key aspect of our campaign for rent controls was to highlight the need for rents to be determined according to factors such as the quality of the property, rather than tying caps only to local market levels or to inflation.

Further, we believe the central affordability problem remains unaddressed: *under such a formula, rent levels cannot be decreased.* Of course, we welcome any curb on spiraling rents. But in a market that is out of control, rents need to come down rather than just rise at a less extreme rate. This will not be achieved easily, and this is in part why we came to imagine Living Rent as a campaigning Union. The bill's limitations highlight the need for tenants to organize beyond providing a better legal framework for individual relationships between a tenant and their landlords. Given an innate imbalance of power between tenant and landlord, better laws are a necessary but not a sufficient condition for improving tenants' rights and regulating rent. We believe a strong tenants' movement can alter the balance of power in the housing sector by building collective power and a multitude of voices to confront the well-organized and powerful landlord lobby.

Despite all these drawbacks, Living Rent has succeeded in getting rent controls onto the agenda for the first time in nearly thirty years. Little more than a year ago the notion was taboo. For Becka and Morag, Living Rent brought the debate about rent controls into the public sphere: 'a year ago, it was a dirty word, politicians [were] not talking about it,' (Morag) and 'groups such as Shelter were never going to bring it up' (Becka). As a result of our intervention, however, the idea has lost much of 'its shock value' (Morag), and it has now entered the realms of political discourse and feasibility. In advance of the 2016 elections, 90 percent of the parties in Holyrood in some way committed to rent controls, with sustained pressure coming from their base. We are winning the argument that the free market cannot deliver affordable housing, and that regulation is both vital and necessary. We have not yet won the rent controls that are sorely needed, but we—along with sister organizations throughout the United Kingdom—have shifted the terms of the debate and made some notable material and political gains with the potential for further generalization.

As the bill has passed we have seen significant debates in the United Kingdom over rent control[7] and over housing-related issues more generally. Rent pressure zones are now also on the agenda in Ireland (see Byrne, this volume). Moreover, after sustained campaigning by Living Rent precursor EPTAG and other groups, the Scottish government has proscribed illegal letting fees (charges other than rent and a refundable deposit). In England, a proposal banning letting agency fees and seeking to 'provide a fairer deal for renters' was forwarded in April 2017 (Department for Communities and Local Government, 2017), and Wales is now considering similar legislation.

THE FUTURE: A SCOTTISH UNION OF TENANTS

The bill provided the ideal focus to engage in lobbying, improve our organizational skills and raise the profile of our core demands. But what next? As mentioned, our ambitions have always outstripped the opportunities afforded to us in the guise of a parliamentary lobbying campaign. Our only limitation is a lack of resources. But after the bill was passed, to win more radical change and further power for tenants, we turned our efforts to building a movement with more members and an increase in local actions. To finance this, we launched Living Rent as a Tenants' Union in July 2016. Through the union, we aim to strengthen our local branches, develop national campaigns with affiliated organizations, fight more local campaigns and involve tenants and activists beyond the electoral and parliamentary calendar.

Internally, we face the difficulties of a change in culture from lobbying to organizing. Many of our members come from a political and lobbying activism background (from political parties, the national student union and charities). To expand this skills base, we trained our members to use more community-organizing methods such as stalls and door-knocking to recruit and engage with new members and follow up and encourage members to seek collective solutions to the housing question. We learned from the experiences and methods of Scottish community organizers, ACORN organizers and from community organizations developing in many English cities (Bristol, Newcastle, London, etc.). Geographically, each local branch has a different history of people organizing, and mobilizing these groupings into a more coherent body is a substantial task that involves a common culture and a common set of tools while also providing sufficient autonomy to each branch as regards specific campaigns.

Externally, we still face the daunting task of building a tenants' union following the virtual collapse of the broader independent housing movement in the United Kingdom. We firmly believe in the potential for alternative forms of political and community organizations, separate from party politics and democratic, active and powerful. But materially we are held back by the familiar limitations of time and money. Our volunteers are overstretched and lack the capacity to put in the time needed to expand the organization. In January 2017, we hired our first part-time member of staff in Glasgow, using our savings and Tenant Union dues. We are currently recruiting a new paid member of staff in Edinburgh. Securing substantial funding is an important target for the near future because it would allow us to employ people full-time to carry out the work necessary to expand the movement. These appointments are and will help to make the movement more accessible, while also helping to diversify the membership beyond just those who have the time to attend regular meetings. As we move away from purely lobbying-based activities and towards a more union-like structure, serious work is needed to ensure that we are accountable to and represent the tenants who join us as members. We have set up a hardship fund, available to all members who face unexpected costs relating to housing. Yet, we remain wary of unions which turn into 'service' providers. Campaigns that only help tenants know and access their legal rights miss the fundamental point that tenants barely have any rights. Raising tenants' awareness and enforcing existing rights is essential, but we believe we need to continue to fight for more rights and organize collectively to challenge the fundamentally exploitative landlord–tenant relationship.

In terms of specific campaigns, we are focusing on three campaigns at different scales. On the national level, the new bill's change in the tribunal system will provide interesting avenues to fight for tenants' rights. We aim to ensure that tenants can take full advantage of the new legislation and that appeals against unfair and unreasonable evictions, and against rip-off rents, can be carried through to fruition. We also campaign to guarantee that the panels influencing these decisions do not just comprise landlords and industry professionals. They should involve actual tenants, involved in the issues, aware of the problems and with a real stake in the outcomes. In addition, we continue to lobby the government for further change in the mandatory grounds for eviction, while campaigning for radical change to the PRS and a national system of quality-linked rent controls.

At the local level, we have continued to develop and encourage campaigns and direct actions against particular landlords and letting agents. In particular, we campaign around the monitoring of illegal premium fees—such as administration fees, change of tenancy fees, cleaning fees and deposit fees—charged by letting agencies, despite being illegal in Scotland since 2012 following successful campaigns by Living Rent and Shelter Scotland. We have been confronting letting agencies to change this situation and ensure that the law is respected. As well as achieving concrete results for tenants, such local battles provide an excellent way of drawing people into the movement and keeping them engaged. We have also helped members fight evictions and confront social housing authorities, as we seek to support all tenants in Scotland.

In the long term, the direction Living Rent takes is to be determined by the organization's members. We have noted the importance of increased funding, but we will not accept money (or political capital) that would bind us to particular goals or force compromise on any of the organization's basic principles. We continue to shift the discourse away from Thatcherite assumptions about the free market and minimal state and fight for rent controls to be in the public consciousness. The Glasgow branch has been mobilizing around the new 'rent pressure zone' legislation, and this is now a national campaign strategy for Living Rent. Ultimately, we seek the decline of the PRS. Surveys consistently show that people do not want to live in private-rented housing. The relationship between landlord and tenant is inherently exploitative and there are limits to how fair it can be made through reform. If we exist only to ameliorate its worst aspects, we will have fallen short of our potential. Our pragmatic steps to challenge the housing situation are also powered by our wish that public housing and genuinely affordable private-rented housing should be available for all. Yet, we know that to achieve both smaller and larger victories, we need sustained collective action on the part of tenants. Such action requires a powerful, well-organized and mass movement: a Scottish Union of Tenants.

NOTES

1. http://eptag.org.uk/.
2. To add a slight nuance, since 2003 PRS homes with more than two households have to abide by House in Multiple Occupancy (HMO) rules. These rules provide neither security nor quality of housing; they mainly cover fire-related improvements in the house.
3. 'National' here refers to Scotland; housing being a devolved issue.
4. The government did accept a number of our suggestions. However, these have been limited and fail to resolve some of the most important problems, such as rising rents.
5. From 15 January 1989, new tenancies were no longer subject to controls established in the Rent Act 1977.
6. For example: Unite, Unison, RMT, GMB, UCU, Acorn, NUS Scotland, Scottish Churches Housing Action, STUC Youth Committee, Scottish Youth Parliament, Zero Tolerance and multiple Students' Unions.
7. Governments have multiplied research into rent controls. For example, the UK government ordered a briefing on the 'historical context of rent control in the private rented sector' to the Library of the House of Commons in 2013; the London Assembly commissioned Cambridge academics on the subject in 2015; and the Scottish government had a briefing on private rents in 2015.

REFERENCES

Bentley, David. 2015. "The Future of Private Renting." January. *London: Civitas*. http://civitas.org.uk/pdf/thefutureofprivaterenting.
Berry, Kate, and Anouk Berthier. 2015. "SPICe Briefing: Private Rents." 15/66, October 15. Edinburgh: Scottish Parliament. http://www.parliament.scot/Research-BriefingsAndFactsheets/S4/SB_15-66_Private_Rents.pdf.

Citylets. 2015. "Oil Cooled Market." *Quarterly Report* 33: https://www.citylets. co.uk/research/reports/pdf/Citylets-Rental-Report-Q1-15.pdf?ref=reports,

Department for Communities and Local Government (DCLG). 2017. Government Action to Ban Letting Agent Fees. https://www.gov.uk/government/news/government-action-to-ban-letting-agent-fees.

Scottish Government. 2014a. Housing Statistics for Scotland—Key Information and Summary Tables. http://www.gov.scot/Topics/Statistics/Browse/Housing-Regeneration/HSfS/KeyInfoTables.

———. 2014b. Private Sector Rent Statistics, Scotland (2010 to 2014). http://www.gov.scot/Publications/2014/11/2313.

Segerberg, A., and W. Lance Bennett. 2011. "Social Media and the Organization of Collective Action: Using Twitter to Explore the Ecologies of Two Climate Change Protests." *Communication Review* 14(3): 197–215.

Chapter 8

'Social Housing Not Social Cleansing'

Contemporary Housing Struggles in London

Paul Watt

This chapter provides an overview of contemporary housing struggles in London, a city that is experiencing a chronic housing crisis. As this crisis has deepened and broadened in terms of insecurity and unaffordability, so London's housing struggles have multiplied. Some idea of the latter's diversity can be gauged by how the Radical Housing Network (RHN)—a London-based umbrella organization 'made up of groups fighting for housing justice' set up in 2013—has twenty-six signed-up campaigns.[1] These include Defend Council Housing, Tower Hamlets Renters, Focus E15, SQUASH (Squatters' Action for Secure Homes), National Bargee Travellers Association, UCL Cut the Rent and Grenfell Action Group. One leitmotif that runs throughout London's housing struggles is 'social housing not social cleansing', a slogan that originated with the Focus E15 campaign in East London but which appears widely across the city (see figure 8.2, for example). As Watt and Minton (2016) argue, social housing in London—consisting of public 'council housing', housing association and cooperative rented properties—has shrunk, consequent on a sustained, decades' long, neoliberal policy assault. Social housing can be regarded as a part of the 'urban commons', which stands in opposition to the logic of commodification (Gillespie et al. 2018; Hodkinson 2012b). The social housing not social cleansing slogan speaks to activists' interlinked demands *for* protecting and expanding the social rental sector and *against* the ever-present spectre of social cleansing for London's poor and working-class residents (i.e., the prospect of displacement away from their neighbourhood to cheaper urban areas or even outside the city altogether) as a result of evictions, demolitions, rent hikes and benefit cuts (Elmer and Dening 2016; Minton 2017; Watt and Minton 2016; Watt 2017). As such, social housing not social cleansing emphasizes the defence and expansion of the urban commons, coupled with the preservation of the 'right to the city' for ordinary Londoners and especially those who are socially marginalized because of classed, racialized and gendered exclusionary processes (Harvey 2012; Watt 2017; Gillespie et al. 2018).

This chapter focuses on research on several London-based housing struggles, including participation in some cases. Each section illustrates social housing not social cleansing, even if this particular wording is of relatively recent origin, as well as the defence of 'our homes and communities', a prominent theme within the UK social-housing tenants' movement (Bradley 2014). The first two sections outline campaigns—against Housing Action Trusts in the late 1980s and against housing stock transfers during the 1990s–2000s—which both emphasized the defence of council housing. The chapter then moves forward to the last decade by first examining the struggle against the demolition of council and housing association estates, which is taking place under the guise of 'regeneration', and, second, those campaigns which focus on challenging planning applications. The penultimate section focuses on resistance to the break-up of short-life housing cooperatives, and the final section examines activists' tactics of temporary occupations and focuses on one such occupation that occurred at a half-empty council estate awaiting regeneration.

'FLATTEN THAT HAT':
THE CAMPAIGN AGAINST HOUSING ACTION TRUSTS

The Margaret Thatcher and Major Conservative governments of the 1980s and 1990s mounted a multistranded neoliberal policy assault on the principle of public housing as a core element of the UK postwar Keynesian welfare state (Hodkinson et al. 2013). These neoliberal policies were designed to privatize and demunicipalize council housing away from public ownership either towards heavily subsidized, individual homeownership via the Right-to-Buy (RTB) in the Housing Act 1980 or towards nonpublic landlords via Housing Action Trusts and Large Scale Voluntary Transfer. The aim of Housing Action Trusts (HATs), introduced in the Housing Act 1988, was to take some of the 'worst estates' out of local authority control for a 5- to 10-year period and put them under the control of a HAT, which would renovate them and then sell them back to either a housing association or private landlord (Tiesdell 2001). The first phase of HATs was led by the central government and targeted six local authority areas: three in London (Lambeth, Southwark and Tower Hamlets) and three elsewhere in England (Tiesdell 2001). The early intention—before the 1988 act was passed—was for HATs to be imposed by central government with no intention of holding a ballot of affected tenants. During this period, strong grassroots tenant

opposition to HATs emerged in all areas alongside widespread local authority opposition (Tiesdell 1999). Tenants of the six affected Tower Hamlets'
estates received a letter in mid-1988 telling them about the proposed HAT.
As Woodward (1991) details, Tower Hamlets' tenants rapidly mobilized
around the preservation of their council homes, with HATs being widely
regarded as a Tory privatization vehicle. The six national HAT areas collabo-
rated. As Beatty, one of the Tower Hamlets' anti-HAT campaigners, said:
'it was the nationwide thing that we joined up with, we had a big massive
meeting at York Hall, we had people come down from up north. So it was a
joined up campaign, it wasn't just one area' (2017 interview).

The anti-HAT campaigns lobbied the House of Commons and House of
Lords and tenants spoke at the latter. Although the government had initially
not wanted a tenant ballot, the House of Lords defeated the government on
this in July 1988 such that a ballot was required by the time the 1988 act was
passed in November (Tiesdell 2001). Not only did the campaign engage in
more 'respectable' lobbying of Parliament, but campaigners from across the
country also travelled to the Cotswold home of Nicholas Ridley, Secretary of
State of the Environment in November 1988, to 'see how he would respond to
having his home taken over by a HAT' (figure 8.1). As Beatty recounts, 'we
just invaded their homes and gardens basically'. This furious campaigning

Figure 8.1   Anti-HAT protest outside Nicholas Ridley's home, November 1988.
Courtesy of Ocean Estate Tenants Association.

paid off because the government abandoned all six initial HATs with most not even getting to the ballot stage (Tiesdell 1999, 2001; Woodward 1991). As Tiesdell (2001, 367) argues, the government had not anticipated the extent of opposition: 'the overarching concerns were about future rent levels and security of tenure. Tenants felt there would be little point in their homes being improved if they could not afford the new rents and/or were displaced during or after improvement'. As Beatty said about Tower Hamlets:

> People were very happy [that the HAT was dropped] because they all kept their secure tenancy. See, the campaign really was about assured tenancy and secure tenancy, and people were just petrified of assured tenancies, they can chuck you out, can't they, if you live with your parents and they both die then you are on your own, on your bike, can't hand down the [tenancy].

HATs evolved over time but only a few went ahead in London (Tiesdell 2001). Far more significant for the city's housing landscape and struggles is housing stock transfer to which I now turn.

'VOTE NO TO PRIVATIZATION': CAMPAIGN AGAINST STOCK TRANSFERS

Large-scale voluntary transfer (LSVT)—the stock transfer process whereby a local authority landlord sells the stock of rented housing to a housing association on the basis of a tenants' ballot—began nationally in 1988, but only became significant in London's housing struggles during the late 1990s–late 2000s. Stock transfer had limited impact in London until 1997, after which it formed a key plank in New Labour's 'modernization' agenda for the welfare state (Watt 2009a, 2009b). In introducing its Decent Homes initiative, New Labour tied local authority funding for improvements to three 'options': stock transfer, Arm's Length Management Organization (ALMO) or Private Finance Initiative (PFI) (Hodkinson et al. 2013). LSVT forms part of the neoliberalization of housing because it ensures marketization, either directly or indirectly, by ruling out direct public investment by councils in their stock, that is, the 'fourth option' (HOCCHG 2009; Hodkinson et al. 2013). Opponents regard stock transfer as the 'privatization of council housing' and argue that—when comparing local authority 'secure' tenancies to housing association 'assured' tenancies—it results in higher rents, lower security and lack of democratic accountability. Large anti-transfer campaigns arose in cities such as Birmingham, Edinburgh and Glasgow, as well as London, while the national Defend Council Housing (DCH) campaign was formed in London during the late 1990s. A cross-party House of Commons Council Housing

Group was formed at which DCH, Austin Mitchell, the Labour Member of Parliament (MP) for Hull and other MPs held a series of meetings at the House of Commons, which provided a forum for council tenants from all over the country to highlight the problems of stock transfer and to argue for, direct public investment in council housing (HOCCHG 2009).

As several London councils put forward proposals to transfer slices of their stock during the late 1990s and early 2000s, so tenants, community and political groups established borough-wide, anti-transfer campaigns. In addition to national concerns regarding rents and security, London anti-transfer campaigns were spurred by the very real potential for transfer to enhance gentrification via 'state-led gentrification' (Watt 2009a). A major part of DCH's grassroots strength lay in London and especially in inner London boroughs such as Camden, Southwark and Tower Hamlets (Watt 2009a, 2009b). Each of these boroughs had prominent successful anti-transfer campaigns. In Southwark, campaigners famously voted against stock transfer at the Aylesbury estate in 2001, whereas fifteen 'no votes' occurred at Tower Hamlets' estates, contributing towards Tower Hamlets Council dropping its transfer programme (Watt 2009b). One-third of all London ballots resulted in 'no votes' with tenants wishing to remain with their council landlord, a higher figure than the one-quarter average for England (Watt 2009b). As the stock transfer programme began to peter out and the Coalition and Conservative Governments broadened out their 'austerity' assault on all forms of state support for housing (via Housing Benefit caps, the Bedroom Tax, cuts to social housing grants, etc.), a wider set of housing struggles has emerged and it is these I now examine.

'SAVE OUR HOMES':
THE FIGHT AGAINST ESTATE DEMOLITIONS

The 'regeneration' of council-built estates via either full or partial demolition is one of the major issues galvanizing London's recent housing struggles along social housing, not social cleansing lines. Estate demolitions date back to the 1970s, but they have accelerated since 2000. Local authorities and housing associations justify demolition by arguing that 'Londoners need more homes and more homes can be built on the footprint of "failed/sink estates" since they are low-density', as suggested in the *City Villages* report by Adonis and Davies (2015). Estate demolitions have been pursued with alacrity by Conservative councils such as Barnet, but also by several Labour councils including Southwark, Newham and Lambeth (see Elmer and Dening 2016; Lees and Ferreri 2016; Minton 2017; Watt and Minton 2016). Such estate demolitions have made low-income Londoners' housing crisis *worse,* not better via displacement and insufficient social housing replacement; a Greater London Authority (GLA) report identified 50 estates which had undergone demolition from 2004 to 2014, resulting in a net loss of around 8,300 social rental homes (cited in Watt and Minton 2016, 212).

Campaigns have sprung up against demolition in numerous social-housing estates across the city: 'Save Cressingham Gardens' in Lambeth, 'Our West Hendon' in Barnet, 'Northumberland Park Decides' in Haringey, 'Save Northwold' in Hackney, and 'Carpenters Against Regeneration Plans' (CARP) in Newham (Watt 2013), to name a few. There are also borough-wide groups contesting estate regeneration/demolition, such as the '35% Campaign' in Southwark and StopHDV (Stop Haringey Development Vehicle) campaign in Haringey, plus citywide networks including Demolition Watch London, RHN and London Tenants Federation. The bulldozing of estates has also prompted considerable political opposition, notably from the Green Party and elements within the Labour Party, as well as from trade unions such as GMB and UNITE. Two groupings of radical architects have also recently formed: Architects 4 Social Housing (ASH) and Architectural Workers. The ASH strategy of 'resistance by design' includes working with residents to provide 'architectural alternatives to council estate demolition through designs for infill, build-over and refurbishment that increase housing capacity on the estates'.[2] ASH has worked closely with several estates facing demolition, notably Central Hill and Knights Walk in Lambeth and West Kensington and Gibbs Green in Hammersmith and Fulham.

Save Cressingham Gardens has been fighting Lambeth Council's 'regeneration' plans, which include demolishing the entire estate, since 2012 (Douglas and Parkes 2016). The Save Cressingham Gardens campaign comprises a coalition of tenants and leaseholders, and it has engaged in a wide range of tactics *in addition to* demonstrations, lobbying the council, and using mainstream and social media (see figure 8.2). These tactics include mounting two legal challenges via Judicial Review, trying to 'list' the estate as being of architectural merit, devising an alternative 'People's Plan', holding a 'Housing Crisis Question Time' debate, taking part in the Open London weekend and holding a resident-led writing project guided by Anne E. Cooper, a Cressingham tenant (Cooper 2017).

Save Cressingham Gardens, one of the most energetic estate-based campaigns in London, has waged an intense, imaginative and protracted struggle to preserve existing homes and the estate as a genuine mixed community (Douglas and Parkes 2016; Cooper 2017). Through participant observation at Cressingham Gardens' estate tours, I have witnessed astonishment on the part of nonresident visitors that the estate is slated for demolition because its small-scale, low-rise aesthetic is as far from the 'sink estate' stereotype as one could imagine (see figure 8.2; Minton 2017). Save Cressingham Gardens

Figure 8.2   Preparing to march to Lambeth Town Hall: Save Cressingham Gardens, October 2014. Paul Watt.

illustrates three aspects of London's estate-based campaigns more broadly. First is how the tenure structure of the average London council-built estate has fundamentally changed since the anti-HATs campaign of the 1980s when estates were largely made up of council tenants. Nearly four decades of the RTB have resulted in considerable numbers of homeowners (leaseholders and freeholders) on many estates, as well as private landlords letting their flats to private tenants (Watt and Minton 2016). Cressingham Gardens has around two-thirds council tenant households, slightly less than one-third homeowners, and a few private and housing association tenants (Douglas and Parkes 2016). Organizing such diverse tenure groups is not easy, as London housing activists readily admit. Nevertheless, Save Cressingham Gardens and other estate campaigns have brought tenants and homeowners together by emphasizing a shared 'resident' place-based identity, rather than a tenure-based 'council tenant' identity as was prominent in the earlier anti-HAT and anti-transfer campaigns. Second is how several recent estate-based struggles have emerged out of the efforts of largely novice housing activists who become galvanized once the full picture of what 'regeneration' entails sinks in (Cooper 2017). This is illustrated in this 2014 group interview with three Cressingham Gardens' leaseholders cum-activists.

PW: Before all this, were you involved in any housing activities at all?

Jeanette: Community groups, not housing as such. Within my local community, yes, not Cressingham, but I was doing a lot of voluntary work for local nurseries.

Mary: No. no. I obviously did Free Nelson Mandela back in the 80s, but haven't really done much since then.

PW: You weren't involved in any sort of housing or regeneration kind of things?

Jeanette: Before? No, you read it on the paper, you talk about it but you don't . . . 'that won't happen here'. It's not for us.

Save Cressingham Gardens has been operating for around five years and as such illustrates a third issue regarding London's estate-based campaigns: the sheer longevity of regeneration programmes. Key examples include the decade-long programmes at the Heygate estate in Southwark (Lees and Ferrari 2016) and at the Carpenters estate in Newham (Watt 2013, 2016). By comparison, the anti-HAT and anti-transfer campaigns were short and sharp; they focused on a relatively narrow set of tenure issues and, moreover, hinged around a ballot at a single point in time, which determined a clear 'winner' and 'loser'. Winning and losing in anti-demolition campaigns is by

Figure 8.3   March against demolition of Aylesbury Estate, March 2015. Paul Watt.

contrast incremental as they are forced to operate on the terrain of a seemingly endless war of attrition. This war involves not only multiple, complex tactics, as Save Cressingham Gardens illustrates, but also manifold phases which can include periodic successes *and* failures—for example, winning the first Judicial Review but losing the second, as at Cressingham Gardens (Douglas and Parkes 2016). Despite its longevity, Save Cressingham Gardens is actually a relative newcomer compared to other estate-based struggles, notably the Aylesbury Estate campaigners in Southwark who have been fighting in defence of their homes and community since 2001 (see figure 8.3).

'PLEASE SIR, WE WANT SOME MORE SOCIAL HOUSING': CHALLENGING PLANNING APPLICATIONS

One important component of London's housing struggles is the scrutiny of developers' planning applications to local authorities, including at regeneration estates, to assess how much 'affordable housing'—or more accurately *how little*—is being created via 'planning obligations'. The latter arise from Section 106 of the Town and Country Planning Act 1990, which allows agreements to be made between a council and developers as part of planning permission. Such obligations include funds from the developer to provide affordable housing, improved transport, and so on, which will mitigate the effects of development and benefit the local community. However, an important aspect of the London housing crisis is how local authorities have routinely not kept faith with *their own* affordable housing targets (Bernstock 2014; Flynn 2016). Hence the main aim of planning-related housing campaigns is to put pressure on local councils to keep to their own affordable housing targets, but often with an emphasis on social housing, the most needed and least profitable element within the thoroughly opaque 'affordable housing' category. These campaigns tend to operate within the boundaries of a single local authority, for example the '35% Campaign' in Southwark (Flynn 2016), even if their members might also participate in citywide networks such as Demolition Watch London and Just Space.

One example of planning-related activism relates to the move by West Ham United Football Club (WHU) from their century-old Boleyn Ground in Upton Park to the new Olympics Stadium, a move which was contentious not only for West Ham fans but also for residents of the London Borough of Newham (Watt and Bernstock 2017). WHU sold the Boleyn Ground site to the upmarket private developer Galliard PLC for an undisclosed sum, a company chosen because of its 'origins in east London [and] "impressive links with the local community"' (Gould 2015). Galliard's original development proposal for the Boleyn Ground site included a mixed-use scheme including 838 new residential homes, only 6 percent of which were 'affordable' and zero social housing. The application proved controversial, not least since it was well below the Labour-controlled Newham Council's core strategy that large developments should have 35 to 50 percent affordable housing of which 60 percent should be social housing. The GLA Planning Committee sent the application back to Newham Council in February 2015 and various further planning iterations were submitted until the final one was approved in March 2016 (*Newham Recorder* 2016).

The tiny affordable housing percentage and absence of social housing in a borough with acute housing needs, notably high levels of homelessness (Watt 2017), prompted two local campaigns, which lobbied the council. The first was organized by 'Newham Citizens' which campaigned for building three hundred 'affordable homes' at the Boleyn Ground development (Jeraj 2016); this equated to 35 percent affordable housing (i.e. at the bottom end of Newham Council's target). Newham Citizens form part of The East London Citizens Organization (TELCO) and Citizens UK. The rationale behind the Newham Citizens' campaign, as explained by a homeless charity manager, was pressurizing the council and local Labour MPs: 'think of the planning permission, "you are going to oppose your own policies of 35 percent affordable housing", so that's what we did, we went after them on their own policies' (2016 interview).

The second 'Campaign for 100% Social Housing for the Boleyn Ground Development' (BOLEYNDEV100, 2016) had the more ambitious goal of 100 percent social housing. As such, it not only moved well beyond Newham Council's planning obligation target, but also directly challenged the Orwellian discursive parameters of 'affordable housing', which is de facto *unaffordable* for low-income east Londoners and even many middle-income residents (Watt and Bernstock 2017). The '100% Campaign' emerged out of the long-standing 'Friends of Queens Market' (FOQM) campaign, which successfully fought to preserve Queens Market near the Boleyn Ground. FOQM saw the Boleyn Ground scheme as a renewed threat to the market, and they called a public meeting in East Ham in March 2015. At this meeting, one female FOQM speaker said, 'we see from the angle of Queens Market that we're worried by this development since regeneration means only one thing: posh housing'. Another said, 'we need 100 percent social housing here to rebalance defects elsewhere [in Newham]. We want a proper Olympics legacy for the people of Newham, enough is enough'. There was unanimous support for a 100 percent social-housing campaign based on a show of hands at the end of the meeting. The subsequent campaign ran a street stall at Queens Market and also gathered names for a petition and objection letters.

The two campaigns came together on the evening of the final planning application on 10 March 2016. Galliard had proposed a revised scheme in partnership with Barrett London. This included an increase of 211 'affordable' homes split between affordable rent and shared ownership, taking the total affordable housing to 25 percent, which Newham Council said it could take up to 35 percent on the basis of investing £18m (*Newham Recorder* 2016). Eleven objectors (including the author) spoke and 542 letters objected to the proposal with just two letters in support (Greater London Authority 2016); most of the letters mentioned the lack of social housing and resulted from the efforts of the 100% Campaign. Despite this weight of objection, the council passed the revised scheme. Although Newham Citizens regarded the affordable housing increase as a vindication of their efforts, the 100% Campaign remained incredulous at how the council could approve such a scheme 'with only 25 percent so-called "affordable housing" and no social housing' (BOLEYNDEV100, 2016). Pouring public money into the scheme to boost the affordable housing numbers goes against the spirit of planning obligations, which are obligations *on the part of the developer to the local authority*. By the time the redevelopment got underway, Galliard had dropped out and the newly named 'Upton Gardens' scheme was solely a Barrett London development. So much for Galliard's 'impressive links with the local community'.

'I FELT I HAD A RIGHT TO STAY THERE': SHORT-LIFE HOUSING COOPERATIVES

Housing cooperatives are an often overlooked element of London's social-housing landscape. In 2017, 150 such cooperatives provided tenant owned and managed homes for around twenty thousand Londoners (London Co-operative Housing Group 2017). Despite current efforts to expand the co-op sector, one element within it—short-life housing cooperatives (SLHCs)—has been subject to waves of incorporations, closures and evictions since their peak in the 1980s (Bowman 2004). Most London SLHCs began their life as squats in the late 1960s and early 1970s when groups of young single people wanted to put a roof over their heads as well as create an alternative lifestyle and city (Vasudevan 2017). At that time, London councils had a surfeit of empty 'hard-to-let' properties that were in such a poor state that families from the waiting list refused to occupy them, and it was these which formed the vast majority of London squats during this period (Kearns 1979). Although a spate of evictions occurred during the 1970s, London squatters also mounted an effective resistance, which 'prompted a volte face by the Conservative administration running the GLC [Greater London Council]' (Vasudevan 2017, 60). The GLC granted an amnesty for squatters in 1977, which most took up, resulting in some gaining GLC tenancies and others licences (Bowman 2004; Vasudevan 2017). The latter is 'a form of legitimization which grants security from sudden eviction' (Kearns 1979, 594), and as such SLHCs have 'the permitted use of empty property owned by local authorities and other public bodies' (Bowman 2004, 2). Squatters thus gained a place to live on an unspecified short-life basis and paid low rents in exchange for taking responsibility for repairs and management at zero cost to councils and hence cutting the latter's reliance on government subsidies. According to Bowman (2004, 261), more than one hundred SLHCs existed by 1986, housing over twenty thousand people, three-quarters of whom were living in council-owned property.

SLHCs declined from their peak in the mid-1980s with many being absorbed into housing associations (Bowman 2004). Although the latter 'formalization' was welcomed by some co-op members because it gave greater security, the dismemberment of SLHCs, which included evictions, also provoked 'fierce campaigns to stay put' (Bowman 2004, 174). Campaigners have emphasized how they have been living in nominally short-life housing for many years (up to forty)—rendering it de facto *long-life*—and how during this lengthy period of time they have looked after their homes, using their labour and resources at nil cost to the councils: 'it wasn't short life because I'd been there for 14 years' (Islington SLHC evictee, cited in Thorpe 2006, 22). The rest of this section outlines campaigns to 'stay put' in Lambeth and Tower Hamlets, two boroughs which historically had large numbers of short-life properties that the councils have more recently aimed to shut down (Kearns 1979).

According to Kate Hoey, a local Labour MP, from the 1990s Lambeth Council embarked on a lengthy, intermittent, confused and 'misguided' policy of evictions from SLHCs (Hansard Online 2011). This policy was rekindled in 2011 as Lambeth Council wanted to sell off its remaining 170 short-life properties via auction to raise funds and in so doing cash in on London's property boom (Hansard Online 2011). Around fifteen co-ops formed the Lambeth United Housing Co-operative (2017 personal communication) to resist evictions and preserve existing homes and communities including social housing. Before being evicted, Micky had lived at his co-op for twelve years and he explained that 'the whole thrust of our campaign was to not sell off the housing, to keep it as social housing, to implement some form of rent which the council never wanted to accept from us because it would have changed our legal status' (2017 interview). Had Lambeth Council accepted rents, the licensees would have become tenants. Other SLHC interviewees had been living in their homes since the early 1980s and had been through lengthy legal processes including multiple court appearances: 'I've been fighting for 10 years' (Sarah, 2017 interview). This fight encompassed demonstrations, lobbying councillors', MPs and celebrities, media campaigns, legal challenges, and at the last resort resisting the bailiffs. As Diane (2017 interview) recalls, 'we had a big eviction resistance on the actual day', with around 100 to 150 people including local politicians.

Diane: The street was packed . . . the street was just jammed with people and all the way down the side so the bailiffs couldn't get near.

Mel: There was one super-flash bailiff, and some police.

Fred: Well, the police didn't do anything, it was the super-flash and he came up and bounced off the six or eight people deep wall. . . . I mean the Old Bill [police] weren't interested in it at all. He [bailiff] came up a couple of times, of course he can't assault you, he can attempt to walk through forcefully in a sense but he can't . . . and the Old Bill were just watching it going 'hmm'.

However, as Mel says: 'most people didn't really fight the Court process and they moved and accepted re-housing'. Many SLHC members have been evicted, including Micky. Their previous homes have been auctioned off to the private market, but as the remaining residents note, several of these have been unused by their new upmarket owners. As Diane observes, pointing to a house in the neighbourhood: 'that was bought by a guy, I talked to him years ago, he said he was a solicitor and he bought it for his daughter and it's been sat empty all that time'. Only a handful of Lambeth short-life co-operators have managed to remain in their homes as a result of their own tenacity and wider community support.

In Tower Hamlets, a similar process of evictions has occurred albeit that, unlike in Lambeth, many of the properties have been refurbished and recycled into social housing. As with Lambeth, however, the lengthy process of how the council dealt with its SLHC stock—and more importantly its resident population of largely single, middle-aged and elderly men—has resulted in community breakups, displacement and psychological stress. It is also under-pinned by the same exponential rise in inner London land values and house prices, as Steve (2017 interview) astutely observes: 'it's mind boggling how property gets value. You plonk it in the 1960s and it's worthless, and you plonk it in the 1980s and it's squatted, and then in the 2000s it's worth 500 grand. You just need a time machine'. According to Steve, many of the Tower Hamlets' SHLC members 'had no stomach for the fight'. For him, 'the fight' was connected to the labour he had put into his home over the many years he had lived there, as well as maintaining the communal relations which existed:

I felt I had a right to stay there if you live in a place for 18 years, it's my home. Just because you don't have the money, does that mean you don't have the right to stay in your home? I put many hours of work and love into my home.

By networking with other east London-based housing campaigns, including Focus E15, Steve set up an online petition, which received more than two thousand signatures, and he also organized a deputation to a council meeting. Despite these efforts, Steve and his fellow co-op members went to court and lost their case. Two were subsequently rehoused into council flats within the borough, but their housemate, who was in his eighties, became hospitalized and died not long after being evicted from his home of thirty years.

'THESE PEOPLE NEED HOMES, THESE HOMES NEED PEOPLE': TEMPORARY OCCUPATIONS

Despite London's proud squatting history, squatting has recently been criminalized in residential buildings via Section 144 of the Legal Aid Sentencing and Punishment of Offenders Act 2012 (Vasudevan 2017). Despite this, as Vasudevan observes, temporary occupations have been an important political tactic in London's housing struggles, as evidenced in the Focus E15 and Sisters Uncut campaigns in east London, and the 2015 occupations of the Sweets Way Estate in north London and Aylesbury Estate in south London. The Focus E15 campaign emerged out of a group of twenty-nine young mothers who were living in a temporary supported hostel for homeless youth in Stratford, Newham, the epicentre of the 2012 Olympic Games 'legacy' (Watt 2016; Watt and Bernstock 2017). Following austerity cuts and changes to the council's allocation policies, the mothers received eviction notices from their parent housing association in September 2013. One of the mums recounts their imminent prospect of being cleansed from the city:

> we were told that we had to be out by October 20, so we had two months to find ourselves accommodation. We was registered officially homeless by the council, but the council said they wouldn't be able to help us, we'd have to look for private rented accommodation ourselves and if we hadn't found anything by October 20 that they would have to find us accommodation, but it would be in somewhere like Manchester, Hastings or Birmingham (Cath, 2014 interview).

Instead of dutifully accepting their allotted individual neoliberal fates, the mothers collectivized and began their social housing not social cleansing campaign to prevent their eviction and remain in London, preferably in social housing. In this they were assisted by the Revolutionary Communist Group who had an anti-cuts' stall in Stratford. The invigorated Focus E15 campaigners embarked on a series of temporary occupations, including the housing association show flat and the council's housing offices, following which they were rehoused in London albeit in the PRS (Watt 2016). In September through to October 2014 (i.e., one year after the mothers had received their eviction notices), they mounted a two-week occupation of a block of flats at the half-empty Carpenters estate, which is endlessly awaiting 'regenera-tion' (Watt 2013; see figure 8.4). Gillespie et al. (2018) discuss the gendered aspects of how the occupation promoted the urban commons. As part of this active 'commoning', the occupiers made strenuous efforts to connect with estate residents and also to counter stereotypes of squatting, politics and council estates, as Eileen (2015 interview) observes:

> It wasn't like an imposing kind of tower block, It had a big square in front of it, It was just absolutely perfect for breaking down stereotypes of squatting, break-ing down stereotypes of what being politicised was, about political occupation. It brought the community who live there in, they were coming in and painting it.

Not being a squat but a political occupation also facilitated the occupiers to leave on their own terms after two weeks and not to be evicted (Gillespie et al. 2018). The creation of an 'open house'—a porous social centre—facilitated encounters between groups who might not otherwise meet, but all of whom were experiencing various aspects of the London housing crisis. Tom went along to the open house having experienced the insecurities, displacements and frustrations which are routine among students and youth in general living in the London PRS: 'I have very little of the problems that people have on

Figure 8.4   Focus E15 occupation at the Carpenters Estate, September 2014. Paul Watt.

the estate, but I have moved at least once a year for the last three years . . . through further moving south east to avoid rent rises' (2014 interview). As a self-identified 'white middle-class student', the occupation facilitated Tom's recognition of *both* his own social privileges and how he was nevertheless experiencing London's housing crisis: 'people have talked about housing as a possibility of cross-class alliance, I think it's true, the housing problems particularly in London, you know, are affecting not only working-class people, but also middle-class people in radically different levels of severity'. As Watt (2016) and Gillespie et al. (2018) discuss, the Carpenters occupation and the actions of Focus E15 generally have not only effectively highlighted London's housing crisis, but also helped to forge new solidarities among the city's sometimes seemingly diffuse housing struggles.

CONCLUSION

The chapter has illustrated various dimensions of how London's housing activists are struggling *for* social housing and *against* social cleansing. This can be seen in the anti-HAT and anti-transfer campaigns as they mounted a defence of council housing, that form of social renting which offers the greatest level of security. It can also be seen in how the multi-tenure, estate-based campaigns are fighting demolition, as well as how the short-life housing cooperatives have tried to preserve their section of the city's social-housing sector. The Boleyn Ground campaigns also illustrate the prominence given to maximizing 'affordable housing' but especially social housing. Finally, the Focus E15 campaign shows how some of those Londoners most at risk of social cleansing—working-class lone mothers—have fought back to remain in London.

There are of course considerable differences in the above campaigns, two of which are worthy of note. First, the earlier anti-HAT and anti-transfer campaigns focused on a particular housing tenure—council housing with secure tenancies—while the later anti-demolition and planning campaigns tend to adopt a less narrow tenure-specific approach. Anti-demolition campaigns are often hinged around alliances between homeowners and tenants, while planning-based campaigns emphasize maximizing social housing, which can include housing association as well as council renting. This is not to say, however, that the defence of council housing has somehow become unimportant in London, as illustrated for example by the Axe the Housing Act campaign against the Housing and Planning Bill 2016. The field of housing struggles has simply broadened out to reflect the multiple strands that London's housing crisis takes. Second, the earlier stock transfer campaigns were able to operate in relation to a statutory ballot. By contrast, a ballot is sorely absent in the case of estate demolition/regeneration and this is something that London housing campaigns, such as Demolition Watch London, are demanding. Unfortunately, holding a ballot in relation to estate demolitions is one thing that the Labour Mayor Sadiq Khan appears reluctant to countenance at the time of writing (Mayor of London 2016, 19).

Running throughout these struggles is the defence of 'our homes and communities', a theme which has long been significant in the UK social-housing tenants' movement as Bradley (2014) discusses. It is noteworthy how such defence of the urban commons in the form of social housing has taken on such a pivotal role in relation to contemporary class struggles, especially in relation to how such struggles are gendered and racialized (Watt 2016; Gillespie et al. 2018). As London's housing market has increasingly become a speculator's domain—a speculation that local councils are all too often willing to partake in—so protecting existing homes and communities becomes ever more significant, but also more challenging. These challenges are illustrated by the sheer longevity of several of the struggles delineated here. The Focus E15 campaign has held a regular Saturday street stall in Stratford since 2013, a testimony to what Laura (2015 interview), one of its members, calls 'the power of collective action': 'you have to be brave, you have to be relentless and you have to be disciplined. If you can do that in a campaign, then it shows you can really achieve something; and that's really exciting'.

Acknowledgements

Thanks to the interviewees who gave so generously of their time and to the following for their insightful comments on drafts of this chapter: Quintin Bradley, Paul Burnham, Neil Gray, Karen Harris and Glyn Robbins. Thanks also to the Ocean Estate Tenants Association for giving me permission to use Figure 8.1.

NOTES

1. Radical Housing Network. http://radicalhousingnetwork.org/.
2. Architects 4 Social Housing (ASH). Manifesto. http://architectsforsocialhousing.co.uk/wordpress/manifesto/.

REFERENCES

Adonis, Andrew, and Bill Davies. 2015. *City Villages: More Homes, Better Communities.* London: IPPR.

Bernstock, Penny. 2014. *Olympic Housing: A Critical Review of London 2012's Legacy*. Farnham: Ashgate Publishing Ltd.

BOLEYNDEV100. 2016. Campaign for 100% Social Housing for the Boleyn Ground Development. https://boleyndev100.wordpress.com.

Bowman, Anna. 2004. "Interim Spaces: Reshaping London—the Role of Short Life Property, 1970 to 2000." PhD diss., University of Bristol.

Bradley, Quintin. 2014. *The Tenants' Movement*. London: Routledge.

Cooper, Anne E. 2017. *306: Living Under the Shadow of Regeneration*. London: Devotion Press.

Douglas, Pam, and Jo Parkes. 2016. "'Regeneration' and 'Consultation' at a Lambeth Council Estate." *City* 20: 287–91.

Elmer, Simon, and Geraldine Dening. 2016. "The London Clearances." *City: Analysis of Urban Trends, Culture, Theory, Policy, Action* 20: 271–77.

Flynn, Jerry. 2016. "Complete Control." *City: Analysis of Urban Trends, Culture, Theory, Policy, Action* 20: 278–86.

Gillespie, Tom, Kate Hardy and Paul Watt. 2018. "Austerity Urbanism and Olympic Counter-Legacies: Gendering, Defending and Expanding the Urban Commons in East London". *Environment and Planning D: Society and Space*. Doi: http://journals.sagepub.com/doi/full/10.1177/0263775817753844.

Gould, Mark. 2015. "Local Residents Angry at Lack of Social Housing at West Ham's Ground." *The Guardian*, February 24. https://www.theguardian.com/society/2015/feb/24/newham-residents-social-housing-west-ham.

Greater London Authority (GLA). 2016. *Planning Report D&P/3399/02, 28 April 2016: West Ham Stadium, Boleyn Ground, Green Street, Upton Park, London E13 9AZ*. London: GLA.

Hansard Online. 2011. "Short-life Homes (Lambeth)", December 6. https://hansard.parliament.uk/Commons/2011-12-06/debates/11120680000002/ShortLifeHomes(Lambeth).

Harvey, David. 2012. *Rebel Cities: From the Right to the City to the Urban Revolution*. London: Verso.

HOCCHG. 2009. *Council Housing—Time to Invest*. London: House of Commons Council Housing Group.

Hodkinson, Stuart. 2012b. "The New Urban Enclosures." *City: Analysis of Urban Trends, Culture, Theory, Policy, Action* 16(4): 500–18.

Hodkinson, Stuart, Paul Watt and Gerry Mooney. 2013. "Neoliberal Housing Policy—Time for a Critical Re-appraisal." *Critical Social Policy* 33: 316.

Jeraj, Esmat. 2016. "Community Demands 300 Homes on the Boleyn Development." *Citizens UK*, February 12. http://www.citizensuk.org/community_demands_300_homes.

Kearns, Kevin C. 1979. "Intraurban Squatting in London." *Annals of the Association of American Geographers* 69: 589–98.

Lees, Loretta, and Mara Ferreri. 2016. "Resisting Gentrification on Its Final Frontiers: Learning from the Heygate Estate in London (1974–2013)." *Cities* 57: 14–24.

London Co-operative Housing Group. 2017. *Co-operate Not Speculate*. London: Co-ops 4 London.

Mayor of London. 2016. *Homes for Londoners: Draft Good Practice Guide to Estate Regeneration*. London: GLA.

Minton, Anna. 2017. *Big Capital: Who Is London For?* London: Penguin.

Newham Recorder. 2016. "Boleyn Ground Development Approved with Minimum of 25% Affordable Housing." *Newham Recorder*, March 11 2016.

Ocean Estate Tenants Association. n.d. *HATS OFF THE OCEAN*. London: Ocean Estate Tenants Association.

Thorpe, Caroline. 2006. "Unfair Dismissal." *Inside Housing*, January 13.

Tiesdell, Steven. 1999. *The Development and Implementation of Housing Action Trust Policy*. PhD diss., University of Nottingham.

———. 2001. "A Forgotten Policy? A Perspective on the Evolution and Transformation of Housing Action Trust Policy, 1987–99." *European Journal of Housing Policy* 1: 357–83.

Vasudevan, Alexander. 2017. *The Autonomous City: A History of Urban Squatting*. London: Verso.

Watt, Paul. 2009a. "Housing Stock Transfers, Regeneration and State-led Gentrification in London." *Urban Policy and Research* 27: 229–42.

———. 2009b. "Social Housing and Regeneration in London". In *Regenerating London*, edited by Rob Imrie, Loretta Lees and Mike Raco, 212–33. London: Routledge.

———. 2013. "'It's Not For Us': Regeneration, the 2012 Olympics and the Gentrification of East London." *City: Analysis of Urban Trends, Culture, Theory, Policy, Action* 17: 99–118.

———. 2016. "A Nomadic War Machine in the Metropolis: En/countering London's 21st Century Housing Crisis with Focus E15." *City: Analysis of Urban Trends, Culture, Theory, Policy, Action* 20: 297–320.

———. 2017. "Gendering the Right to Housing in the City: Homeless Female Lone Parents in Post-Olympics, Austerity East London." *Cities*. doi: http://www.sciencedirect.com/science/article/pii/S0264275116302165.

Watt, Paul, and Penny Bernstock. 2017. "Legacy for Whom? Housing in Post-Olympics East London." In *London 2012 and the Post-Olympics City: A Hollow Legacy?* edited by Phil Cohen and Paul Watt, 91–138. Basingstoke: Palgrave Macmillan.

Watt, Paul, and Anna Minton. 2016. "London's Housing Crisis and Its Activisms." *City: Analysis of Urban Trends, Culture, Theory, Policy, Action* 20: 204–21.

Woodward, Rachel. 1991. "Mobilising Opposition: The Campaign against Housing Action Trusts in Tower Hamlets." *Housing Studies* 6: 44–56.

Part III

RETHINKING
THE HOUSING QUESTION:
THEORIES, AIMS, TACTICS AND
STRATEGIES FOR TODAY

Chapter 9

The Myths and Realities of Rent Control

Hamish Kallin and Tom Slater

In September 2015, when it became clear that the Scottish National Party (SNP) was taking seriously the idea of introducing a form of rent control for the private-rented sector (PRS), the response by representatives of those who profit most from renting was immediate and blunt. 'If the Scottish Government wants to increase housing supply' wrote David Melhuish, director of the *Scottish Property Federation*, 'then the introduction of rent controls is not the way to do it' (*Scottish Housing News* 2015, n.p.). His claim was simple: that curtailing the potential profits to be made from private renting would discourage developers from building more housing for private rent. For Melhuish, the eventual consequence would be a decline in the supply of places to live, resulting in a more severe housing crisis. This line of attack has become routine, with *PRS4Scotland* (a lobby group representing landlords, agents, and investors) staking their objection on similar grounds (Renshaw 2015). Both echo a broader neoliberal promise: that rent controls—in any form, in any context—will eventually hurt those on whose behalf they are supposedly introduced (people struggling to find somewhere affordable to live). This is an old argument, grounded in deep contempt for state regulation and a veneration of the supposed 'efficiency' of the 'free' market (Hayek 1972). It is an argument that has failed, on a spectacular level, across the world.

Between our current situation (a mercilessly unfair and inefficient way of organizing rented housing) and our desired situation (in which everyone can afford a decent place to live), there lies a barrier made of weak arguments like those replicated above. These are then repeated ad nauseam until they take on the sheen of 'truth'. In this chapter, we begin by discussing a concept called *agnotology*, or the production of ignorance. The justification of what is built, who profits from it and who gets to live in it is continuously reinforced by a powerful set of claims about the 'naturalness' of private property, the 'efficiency' of the market and the peril of upsetting both. Attention to the production of ignorance helps to explain why these myths are so rarely challenged. We then move on to discuss and dismiss three of the prevalent myths around rent control: (1) that it negatively affects the condition of rented properties; (2) that it negatively affects the supply of housing; and (3) that it is an 'inefficient' way of organizing the housing market.

THE POWER OF STORIES

> By 'ideology' I mean a system of ideas which purports to explain
> to people the real conditions of their social existence. That is to say,
> ideology supplies people with ready-made explanations of everyday
> life. These include well-known statements typically prefaced by such
> remarks as 'everybody knows', 'of course' and 'naturally'.
>
> —Seán Damer (1989, 23)

There are many ways in which our homes are suffused with ideology (the gender politics of roles within the home, the idea that ownership is aspirational, the aesthetics of looking traditional, the division of who lives where and so on). In this chapter, we want to focus on one specific issue: how is it that something akin to a *consensus* is created that tells us that rent controls are a threat that will hurt the economy, hurt people looking for homes, hurt sitting tenants and, of course, hurt landlords? At the same time, how is it that we are *still* told to believe that 'the market' is the most efficient way of organizing the provision of housing, when we have scant evidence, historically or in the present, that this is anywhere close to being true? It is here that the notion of agnotology becomes important.

The term was coined by Robert Proctor, a historian of science. It refers to 'the study of ignorance making' where we decide to focus on 'knowledge that could have been but wasn't, or should be but isn't' (Proctor and Schiebinger 2008, vii). It was while investigating the tobacco industry's efforts to manufacture doubt about the health hazards of smoking that Proctor began to see the scientific and political urgency in researching how ignorance is made, maintained and, manipulated by powerful institutions to suit their own ends. Here the guiding research question becomes, 'Why don't we know what we don't know?' As he discovered, the industry went to great lengths to give the impression that the cancer risks of smoking were still an open question even when the scientific evidence was overwhelming. Numerous tactics were deployed by the tobacco industry to divert attention from cancer risks, such as the production of duplicitous press releases, the publication of 'nobody knows the answers' white papers and the generous funding of decoy or red-herring research that 'would seem to be addressing tobacco and health, while really doing nothing of the sort' (Proctor and Schiebinger 2008,14). The tobacco industry actually produced research about everything except tobacco hazards to exploit public uncertainty (researchers knew from the beginning what they were supposed to find and not find), and the very fact of research being funded allowed the industry to say it was studying the problem.

Agnotology is a useful approach to the housing question because it helps us trace the practices of the powerful institutions and corporations that *do not want certain things to be known* because widely circulating knowledge might call into question the very ideology on which their power is built. It helps to show how vested interests have hijacked the debate by deliberately avoiding particular bodies of knowledge and producing noisy disinformation distilled into readily accessible sound bites that translate seamlessly from the realm of ideas to the realm of policy. Here is one of numerous examples: a UK parliamentary briefing paper prepared in the dying months of Gordon Brown's reign tells us that 'many consider rent control to have been a major contributory factor to the subsequent decay of much of the inner city housing stock' (HM Treasury 2010, 21). The sole reference here is to Peter King's (2006) *Choice and the End of Social Housing*, a polemic published by the Institute of Economic Affairs (IEA), the free-market think tank founded on the gospel according to Friedrich von Hayek, and a driving force behind the Thatcherite Conservative Party revolution of the 1980s. The main thrust of King's argument was to deregulate into non-existence that which remained of 'social housing', garbed in the usual verbiage of 'choice' and 'efficiency'. In the transfer from one (the ideologue) to the other (the policy maker), a political *truth* was created, which was then regurgitated word-for-word in a 2017 parliamentary briefing on rent controls (Wilson 2017).

In *Geography and Social Justice*, David M. Smith puts forward a case for seeing (and enacting) social justice as a process of *equalization*, through which we seek to ameliorate and overcome the gross inequalities generated by 'market forces'. But as Smith points out, arguing in this vein will:

> inevitably face opposition from the vested interests who gain from inequality, who have been able to marshal so much reverence for market outcomes and their association with social justice. Neoclassical economics has performed a powerful ideological role, in the hands of those whose primary purpose seems to have been to *deflect criticism* of distributional inequalities. (Smith 1994, 158, emphasis added)

Almost two decades into the twenty-first century and the state of 'the housing market' across the United Kingdom presents no shortage of reasons to *aim criticism* at a system in which homelessness is rising, indebtedness is rising, in-work poverty is rising and, put bluntly, 'housing has become a problem for everyone' (Dorling 2014, 2). An awful lot of *deflection* has to go on to ensure that profits can continue to be siphoned off by those who speculate on property in such a context.

In the 'overheated' housing market of the South East—which reaches an inhumane zenith in London—acute overcrowding is reaching levels that seem Victorian in their squalor. Renters are increasingly crowded into bunkbeds, garden sheds, lofts and cellars, with weak or rarely enforced legislation to protect them. Evidence has emerged of renters taking turns to sleep or sharing beds to cut the cost of living, while almost a quarter of children in the capital now live in homes officially classified as 'overcrowded'. The average tenant in England is now spending almost 50 percent of their take-home pay on rent alone, a figure which rises to more than 70 percent in London (Osborne 2015). Across the United Kingdom, household debt has risen to £1.5 trillion for the first time, of which the vast majority (some 87 percent) is tied up in mortgages (Richardson 2016). At the same time, the debt levels of private renters continue to climb and eviction levels have risen to 170 a day across the United Kingdom, a figure closely linked to the rise in those unable to keep up with rent payments (Cooper and Paton, this volume). In Scotland, the rising cost of housing has pushed an extra 70,000 children into poverty (Shelter Scotland 2017, 1). As a report for The Scotland Institute (2016, 15) shows, a further 200,000 adults have been pushed into relative poverty as the direct result of unaffordable housing costs because 'at a time when household incomes have mostly been static, rents for all types of property have steadily increased'. Without getting bogged down in a list of depressing statistics, one thing is clear: we are in a serious housing crisis. So who is doing the ideological groundwork to normalize this debt explosion and defuse the scandal of high housing costs?

As Slater (2016a, 2016b) has explained elsewhere, there are a certain number of influential free-market think tanks that continue to churn out reports on proposed solutions to the housing crisis. Here is one example: in the summer of 2016, the Communication Workers Union (CWU) published a report by Alexander Hilton (2016) on the housing crisis that proposed the reintroduction of rent controls as part of a range of measures that might help. Two months later, and the IEA dutifully published a response by extreme libertarian Kristian Niemietz (2016, 7), which sought to prove emphatically that 'rent controls are not and could not be a solution to the UK's housing crisis'. The problem with Niemietz's analysis is that it uncritically reproduces tropes from neoclassical economics that are simply incapable of describing the real world. We are told, for example, that the only reason housing is expensive is because there is not enough of it—despite the fact that estimates suggest we have a higher ratio of bedrooms per person than at any point since the late medieval period and there are more than 730,000 empty homes across the United Kingdom (Dorling 2014, 67). Then we are told that the only reason housebuilding has slowed down is because of postwar legislation—ignoring the fact that 'private housebuilders have never been able to deliver all of the country's housing needs' (Bentley 2016, 3). Indeed, the only period at which housing shortages were overcome is when local authorities were building the majority of new homes (which was, incidentally, also the period with the strongest planning regulations). But this is an inconvenient truth, and so the argument is presented in an ahistorical vacuum. Again and again we are returned to that most utopian of promises: that a free market in land and housing, unbridled by tiresome legislation, would manage to provide sufficient high quality homes for all. Except it never has, and it never could do because free-market capitalism cannot exist without housing inequality.

Such a vision sees the housing crisis as a simple problem of supply and demand. Were restrictions lifted, we are promised, supply would increase and prices would fall. Such a formula ignores the myriad reasons for this crisis, which is not caused by legislative *barriers to profit*, but rampant speculation itself, while remaining blind to rising levels of inequality. An accurate explanation of the housing crisis would have to attend to the continued eradication of affordable housing legislation, the privatization of public housing, speculation on empty properties, tax evasion through hoarded land, the profitability of securitized mortgage assets, consistently low interest rates and so on (Dorling 2014; Marcuse and Madden 2016). These are the fruits of too much profiteering, not too little. Moreover, the 'top end' of the housing crisis is characterized by hyperinvestment in the most expensive parts of the city (Minton 2017). 'Demand' in this context bears no rational relation to 'supply' because the housing is not being bought to be lived in, but purely as a financial asset. The supply and demand narrative is 'wholly unsatisfactory' (Bone and O'Reilly 2010, 234) because it cannot explain the role of financialization and the rise in prices far, far beyond levels of affordability. Research by the estate agent Savills (2017, 5) also (unwittingly) demonstrates that 'supply' follows the money, not the need; in London there is a *surplus* of housing in the upper end of the market—'ready for increased international demand' to use their positive spin—but as you work your way down the affordability ladder the surplus-to-demand ratio diminishes to the point of crisis. The idea that building more in the upper end will help those with less money is a fantasy. The opposite is now demonstrably true. It is the price inflation at the upper end that 'trickles down' the housing ladder, not the surplus (Minton 2017). Furthermore, housing wealth does not trickle down; it flows upwards, into the hands of rentiers, lenders, investors, speculators, developers and housebuilding corporations.

Looking to Ireland or Spain shows dramatically how 'supply' waits for profit, and in the dehumanizing fallout from the financial crisis, empty homes offer more potential profit than affordable ones. As Kitchin, O'Callaghan and Gleeson (2014, 1069) show, between 1991 and 2011 the housing stock in Ireland increased by 834,596 units, with prices rising *at the same time* by 382 percent for the country as a whole. Now around 13 percent of the country's housing stock lies empty—much of which is brand new, constructed in the precrash boom and never occupied—but a crisis of affordability endures nonetheless (McCárthaigh 2016). Meanwhile, in Spain, US private equity firms (most prominently Blackstone and Goldman Sachs) have been hoovering up housing for rock-bottom prices and, in some cases, raising rents by around 900 percent in a country with enough empty homes (3.4 million) to comfortably house all the homeless people in Europe (Neate 2014). Put bluntly, the logic of supply and demand is useless to explain the housing crisis because people demand homes to *live in*, but the driving force of financialization ensures that any link between what a home is used for and what it is sold for has been utterly broken (Rolnik 2013).

The idea that we can simply build our way out of this crisis remains blind to the impact of growing levels of inequality. Dorling (2014) points out that after the last great depression in the 1930s, building more homes worked because inequality was falling drastically at the same time (as a result of a whole host of other policy initiatives) and so people could increasingly *afford* to buy housing. But in an era where inequality is growing consistently (Piketty 2014) and housing itself generates 'an upward distribution of wealth' (Bone and O'Reilly 2010, 234), this is the most obvious flaw with the supply-and-demand model. It is those who *need* affordable housing the most who are least able to 'demand' housing through economic clout. And—as those Glasgow rent strikers knew all too well a century ago—this means that they must 'demand' it through *political* clout.

A TRILOGY OF MYTHS:
QUALITY, SUPPLY AND EFFICIENCY

As is probably quite clear, we are in favour of rent controls. We believe that the profit motive fundamentally leads to a *fall* in housing standards and a *shortage* of housing. Before we can assert that with confidence, however, we will refute three prevalent myths replicated in arguments against rent controls. In a volume dedicated to the memory of the Glasgow Rent Strikes—and the lessons to be learned from them—it seems fitting to note that on one level these arguments have already been debunked by common knowledge. The increased campaigning around housing (whether through the Living Rent campaign in Scotland, the Radical Housing Network in London, the FOCUS E15 mums, the agitation within political parties and so on) demonstrates how inept the logic of 'more of the same' already sounds. The political function of a rent strike, or even the *threat* of one, is to assert a simple truth: that it is those who live in housing who know what is wrong with it and have to live with the consequences, to a much greater extent than those who own that housing. Here we seek to add our voice to these movements by disputing the myth that rent controls will threaten the quality, supply and efficiency of the housing sector.

The *quality* argument goes as follows: rent controls would negatively affect the standard of homes on offer, because if a landlord cannot raise rents as much as they want to, they are likely to skimp on maintenance or—even worse—have insufficient funds to carry out necessary maintenance, even if they wanted to. The most obvious flaw with such an argument is that housing quality within the PRS is *already* atrocious. Indeed, it is the worst of all tenures, with the most sophisticated surveys of poverty showing that one in three tenants in the PRS live in structurally inadequate housing (Lansley and Mack 2015). This is confirmed by the government's own reports: almost one-third of privately rented accommodation fails to meet the government's standards for decent homes (UK Parliament 2016). The housing charity Shelter (2014, 7) reports that:

> over 6 in 10 renters (61 percent) have experienced at least one of the following problems in their [privately rented] home over the last 12 months: damp, mould, leaking roofs or windows, electrical hazards, animal infestations and gas leaks. Ten per cent of renters said their health had been affected because of their landlord not dealing with repairs and poor conditions in their property in the last year, and 9 percent of private-renting parents said their children's health had been affected.

Moreover, in the decades before state intervention in housing (when the vast majority of the UK population were privately renting), standards were *far worse*. The historical record of 'laissez-faire' liberalism on housing standards was simply terrible, with slum conditions and overcrowding commonplace in British cities, where chronic poverty would siphon wealth upwards through rent (Rodger 1989). Those arguing that rent controls would worsen housing quality cannot have it both ways: whenever there has been little or no regulation, rental housing quality has been appalling. John Wheatley expressed this neatly in 1923, the year before he introduced an act of Parliament which funded the construction of more than half a million local authority houses: 'If private enterprise could have given you clean or healthy cities and a healthy people, you would have nothing but healthy clean cities and healthy people because you have never had anything *but* private enterprise' (cited in Damer 2000a, 95).

Wheatley knew first-hand that conditions in the slum tenements of the Clyde region were dehumanizing. Overcrowding in Scottish cities in the early twentieth century (before the 'red tape' of state regulation interfered) was chronic, housebuilding was inefficient and evictions were common (Rodger 1989). Glasgow in 1900 was as close to the conditions of a 'perfect free market' in housing as the likes of Niemietz could possibly desire—no public housing, no regulated standards of accommodation, a lack of monopoly in the hands of any single owner and virtually no protection of tenants' rights. But rents were high and conditions were appalling (McCrone and Elliot 1989), with slum landlords cramming tenants into stairwells, courtyards and alleys; denying them access to light, water or dignity (Gauldie 1976). The 'luxuries' of fire safety, running water, central heating, indoor toilets, watertight roofing and so on were won through political struggle over the decades that followed and only normalized through legislation. And, as the fire at Grenfell Tower in the summer of 2016 so horrifically demonstrated, the 'profit motive' cuts corners wherever it can. Only regulation—effectively enforced—can uphold decent housing standards. It is absurd to say that introducing even modest rent regulation would make that quality problem worse. This is abundantly clear in the case of the Netherlands, where the amount a landlord is allowed to increase rent on an annual basis is conditional upon the standard of the property they are leasing. The result is a rental housing stock in far better shape than in countries that have no rent control (Olsen 1988; Anas 1997; Kutty 1996).

The second myth we want to tackle concerns the question of *supply*. Were rents to be capped, we are told, then fewer people would bother to become landlords, existing landlords would withdraw their properties from the market, and fewer developers would bother to build. The result would be a restriction in the supply of new housing for rent, which would lead to the housing crisis getting even worse. This is neoclassical logic writ large and a profoundly troubling argument for two reasons. First, it is an unconscious admission that the PRS is only viable so long as it can exploit people far beyond their means; a formula based on parasitic greed. Second, it implies that any curtailing of the profits to be made from a sector will simply stop people investing in it. This is akin to believing that the minimum wage means companies stop employing people, that VAT means nobody sells anything anymore or that Fuel Duty means nobody drives nowadays; it is, in other words, a fantastical formula because it is based on the notion that people will only seek to make money in conditions of totally unhampered profitability. Such a hypothesis is, once again, an ahistorical utopia (it has never existed). The precipitous decline of the PRS in Britain over much of the twentieth century—from near 90 percent at its start down to 14 percent by the 1970s (Stafford 1976, 3)—was clearly influenced by rent controls, but it would be simplistic to say this was the sole cause. The PRS was squeezed on two fronts: investment in public housing (after decades of organized struggle) offered many working-class tenants their first decent homes, while the incessant emphasis on the 'naturalness' of homeownership legitimized (and helped to finance) middle-class aspirations. To then suggest that any decline of the PRS in and of itself is a crisis is misplaced. Similarly, it is inaccurate to suggest that the massive expansion of the PRS in recent decades has been caused *solely* by the abolition of rent regulation. It is well documented that decades of drastically reducing the affordable housing stock alongside the stagnation of wages and the rise in house prices has left people with few alternative options (Meek 2014). In other words, the growth of the PRS is a symptom of the current housing crisis not its solution.

It therefore stands to reason that we question the existence of the PRS itself. If the most strident critique of rent controls is that it will lead to a reduction of the sector, it is sorely tempting to respond by saying, 'Sounds good!' As an innately exploitative relation, private renting is a parasitic form of accumulation which funnels wealth up. It fuels rising inequality and lends it a cruel generational permanence. In this light, a downsizing of the PRS can hardly be considered a humanitarian tragedy if it makes decommodified forms of housing provision an urgent necessity. The 'supply' argument only makes sense if it denies all other forms of housebuilding and tenures and ignores the possibility of collective ownership. Unfortunately, just hearing the words 'rent control' is deeply unsettling to people who believe in so-called 'free' and competitive markets, in private property rights and in the logic of trickle down. The vast majority of economists, even some on the left like Paul Krugman (who famously trashed rent control in a *New York Times* column in 2000), are trained to think in the neoclassical way, striving for equilibrium through supply and demand. This perspective has become so hegemonic that neoclassical economists were quick to frame the fallout from the 2008 financial crisis as a time of 'recovery', rather than a time for any major structural/institutional changes (Mirowski 2013).

Finally, we come to the holy grail of 'efficiency.' For neoclassical economists, something is inefficient if it 'artificially' interferes with the 'natural' operation of the price mechanism of the market. Rent control is viewed as a form of price fixing, which will have deleterious consequences in terms of encouraging the problem of 'sitting tenants' who will (a) block outsiders to the rental property market from gaining a foothold in it and (b) affect the functioning of a 'dynamic' labour market as they will refuse to move house to take any offer of employment elsewhere (as they would have to give up their low-cost rental housing if they did). An example of this kind of reasoning comes from the behind-the-scenes ignorance production industry in the run up to the 2015 UK general election. In the context of the Labour Party taking high housing costs more seriously than in its recent history and proposing an upper limit on rent increases within tenancies in the PRS, the IEA published a report titled *The Flaws in Rent Ceilings* (Bourne 2014). A crusade against all forms of rent regulation anywhere, the report argued that 'under rent control there is less incentive for families to reduce their accommodation demands, therefore exacerbating the shortage of properties for others' (Bourne 2014, 16). The tenor of the document reaches a crescendo a few pages later in the spectacular assertion that 'the truth would appear to be that tenants are unwilling to pay for increased security' (Bourne 2014, 25), leading to the conclusion that any 'extra security' for tenants [in the form of rent controls] 'comes at the expense of reduced economic efficiency' (Bourne 2014, 35). The proposed 'solution' was to increase housing supply by stopping any and all government interference in the competitive housing market, which must be allowed to operate free of cumbersome restrictions to provide incentives for producers and consumers to 'optimize' their behaviour and push the market towards equilibrium, while yielding the maximum amount of utility for the maximum number of people.

The problem with this efficiency argument is not only the quite breathtaking assumption that low-income consumers have the freedom to 'rationally choose' where they want to live, without any kind of structural constraints in their lives, but the way it is skewed towards the interests of landlords: 'landlords in a secure tenancy framework would face the prospect of 'problem tenants' enjoying greater security of tenure, making the management of risk through turnover more difficult.' (Bourne 2014, 25). Language matters: the 'management of risk through turnover' is a very polite way of describing evictions, and a 'problem tenant' is someone who cannot afford to pay the rent. If we are interested in housing as a question of social justice, then 'economic efficiency' arguments are to be treated with the utmost caution. Real 'efficiency' is surely not achieved when rental housing costs have reached 50 percent of household incomes, when households have less money to spend on other necessities (and luxuries), and when the state haemorrhages £35 billion a year on subsidies to private landlords through housing benefit. In choosing between fears over price-fixing and concerns for human well-being, the basis of a humane and sensible housing policy must side with the latter.

CONCLUSION

In this chapter we have shown how the idea that rent controls simply *fail* is based more on ideology than fact. We have argued that supply and demand is an inept theory because it only works in an ideal city that has never existed;

that deregulation leads to a fall in housing standards; that the profit motive will never deliver enough homes for everyone; and that the cruellest sign of an 'inefficient' system is one that feeds off a growing rate of inequality. These arguments stem from a different way of viewing solutions to the housing crisis—where the quality of life of those who live in houses, not the profit rate, is our measure of success—and this immediately asks different questions. Why is it considered morally acceptable for a tiny number of people to grow rich off owning buildings, while a major section of the public grows poor through paying for a place to live? Are we willing to tolerate a city that has decanted its poor to the suburbs, where all of space is valued only for the money it generates? Will we continue to believe the same old stories about the equilibrium of the market while inequality continues to rise? These are urgent questions, and they will be answered one way or another—in arguments, in ballot boxes, on the streets—for each of them seems to represent a point of tension close to breaking.

The agitation in Glasgow a century ago is the most celebrated moment of political action around rent controls. But Cowley (1979, 137) reminds us that in Birkenhead around the same time, some two thousand women marched on the Town Hall singing 'Father is fighting in Flanders, we are fighting the landlords here.' Twenty years later in Stepney, East London, tenants appalled at their conditions went out on strike and won. They were copied in Birmingham where, once again, women were at the forefront of the struggle. In 1968 tenants across London formed the United Tenants Action Group, whose members withheld the increase in their rent and won. From 1972 to 1974, tenants throughout the country took part in pickets, marches, partial and complete rent strikes. They were protesting against the Housing Finance Act, which, reminiscent of the contemporary crisis, sought to force local authorities into housing the homeless in temporary accommodation, but gave them no extra funds to do so, and heavily stigmatized those families who had nowhere else to go. In Kirkby, Lancashire, some five hundred tenants paid no rent and no rates for an entire year. Their agitation helped to weaken the incumbent Tory government, which collapsed in 1974. In other words, while we should celebrate and remember the Glasgow Rent Strikes, we should not see them as an isolated event. Housing has never occupied as prominent a role in working-class consciousness as the workplace, but private tenants are historically not strangers to revolt. With the housing crisis across the United Kingdom—and particularly in London—reaching new levels, and with the percentage of us forced to rent privately growing year on year, there is no doubt that tenants will not remain placid forever. And at that point, those petty fantasies about 'supply and demand' disappear because real demands are louder.

REFERENCES

Anas, Alex. 1997. "Rent Control with Matching Economies: A Model of European Housing Market Regulation." *Journal of Real Estate Finance and Economics* 15: 111–37.

Bentley, David. 2016. "The Housing Question: Overcoming the Shortage of Homes." London: *Civitas*. http://www.civitas.org.uk/content/files/thehousingquestion.pdf.

Bone, John, and O'Reilly, Karen. 2010. "No Place Called Home: The Causes and Social Consequences of the UK Housing 'Bubble.'" *British Journal of Sociology* 61: 231–55.

Bourne, Ryan. 2014. *The Flaw in Rent Ceilings*. London: Institute of Economic Affairs.

Cowley, John. 1979. *Housing For People or For Profit?* London: Stage 1.

Damer, Seán. 1989. *From Moorepark to 'Wine Alley': The Rise and Fall of a Glasgow Housing Scheme*. Edinburgh: Edinburgh University Press.

———. 2000a. "The Clyde Rent War! The Clydebank Rent Strike of the 1920s." In *Class Struggle and Social Welfare*, edited by Michael Lavalette and Gerry Mooney, 71–95. London: Routledge.

Dorling, Danny. 2014. *All That Is Solid: The Great Housing Disaster*. London: Penguin Books.

Gauldie, Enid. 1976. "The Middle Class and the Working Class Housing in the Nineteenth Century." In *Social Class in Scotland: Past and Present*, edited by Allan MacLaren, 12–35. Edinburgh: John Donald Publishers Ltd.

Hayek, Friedrich Von. 1972. "The Repercussions of Rent Restrictions." In *Verdict on Rent Control*. London: Institute of Economic Affairs.

Hilton, Alexander. 2016. "How to Repair the Housing Market Quickly—A Crisis Response." *Communication Workers Union*. http://www.devolved.org.uk/HousingReport.pdf.

HM Treasury. 2010. *Investment in the UK Private Rented Sector*. London: UK Treasury.

King, Peter. 2006. *Choice and the End of Social Housing*. London: Institute of Economic Affairs.

Kitchin, Rob, Cian O'Callaghan and Justin Gleeson. 2014. "The New Ruins of Ireland? Unfinished Estates in the Post-Celtic Tiger Era." *International Journal of Urban and Regional Research* 38: 1069–80.

Kutty, Nandinee. 1996. "The Impact of Rent Control on Housing Maintenance: A Dynamic Analysis Incorporating European and North American Rent Regulations." *Housing Studies* 11: 69–88.

Lansley, Stewart, and Joanna Mack. 2015. *Breadline Britain: The Rise of Mass Poverty*. London: Oneworld Books.

Marcuse, Peter, and Madden, Peter. 2016. *In Defense of Housing*. New York: Verso.

McCárthaigh, Seán. 2016. "200,000 Homes Empty Amid Housing Crisis." *The Times*. https://www.thetimes.co.uk/edition/ireland/200-000-homes-empty-amid-housing-crisis-dvqjwprcc.

McCrone, David, and Brian Elliot. 1989. *Property and Power in a City: The Socio-logical Significance of Landlordism*. Basingstoke: MacMillan Press.

Meek, James. 2014. "Where Will We Live?" *London Review of Books* 36: 7–16.

Minton, Anna. 2017. *Big Capital: Who Is London For?* London: Penguin Books.

Mirowski, Philip. 2013. *Never Let a Serious Crisis Go to Waste*. London: Verso.

Neate, Rupert. 2014. "Scandal of Europe's 11m Empty Homes." *The Guardian*, February 23. https://www.theguardian.com/society/2014/feb/23/europe-11m-empty-properties-enough-house-homeless-continent-twice.

Niemietz, Kristian. 2016. *The Key to Affordable Housing: A Critique of the Communication Workers Union's Rent Control Proposals*. London: Institute of Economic Affairs.

Olsen, Edgar. 1988. "What Do Economists Know about the Effect of Rent Control on Housing Maintenance?" *Journal of Real Estate Finance and Economics* 1: 295–307.

Osborne, Hilary. 2015. "Tenants in England Spend Half their Pay on Rent." *The Guardian*, July 16. https://www.theguardian.com/money/2015/jul/16/tenants-in-england-spend-half-their-pay-on-rent.

Piketty, Thomas. 2014. *Capital in the 21st Century*. Cambridge, MA: Harvard University Press.

Proctor, Robert, and Londa Schiebinger. 2008. *Agnotology: The Making and Unmaking of Ignorance*. Stanford: Stanford University Press.

Renshaw, Rosalind. 2015. "Agents and Landlords Mobilise in Scotland as Rent Controls Draw Nearer." *Property Industry Eye,* October 1. http://www.propertyindustryeye.com/agents-and-landlords-mobilise-in-scotland-as-rent-controls-draw-nearer/.

Richardson, Hannah. 2016. "Warning as Household Debts Rise to Top £1.5 trillion." *BBC*, November 7. http://www.bbc.co.uk/news/uk-37873825.

Rodger, Richard. 1989. "Crisis and Confrontation in Scottish housing 1880–1914." In *Scottish Housing in the Twentieth Century*, edited by Richard Rodger, 25–53. Leicester: Leicester University Press.

Rolnik, Raquel. 2013. "Late Neoliberalism: The Financialization of Homeownership and Housing Rights." *International Journal of Urban and Regional Research* 37: 1058–66.

Savills. 2017. *London's Future Homes and Workplaces—The Next Five Years*. London: Savills World Research.

Scottish Housing News. 2015. "Rent Control Plans 'Threaten Scotland's Burgeoning PRS Market'." September 2. http://www.scottishhousingnews.com/5216/rent-control-plans-threaten-scotlands-burgeoning-prs-market/.

Shelter. 2014. *Safe and Decent Homes: Solutions for a Better Private Rented Sector*. http://england.shelter.org.uk/__data/assets/pdf_file/0003/1039530/FINAL_SAFE_AND_DECENT_HOMES_REPORT-_USE_FOR_LAUNCH.pdf.

Shelter Scotland. 2017. *Shelter Scotland Written Evidence on the General Principles of the Child Poverty (Scotland) Bill (March 2017)*. http://scotland.shelter.org.uk/__data/assets/pdf_file/0008/1357577/Shelter_Scotlands_written_evidence_on_the_Child_Poverty_Scotland_Bill.pdf/_nocache.

Slater, Tom. 2016a. "The Housing Crisis in Neoliberal Britain: Free Market Think Tanks and the Production of Ignorance." In, *The Handbook of Neoliberalism*, edited by Simon Springer, Kean Birch and Julie Macleavy, 370–82. London: Routledge.

———. 2016b. "Revanchism, Stigma, and the Production of Ignorance: Housing Struggles in Austerity Britain." In *Risking Capitalism*, edited by Susan Soederberg, 23–48. Bingley, Emerald Group Publishing Limited.

Smith, David M. 1994. *Geography and Social Justice*. Oxford: Blackwell Publishers Ltd.

Stafford, David C. 1976. "The Final Economic Demise of the Private Landlord?" *Social and Economic Administration* 10: 3–14.

The Scotland Institute. 2016. *Housing Costs, Poverty and Homelessness in Scotland*. Glasgow: The Scotland Institute.

UK Parliament. 2016. *Housing and Planning Bill: Written Evidence Submitted by Crisis*. https://www.publications.parliament.uk/pa/cm201516/cmpublic/housingplanning/memo/hpb04.htm.

Wilson, Wendy. 2017. "Private Rented Housing: The Rent Control Debate." *House of Commons Library*. http://www.researchbriefings.files.parliament.uk/documents/SN06760/SN06760.pdf.

Chapter 10

The Relational Articulation of Housing Crisis and Activism in Post-Crash Dublin, Ireland

Rory Hearne, Cian O'Callaghan,
Cesare Di Feliciantonio and Rob Kitchin

In this chapter, we look at the evolving relationships between the commodification of housing and the role of activism in the Irish context. We draw on the periodizations of Manuel Aalbers (2015), with respect to the changing role of housing, and Margit Mayer (2013), with respect to social movements as shaped by neoliberalism, to unpack the ways in which the particular character of housing systems both creates specific crises and necessitates specific contingent and conjunctural responses from activist movements. In line with her long-standing interest in urban social movements and politics, urban scholar Mayer (2013, 5) has suggested the need to consider how contemporary activism responds to, and is shaped by, the impact of the different waves of the neoliberalization of cities because 'urban protests and the claims made on urban development address—and correspond with—specifically neoliberal designs and enclosures'. In her periodization, she highlights four phases: Fordist/Keynesian norms (up to the early 1980s); roll-back neoliberalization in the 1980s; roll-out neoliberalization in the 1990s; and the current phase marked by the triumph of austerity and the financialization of the economy. Building on Mayer's argument, we analyse the strategies developed by housing activists in Ireland as a response to different waves (and crises) in the neoliberalization of housing. To account for the evolution of the housing sector, we also draw upon the periodization of housing developments proposed by Aalbers (2015) who distinguishes between (a) the pre-modern period; (b) the modern/Fordist period; (c) the flexible neoliberal period; and (d) the late neoliberal/postcrisis one.

The importance of processes of capital accumulation in shaping urban space has, of course, been a long-standing interest of critical geographers (Harvey 1982). The built environment has provided a 'safety valve' for the overaccumulation of capital (Harvey 1982), whereas the 'abstraction' of space from the social conditions of its production is a core component in the material-ideological work of capitalism (Lefebvre 1991). As such, the production of urban space is intrinsically tied in with political economic processes happening across spatial scales (Brenner and Theodore 2002). However, urban space is also, as Lefebvre (1991) argues, an *oeuvre* produced out of the everyday life of the city's inhabitants. The politics of urban space is shaped, in part, out of this intersection of the city as a site for capital accumulation and what Wood (2017) calls 'the city as inhabited'. Moreover, from the late 1970s with the advent of neoliberalism, the urbanization of capital has become a more central component of the global economy. Housing has been key to these political economic shifts and to the activist struggles that emerge as a response to the material changes wrought by these transformations (Aalbers and Christophers 2014; Di Feliciantonio 2016).

The choice to focus on housing is based on a double set of considerations. The first one concerns the main role of housing (and real estate) in the contemporary economic history of Ireland and the profound neoliberalization and financialization of housing. During the 'Celtic Tiger' period, construction and real estate registered a massive well-documented boom (e.g., Kitchin et al. 2012; Memery, 2001), followed by the collapse of the sector after 2008, marked by the proliferation of what Kitchin et al. (2014) have defined as 'the new ruins of Ireland' (i.e., unfinished estates). However, since 2013 real estate has registered a spectacular recovery (combined with further financialization of the urban environment), especially in Dublin (see Byrne 2016). The second concern relates to the interscalar character of housing (Aalbers 2015); although typically considered as local because of its fixity, housing is deeply influenced by national laws, regulations and investments (especially in a small country like Ireland), and in recent years, it has registered the massive entrance of 'global players' as investors and landlords (Byrne 2016). So, housing highlights the multiscalar working of 'actually existing neoliberalism' (Brenner and Theodore 2002).

Our argument is that housing activism has been shaped by, and has acted as a response to, the main characteristics of each period and the different crises generated by them. We do not consider the 'pre-modern' and 'modern/Fordist' periods, our analysis beginning with the 'Celtic Tiger' years (corresponding to the third phase in Aalbers's conceptualization) and focusing mainly on the current postcrash period, characterized by austerity politics and rapidly deepening financialization. Our aim here is to use the periodizations offered by Aalbers and Mayer as a heuristic device to better frame the changes in the Irish housing sector and the responses provided by different social actors (e.g., new anti-austerity and community housing activism, nongovernmental organizations, unions, older 'social housing' community groups, lone parents and Left political parties) to different types of housing crises. Methodologically the chapter draws from a number of different research projects carried out since 2010, including academic, policy and activist, using several research methods (participant observation, interviews, policy analysis and activist praxis).

NEOLIBERALIZATION AND IRELAND'S HOUSING CRISIS

As Kitchin et al. (2012) have argued, Ireland's encounter with neoliberalism does not easily map onto paradigmatic cases of roll-back and roll-out neoliberalization. They attribute this to a range of factors, including Ireland's status as a postcolonial nation (which meant that the Fordist welfare state had not developed to a similar level to that of, for example, the United Kingdom), that major neoliberal reforms were first introduced during a period of economic growth (the first phase of the Celtic Tiger), and that these were rolled out in combination with an expansive programme of 'social partnership' (in which trade unions traded pay increments for commitments not to engage in industrial action). In combination, these conditions meant that neoliberal reforms were introduced initially in a 'commonsense' and noncontentious manner. However, the weak state apparatus and Ireland's embrace of globalization, combined with the importance of property developers as a component of the local elite, made Ireland a perfect testbed of neoliberal housing policies. In this regard, Kitchin et al. (2012) argue that Irish neoliberalization was characterized by a form of 'path amplification', particularly with regard to housing. This led eventually to the housing crisis and a particularly extreme version of neoliberalism emerging in and through its wake.

During the so-called Celtic Tiger era (1993–2007), export-led growth throughout the 1990s was followed in the 2000s by growth predicated on a debt-fuelled property bubble. Between 1991 and 2006, 762,541 housing units were built nationally, while house prices rose by 429 percent in Dublin and 382 percent in the country as a whole (Kitchin et al. 2012). From 2007 onwards, Ireland's economic boom collapsed along with the global financial system, resulting in a dramatic and severe housing and financial crisis and recession. House prices fell by 57.4 percent in Dublin and 48.7 percent in the rest of the country (Central Statistics Office [CSO], 2015). Unemployment soared from a low of 4 percent in 2004 to a peak of more than 15 percent by 2011 (Kitchin et al. 2012). In late 2010, the Fianna Fáil government agreed

to an 85 billion IMF-EU-ECB bailout programme, and successive governments responded with a series of harsh austerity budgets in the ensuing years
(Hearne 2014). As noted previously, one outcome of the property crash was a
landscape of unfinished and vacant residential and commercial developments.
The National Survey of Housing Developments in 2010 documented 2,846
unfinished estates in Ireland, present in every local authority, of which only
429 still had active construction happening on them (Housing Agency 2010).
The extent of oversupply was clarified in the 2011 census, which reported
that 230,086 units were vacant (excluding holiday homes), 168,457 houses
and 61,629 apartments out of a total housing stock of 1,994,845 (CSO 2012).
This was combined with growing levels of mortgage arrears, which peaked
in Q3 of 2013 at 12.9 percent of all principal residence mortgages (99,189)
in arrears of more than ninety days (Central Bank 2016).

Notwithstanding the particular trajectory of neoliberalism in the Irish context, the transformation of Ireland's housing system over the course of the
property bubble conforms to many aspects of Aalbers (2015) periodization of
the flexible neoliberal/Post-Fordist period. These include the shift to promoting mortgaged homeownership, the withdrawal of state-provided affordable
ownership and social rental housing provision and the promotion of housing as a financialized asset. The collapse of this model of housing provision
resulted in a wrecked national banking system and dysfunctional housing
market, which has left many thousands of households struggling with debt
(Waldron and Redmond 2016).

THE NEW HOUSING AND HOMELESSNESS CRISIS

From 2013, Ireland's property market has substantially recovered in specific
parts of the country. In Dublin in particular, the 'contradiction' between a
robust urban economy and the proliferation of 'distressed assets' has created
a favourable climate for international capital investors (Byrne 2016). This
influx of international capital, in combination with the policy response of
successive governments to the crisis, has created a new housing and homelessness crisis, which stems from the structural problems of the system as
it has evolved over the boom-and-bust years (Kitchin et al. 2016; Hearne
2017). In line with Aalbers' (2015) periodization, during the Celtic Tiger
years, Irish housing policy moved away from the state provision of social
housing and outsourced it to the private sector, making it dependent on procyclical forces (Byrne and Norris 2017). The Celtic Tiger years also saw the
creation of public-private partnerships (PPPs) to regenerate existing older
social housing estates, which would also include new private housing units.
However, the majority of these schemes collapsed when developers were hit

by the property crash (Hearne 2011). The state, moreover, initiated a policy of housing tens of thousands of social housing tenants in the private-rental sector (PRS) through the payment of a state-subsidy (Rent Supplement, recently renamed the Housing Assistance Payment [HAP] to landlords). Between 1994 and 2004, Rent Supplement claimant numbers increased by 101 percent, in comparison to a 15.2 percent increase in mainstream social housing tenants (Byrne and Norris 2017, 8).

Although the overwhelming policy drive during the Celtic Tiger was towards homeownership, homeownership rates actually fell from 81 percent in 1991 to 76 percent in 2006, whereas the proportion of households in the PRS increased from 9.9 percent in 2006 (145,317) to 18.5 percent in 2011 (305,377) (Hearne 2017). This was the outcome of a number of factors, including the growth of buy-to-let investors and increased immigrant populations, who were often limited in their accommodation choices because of the need to be close to work in city centre areas (see Gilmartin 2014). Moreover, the PRS remains underregulated in the Irish context (Sirr 2014), resulting in various problems for tenants in terms of affordability, security of tenure and living conditions (see Byrne, this collection).

Furthermore, following the crash, as part of a series of severe national austerity budgets from 2008 to 2013, exchequer capital funding for newly built social housing was cut by 90 percent, resulting in an almost complete cessation of new supply by the principal state provider, local authorities. Hearne (2017) has calculated that, had existing levels of capital funding been sustained, an additional 31,136 social-housing units would have been delivered over the period 2010 to 2016. Meanwhile, the PRS is under increased pressure. The lack of new private-sector supply, coupled with more stringent regulations on mortgage lending, has led to higher-income households renting for longer periods, whereas households who previously would have accessed social-housing units are instead being pushed into the PRS (through the HAP payment). Rents have increased at a rate of 13.5 percent on an annual basis nationally, and rents in Dublin have risen by 15 percent per year (a 65 percent increase from their lowest point in 2010) (Daft 2016).

The introduction of 'global players', such as vulture funds and private equity funds, to Dublin's housing market has also served to increase both property prices and rents. Facilitated by the National Asset Management Agency (NAMA)—the 'bad bank' established by the Irish state in 2009 as a mechanism to resolve the country's financial crisis by taking on 74 billion of distressed property loans associated with the five main Irish banks (Byrne 2016)—these funds have bought up ninety thousand properties and hold at least 10.3 billion worth of assets in Ireland (RTE 2017). Sales of properties to investors have increased from 22 percent of all purchases in 2010 (5,194 properties) to 36 percent of all purchases in 2016 (16,999 properties) (Hearne

2017). These factors have combined to create a new housing and homelessness crisis. Homelessness has increased dramatically in Ireland in recent years as a result of evictions from the PRS. Family homelessness emerged as a major issue from 2014 onwards. A majority of these families are lone parents (e.g., this group comprises 70 percent of families in 'emergency accommodation' including commercial hotels). This is reflective of the challenges faced by low-income households as a result of rising rents and inadequate social housing supports. The number of people homeless in Ireland more than doubled from 3,226 to 7,421 between July 2014 and December 2016. In Dublin, the epicentre of this new crisis, 5,480 adults accessed homeless accommodation in 2015, increasing to 6,314 for 2016 (Dublin Region Homeless Executive 2016). The number of homeless families has likewise grown from 598 in March 2016 to 1,091 (comprising 1,465 adults and 2,262 children) in April 2017 (Dublin Region Homeless Executive 2017).

NEW HOUSING MOVEMENTS

These specific material changes to the Irish housing system have influenced the form that movements have taken following the crash. In contrast to countries such as Spain, which followed a similar trajectory in terms of the property bubble (García-Lamarca and Kaika 2016), the issue of mortgage debt was not politicized to the same degree in postcrash Ireland. The dominant, if contested, narrative of the crisis framed the property bubble as the responsibility of homeowners (O'Callaghan et al. 2014). Moreover, Ireland's mortgage arrears crisis only reached its peak in 2013, five years after the initial 'crisis'. Despite having one of the highest mortgage default rates in Europe—with almost a quarter of all Principal Dwelling House (PDH) mortgages in arrears, and a fifth (21.7 percent) of all Buy-to-Let (BTL) mortgages in arrears—Ireland has had a comparatively low repossession rate. There were 600 PDH repossessions in 2012 and 5,568 repossessions in the period 2012–2016, although, repossessions did show an increase in 2016 (Hearne 2017). This contrasts with 570,000 foreclosures in Spain between 2008 and 2014 (García-Lamarca and Kaika 2016). In line with the new postcrisis transformations outlined, the principal source of evictions in Ireland has been of tenants in the PRS. In the first instance, this occurred when rent receivers were appointed by financial institutions recovering BTL properties in arrears. During the first quarter of 2015, rent receivers were appointed to 886 BTL properties, bringing the stock of accounts with rent receivers appointed to 5,965, up from just 566 in 2012. As the property market in the major cities began to recover, a new wave of economic evictions because of escalating rents followed.

The upshot of these factors was that new housing movements did not emerge immediately following the crisis. And indeed, rather than indebtedness forming the main political antagonism (e.g., see Di Feliciantonio 2016), the issue of family homelessness, stemming from evictions in the PRS, became the focus of new movements. As such, postcrisis housing movements in Ireland follow a different trajectory to that of paradigmatic cases like Spain. Here, we periodise the emergence of postcrisis Irish housing movements in two phases.

During the first phase (2008–2014), housing movements emerged out of preexisting struggles of disadvantaged communities during the period of the boom (corresponding to the phase of 'roll-out neoliberalization' in Mayer's conceptualization). Although the Celtic Tiger brought increased levels of wealth for a broad section of the population, there were also communities and sections of society that saw little benefit from the economic boom. Communities in social-housing estates, in particular, found themselves caught in the crosshairs between the state and the Local Authority's policy retrenchments on social housing, and 'regeneration' plans based on inflating land values of the estates. Such urban regeneration schemes, implemented through Integrated Area Plans (IAPs) and PPPs, resulted in conflict when communities felt their concerns were not being taken into account (Attuyer 2015; Hearne 2011). During the boom, social-housing communities in the south inner-city of Dublin—such as St. Michael's Estate, Fatima Mansions and Dolphin House—mobilized anti-displacement campaigns in response to state 'regeneration' plans, engaging in public advocacy, and linking together to form a cross-city tenants' alliance, Tenants First, in 2003 (Bissett 2008). The collapse of PPP schemes following the crash coalesced action in these communities at an individual estate level and at a city scale with public protest marches to the City Council offices organized by Tenants First (Hearne 2014). The austerity budgets also had an immediate and devastating effect on these communities with large cuts to regeneration, community development, the Drugs Task Force and Traveller programmes prominent.

The communities participated in a national alliance, with some support from the trade unions SIPTU and Unite, to hold one of the first national anti-austerity protests in September 2009, with twelve thousand attending. Weekly vociferous protests were held by community activists at the local offices of government ministers until January 2010 when the government removed the majority of funding and autonomy of local community organizations. Some of the community groups regrouped and created a new movement with artists, the Spectacle of Defiance and Hope, against the community cuts. These linked with other small-scale anti-austerity protests (Hearne 2014). Although some victories were achieved (see Hearne and Kenna 2014), the cuts to

community development and youth supports resulted in an effective dismantling and silencing of much of the community infrastructure.

As such, these community-led campaigns were at the forefront of early
anti-austerity protests, which also formed the first wave of housing movement
response. Thus, the first phase of postcrisis housing movements was born out
of preexisting community-based movements contesting the course of regeneration during the boom. These campaigns were taken to another level in
response to both the immediate collapse of PPPs and the emerging politics of
austerity. However, they remained relatively isolated, in part, because of the
subdued nature of the initial anti-austerity response in Ireland before 2014,
and were (partially) defeated. In this sense, the first phase of movements was
a reaction to austerity from communities already suffering from housing dis-
advantage during the boom. If we connect to Mayer's periodization discussed
in the introduction, this phase can be seen as marking the shift from the third
(roll-out neoliberalization) to the fourth phase (characterized by austerity and
financialization).

A second phase of housing movements (2014–present) began to emerge
as the initial period of the crisis gave way to the new housing crisis. These
movements explicitly emerged in response to crises in the PRS and in particular the burgeoning homelessness emergency. The character of these new
groups was diverse. Groups like Housing Action Now attempted to bring
together the older social-housing community and newer housing and anti-austerity activists, while the Dublin Tenants Organization aimed to create a tenants' union to mobilize and advocate for those in the PRS, seeking to create
a broader political platform for housing struggles (see Byrne, this collection).
But many new groups were more circumscribed in their focus: they emerged
at the grassroots level as a direct response to the threat of homelessness.

However, a wider, more politicized, housing movement would coalesce
around these groups. A number of conjunctural factors contributed to this.
Firstly, activists became inspired by a range of new tactics and strategies
emerging both in Ireland and internationally. Internationally, the notoriety of
the main housing movement in Spain, the *Plataforma de los Afectados por
la Hipoteca* (PAH), was spreading in activist circles. Promoting contentious
direct actions including the picketing of banks and politicians in their personal homes, along with occupying empty buildings, the PAH has been able
to challenge the cultural and political hegemony of homeownership, making
squatting a widespread practice (Di Feliciantonio 2017). Members of the
PAH were invited by local activists to give a talk and workshop in Dublin in
December 2014, which was highly influential in subsequent housing movements in the city. At the national level, the Right2Water movement (an alliance of local independent community groups, left-wing political parties and
anti-austerity trade unions such as Unite and Mandate) had mobilized massive

sections of the population (Hearne 2015). At the local level, the Right2Water movement was instrumental in politicizing people, some of whom later transitioned into housing activism. Direct actions by some grassroots groups such as the North Dublin Bay Housing Crisis Committee (who were a group of parents and families affected by the housing crisis who occupied the offices of the Local Authority until demands for housing were listened to) were influential in paving the way for more radical tactics. The latter also underscores the importance of women to recent housing movements in the Irish context. Women, and lone parents in particular, have been disproportionately affected by the new forms of family homelessness, but they have also been at the forefront of new housing movements in response. As such, the particular material conditions of the new housing crisis resulted in new movements forming in the communities and sections of society hit hardest. The specificities of those affected, in combination with the influence of new movements internationally, also began to shape the types of discourses, strategies and tactics of this new set of actors.

Pivotal to the coalescing of these new housing movement politics was the formation of the Irish Housing Network (IHN), an umbrella network for a number of grassroots housing action groups, in 2015. The IHN have been heavily influenced by models developed by the PAH in Spain, which emphasize the importance of those affected by the housing crisis leading struggles (Di Feliciantonio 2017). Their activist strategy has consisted of building a horizontal activist-led network structure of organization (excluding formal representation of political parties, trade unions, etc.), direct actions that target particular issues, capacity building among communities affected by housing inequality and building a counternarrative on the housing crisis. This has included exposing the paradox between high levels of housing vacancy and growing homelessness, conducting walking tours of the city showing the location of vacant buildings and in a number of cases, engaging in direct actions including the occupation of vacant buildings. In the case of walking tours, activists explain to the audience the history of vacant sites, including the details on property and how long they have been vacant, thus spreading awareness about their speculative nature. A similar goal is pursued in the case of the occupation of vacant buildings, when activists show the public how vacant buildings could be used to respond to the primary needs of an increasing number of people. The practice of occupation also challenges the increasing institutional response based on providing homeless emergency accommodation in hotels and bed and breakfasts, an extremely expensive solution that does not offer any stability to people in need.

In this sense, the second phase of movements was more explicitly an activist response largely shaped around homelessness but which encompassed a wider vision for housing. In the absence of other movements emerging in response to the wider housing and property crash, and with the homelessness crisis growing steadily worse from 2014 onwards, homelessness became a unifying signifier enabling a broad unity. In particular, campaigners and activist groups made visible new forms of family homelessness which placed the issue firmly on the political radar and in public discourse.

THE CHALLENGE OF BUILDING AN
IRISH HOUSING MOVEMENT

Here we offer some factors to help explain the apparent contradiction of a prolonged and escalating crisis and increased housing activism but an absence of a major social movement in housing. We do this by exploring some of the recent actions that attempted to build cross-group alliance campaigns and in particular drawing out factors such as the approach taken by different actors, how they positioned themselves in relation to claims and the particular context of the Irish civil society landscape. We focus briefly on three recent actions/campaigns: (a) 'The rent crisis must be stopped' campaign to improve tenants' rights and introduce rent regulation, (b) the occupation of Apollo House and (c) the campaign to stop the sale of public land for 'strategic development and regeneration' under PPP schemes.

During 2016, trade unions (SIPTU, IMPACT, Mandate, Unite) involved in the National Homeless and Housing Coalition (NHHC) organized 'The Rent Crisis Must Be Stopped' campaign. The NHHC was set up in 2015 as an attempt to bring the various housing nongovernmental organizations (NGOs), left political parties, trade unions and housing groups together to form a united campaign. The IHN participated at certain points in this campaign, but there was some tension over how it would be represented given its network nature. Organized as a traditional political alliance-type campaign, it called for the government to declare a housing emergency, build social housing, introduce rent control and secure tenancies. Despite considerable resources and effort, their organized marches had no more than five hundred to two thousand in attendance. Nevertheless, the campaign is seen as having some influence on the implementation of a limited form of rent control by the government in late 2016.

The campaign suffered, in part, from the depoliticizing effects of social partnership during the Celtic Tiger, which had resulted in a demobilized and passive trade union sector. Furthermore, NGOs and charities have played a central role in delivering Irish housing and welfare services and are heavily reliant on state funding. The state has used this as leverage to silence potential dissent through 'service level agreements' with NGOs that forbid public advocacy or protest as a condition of service delivery. Thus, housing NGOs dominate the 'homelessness' space (particularly public debate), but their public critique of government policy is tempered. As such, there was a tension in terms of organizational approach between trade unions and the NGO sector on the one hand, who pursued a public advocacy campaign, and newer housing movements on the other hand, who sought to align themselves with more radical, rather than reformist, demands. Although the campaign constituted a re-politicization of the trade union and NGO sector, for some sections of new housing movements, there was a perception that the approach was not radical enough to address the crisis.

Between December 2016 and January 2017, the direct action taken to occupy Apollo House, a NAMA-controlled office building in Dublin city centre, brought together a wide coalition of actors. Operating under the name 'Home Sweet Home', the coalition included activists from the IHN, trade unionists from Unite and high-profile artists including Glen Hansard and Jim Sheridan. Within two days of occupying the building, Home Sweet Home opened Apollo House as a dry hostel for the homeless. The campaign captured the public imagination and through its 'Go Fund Me' page, received 160,000 in donations, along with widespread public support, volunteer work and donations from thousands of people across the country. Through fighting an injunction served by receivers appointed by NAMA in the courts, and through a media campaign in support of the occupation, Home Sweet Home was successful in making visible and politicizing the homelessness crisis. During this period of the occupation, the group put pressure on the Housing Minister, Simon Coveney, to deliver new emergency provisions and address the crisis. After commitments to improving basic standards were made by the Minister, the group left the occupation on January 12, 2017, in compliance with a court injunction.

Although the action opened up the possibilities for the formation of new political subjectivities, the restricted focus on homelessness failed to connect up with the wider impacts of the housing crisis. The positioning of homelessness and particularly the centring of the most vulnerable subjects of society (e.g., rough sleepers, people with addictions) in campaigns, seemed to prevent the average 'indebted wo/men' (Di Feliciantonio 2016) from actively identifying with them, albeit being generally sympathetic. The focus on homeless families and individuals also placed pressure on vulnerable individuals to become key actors in movements. However, these groups are often reluctant to engage in public action because of the stigma attached to homelessness and the reality of their traumatic and chaotic circumstances. As such, despite the emphasis on affected-led struggles, the sensitive and difficult nature of the action meant that Home Sweet Home activists were often obligated to speak on behalf of homeless individuals. In terms of the overarching aim of new movements to transform the hegemonic narrative around housing, the focus on homelessness runs the risk of limiting the narrative to that particular issue. The case of the Apollo House has shown this: hundreds of people supported the occupation of the vacant building for homeless people in central Dublin through volunteer work or donations, but then no broader mobilization followed the direct action.

In April 2017, an announcement was made by then Housing Minister Simon Coveney to sell four parcels of public land in Dublin earmarked for 'strategic development and regeneration', with advertisements placed in national newspapers. This constituted the revival of failed Celtic Tiger policies to deliver new social and private housing through PPP schemes (Hearne 2011). Community organizations in the old social-housing estates, such as St. Michael's Estate, had already begun to organize against this partial privatization through holding local public meetings in the first half of 2017. Newer groups such as the North Dublin Bay Crisis Committee organized against similar plans in their area, whereas Dublin Central Housing Action (a group within the IHN) campaigned at a local level on the issue. The issue also attracted support from left political parties, such as the Workers Party, which proposed a costed plan to deliver mixed-income social housing on the sites. Sinn Féin, which has positioned itself as the main anti-austerity left party in the postcrisis period, was initially supportive of the Workers Party proposals but later consented to the government plans on the basis that 30 percent of units on the regenerated estates would be designated for social housing.

These campaigns marked a point of intersection between first- and second-phase housing movements. In their respective campaigns, these groups have tried to connect the privatization of the public land to the wider housing crisis by mobilizing locally for affordable housing. Yet despite the parity of their agenda, there were some tensions between the different groups involved. For first-phase groups, the campaign constituted a continuation of years of struggle around an issue that they had built up considerable social movement capacity in addressing. For second-phase groups, the land being sold constituted one of the last available resources to build social housing on a large scale in Dublin city centre and to stem what they viewed as the 'social cleansing' of the urban core. However, these different campaigns failed to link up into a wider platform. Newer groups have at times ended up reproducing some of the strategies of older movements but without also reflecting on the successes or failures that these movements experienced. Although the haste at which campaigns are launched is understandable, given the severity of the current crisis, it nevertheless speaks to the absence of social movement infrastructure and history in the Irish context.

CONCLUSION

In this chapter, we have built upon the periodizations of Aalbers, with respect to the changing role of housing, and Mayer, with respect to social movements as shaped by neoliberalism, to account for the changing forms of housing activism in Ireland after the collapse of the economy. We have identified two phases: the first one (2008–2014) strictly connected to the struggles carried by the disadvantaged groups during the years of the Celtic Tiger and the initial phase of austerity (corresponding to the phase of 'roll-out neoliberalization' in Mayer's periodization); the second one, started in 2014, characterized by new grassroots groups and national alliances, partially shaped by transnational solidarity, aiming to respond to the increasing polarization of Irish society and the housing market.

As Aalbers, Mayer and others have demonstrated, in late capitalism housing has become a more pivotal component of the global economy, and therefore more central to the analysis of political economy (Aalbers and Christophers 2014). The deep infiltration of finance capital in housing has profoundly affected the nature of urban space and transformed everyday life at a biopolitical level (García-Lamarca and Kaika 2016). Although these transformations are characterized by a level of convergence internationally (Aalbers 2015), we argue that it is also necessary to consider the relational ways that local material conditions mediate and shape these processes. We conclude that viewing the neoliberalization of housing conjuncturally requires us to examine how housing crises make specific types of activism both possible and necessary and how activism creates possibilities for addressing the structural problems of housing systems in contextually specific ways.

Overall, our analysis demonstrates a contradictory moment in Irish housing movements. On the one hand, new movements and campaigns appear to be speaking to a residual section of society through a core focus on homelessness, much like older movements centred on social housing. Alongside this, the general population has been incorporated into the hegemonic narrative of economic recovery whereby a sizeable proportion of the middle classes 'gain' from rising property prices. Thus far, the housing movement has failed to transform the hegemonic narrative that this broad group identifies with. On the other hand, the postcrisis period has witnessed a series of radical transformations in housing movement politics that, though in their infancy, suggest the emergence of a new base in the social movement infrastructure. The emergence of a range of new groups, the reigniting of older community-based campaigns, and the shift in the political position of NGOs and trade unions all testify to this. In this sense, housing could become a key signifier of the deeply unequal 'recovery' and a rallying point around which civil society unites for social justice.

REFERENCES

Aalbers, Manuel B. 2015. "The Great Moderation, the Great Excess and the Global Housing Crisis." *International Journal of Housing Policy* 15(1): 43–60.

Aalbers, Manuel. B., and Brett Christophers. 2014. "Centring Housing in Political Economy." *Housing, Theory and Society* 31(4): 373–94.

Attuyer, Katia. 2015. "When Conflict Strikes: Contesting Neoliberal Urbanism outside Participatory Structures in Inner-city Dublin." *International Journal of Urban and Regional Research* 39(4): 807–23.

Bissett, John. 2008. *Regeneration: Public Good or Private Profit?* Dublin: Tasc at New Island.

Brenner, Neil, and Nik Theodore. 2002. "Cities and the Geographies of 'Actually Existing Neoliberalism.'" *Antipode* 34(3): 349–79.

Byrne, Michael. 2016. "'Asset Price Urbanism' and Financialization after the Crisis: Ireland's National Asset Management Agency." *International Journal of Urban and Regional Research* 40(1): 31–45.

Byrne, Michael, and Michelle Norris. 2017. "Procyclical Social Housing and the Crisis of Irish Housing Policy: Marketization, Social Housing, and the Property Boom and Bust." *Housing Policy Debate*: 1–14.

Central Bank. 2016. 'Residential mortgage arrears and repossession statistics'. Available at: https://www.centralbank.ie/docs/default-source/statistics/credit-and-banking-statistics/mortgage-arrears/gns-6-2-2-4-2016q1_ie_mortgage_arrears_statistics.pdf?sfvrsn=8.

Central Statistics Office (CSO). 2012. "Profile 4: A Roof over Our Heads." http://www.cso.ie/en/media/csoie/census/documents/census2011profile4/Profile_4_The_Roof_over_our_Heads_Full_doc_sig_amended.pdf.

———. 2015. "Residential Property Price Index." http://www.cso.ie/en/releasesandpublications/er/rppi/residentialpropertypriceindexdecember2015/

Daft. 2016. "The Daft.ie Rental Price Report 2016". http://www.daft.ie/report/2016-q4-rental-daft-report.pdf.

Dublin Region Homeless Executive. 2016. [Accommodation usage annual infographic]. http://www.homelessdublin.ie/accommodation-usage.

———. 2017. [Homeless families]. http://www.homelessdublin.ie/homeless-families.

Di Feliciantonio, Cesare. 2016. "Subjectification in Times of Indebtedness and Neoliberal/Austerity Urbanism." *Antipode* 48(5): 1206–27.

———. 2017. "Social Movements and Alternative Housing Models: Practicing the 'Politics of Possibilities' in Spain." *Housing, Theory and Society* 34(1): 38–56.

García-Lamarca, Melissa, and Maria Kaika. 2016. "'Mortgaged Lives': The Biopolitics of Debt and Housing Financialization." *Transactions of the Institute of British Geographers* 41(3): 313–27.

Gilmartin, Mary. 2014. "Immigration and Spatial Justice in Contemporary Ireland." In *Spatial Justice and the Irish Crisis*, edited by Gerry Kearns, David Meredith and John Morrissey, 161–76. Dublin: Royal Irish Academy.

Harvey, David. 1982. *The Limits to Capital*. Oxford: Blackwell.

Hearne, Rory. 2011. *Public Private Partnerships in Ireland: Failed Experiment or the Way Forward for the State*. Manchester: Manchester University Press.

———. 2014. "Achieving a Right to the City in Practice: Reflections on Community Struggles in Dublin." *Human Geography* 7(3): 14–25.

———. 2015. "The Irish Water War." *Interface: A Journal for and about Social Movements* 7(1): 309–21.

———. 2017. "A Home or a Wealth Generator? Inequality, Financialization and the Irish Housing Crisis." Dublin: TASC. https://www.tasc.ie/download/pdf/a_home_or_a_wealth_generator_inequality_financialization_and_the_irish_housing_crisis.pdf

Hearne, Rory, and Padraic Kenna. 2014 "Using the Human Rights Based Approach to Tackle Housing Deprivation in an Irish Urban Housing Estate." *Journal of Human Rights Practice* 6(1): 1–25.

Housing Agency. 2010. "2010 National Housing Survey." http://www.housing.ie/Our-Services/Unfinished-Housing-Developments/2010-National-Housing-Survey.

Kitchin, Rob, Cian O'Callaghan and Justin Gleeson. 2014. "The New Ruins of Ireland? Unfinished Estates in the Post-Celtic Tiger Era." *International Journal of Urban and Regional Research* 38(3): 1069–80.

Kitchin, Rob, Cian O'Callaghan, Mark Boyle, Justin Gleeson and Karen Keaveney. 2012. "Placing Neoliberalism: The Rise and Fall of Ireland's Celtic Tiger." *Environment and Planning A* 44(6): 1302–26.

Kitchin, Rob, Rory Hearne and Cian O'Callaghan. 2016. "Housing." In *Austerity and Recovery in Ireland: Europe's Poster Child and the Great Recession*, edited by William K. Roche, Philip J. O'Connell and Andrea Prothero, 272–89. Oxford: Oxford University Press.

Lefebvre, Henri. 1991. *The Production of Space*. Oxford: Blackwell.

Mayer, Margit. 2013. "First World Urban Activism." *City: Analysis of Urban Trends, Culture, Theory, Policy, Action* 17(1): 5–19.

Memery, Clodagh. 2001. "The Housing System and the Celtic Tiger: The State Response to a Housing Crisis of Affordability and Access." *International Journal of Housing Policy* 1(1): 79–104.

O'Callaghan, Cian, Mark Boyle and Rob Kitchin. 2014. "Post-Politics, Crisis, and Ireland's 'Ghost Estates.'" *Political Geography* 42: 121–33.

RTÉ. 2017. *The Great Irish Sell Off. RTE Television.* Monday January 9.

Sirr, Lorcan. 2014. *Renting in Ireland: The Social, Voluntary, and Private Sectors.* Dublin: Institute of Public Administration.

Waldron, Richard, and Declan Redmond. 2016. "Stress in Suburbia: Counting the Costs of Ireland's Property Crash and Mortgage Arrears Crisis." *Tijdschrift voor Economische en Sociale Geografie* 107(4): 484–501.

Wood, Patricia Burke. 2017. *Citizenship, Activism and the City: The Invisible and the Impossible*. Oxon: Routledge.

Chapter 11

'Only Alternative Municipal Housing'

Making the Case for Public Housing Then and Now

Sarah Glynn

It is spelled out clearly on the big banner held aloft by the tenants of Partick at the centre of one of those much-reproduced black-and-white photographs from the 1915 Glasgow Rent Strike: 'only alternative MUNICIPAL HOUS-ING'. And although the immediate demand of the 1915 rent strikers was for rent control, the resulting 1915 Rent Restriction Act, together with the extensive tenant unrest, served as the catalyst that helped to break down government resistance to subsidized public housing and to establish council housing's place in British working-class life. This happened because munici-pal housing had already become a central demand of Left politics, in fact, a demand that had begun to enter mainstream debate and be given reluctant consideration as a temporary solution by politicians whose views were very far from socialist.

This chapter begins by looking at how government resistance to state-subsidized housing was broken down historically by a combination of ten-ant campaigns and wider socialist action, in the face of the clear failure of private developers and landlords to provide decent working-class homes. But reluctant acceptance of public housing was not enough. The following sections look at the intrinsic problems with a system that was almost always considered of second-class status and at how these problems helped open the door to the neoliberal revolution and the return of many of the old evils of private renting. This then raises the issue of demands for today's housing campaigners, fighting those same evils. Like the tenants of Partick, campaign-ers need to combine immediate demands for more affordable rents and better conditions, with demands for more long-term structural changes that will get rid of housing problems at the source. The primary purpose of this chapter is to suggest practical long-term demands that would make that fundamental and sustained difference. It argues for a new investment in public housing that learns from past mistakes, public housing that would be as desirable as other housing tenures, and would be managed locally with maximum tenant involvement. Housing does not exist in isolation, and campaigns for better housing are intimately linked to campaigns for wider social change: greener planning, genuine local democracy and ultimately a revaluation of societal aims. This chapter looks at improvements in housing as part of a much bigger shift towards an ecosocialist future and puts forward practical reforms for step changes that will help move us in that direction.

Although some of the changes proposed here may seem a long way from current thinking, recent developments in Scottish housing policy provide some grounds for optimism, especially the boost given to social housing by ending the Right-to-Buy and increasing investment in council housing. And while housing policy in England is moving in the opposite direction, the scale of the crisis this is creating is impacting on the public consciousness, especially since the Grenfell fire drew the veil from a world that many had learned to ignore. More generally, both the Scottish Independence campaign and Labour's Momentum have demonstrated the growing hunger for a more socialist approach. As the 1915 rent strikers discovered, change happens when ordinary people show that they will no longer tolerate a housing crisis, and then what was once dismissed as impossible soon becomes normal. Alternative policies would remain on the shelf without pressure from below to prove that the status quo will no longer be accepted, but grassroots action needs workable alternatives to aim for. This chapter is about preparing to build on the movement for change.

THE GROWTH OF AN IDEA

Despite a general assumption on behalf of the ruling classes that government should not intervene to alter the balance of market forces, and that unearned help encouraged dependency and fecklessness, it was impossible for them to ignore the housing needs of the workers who crowded into the Victorian industrial cities. Slums were feared as a breeding ground for disease and criminality; better homes were regarded as a prerequisite for a healthier, more efficient workforce; and poor housing conditions could prove a trigger for unrest at a time of a growing labour movement and revolutionary developments across the English Channel. By the start of the First World War, this situation had already led to interventions by national and local government, as well as by various forms of semi-philanthropic groups anxious to demonstrate that the provision of quality working-class homes was compatible with making a small but comfortable profit. There were already many examples of housing built by the municipalities, especially following the 1890 Housing Act. The hope was that these would eventually bring in a return on the initial investment. However, local authorities increasingly had to resort to raising a portion of their running costs, as well as loan repayments, through the rates—the local property tax. Despite this creeping acceptance of limited government action, resistance to government interference in the market through subsidy remained strong, and the overall impact of what had been done was woefully inadequate.

The Social Democratic Federation (SDF) had argued for municipal involvement in nonprofit housing from 1885; the Workmen's National Housing Council, which was founded by three SDF members in 1898, played an important role in arguing for state intervention in rents and housing supply; and from the early 1900s, Labour Party branches were demanding subsidized municipal housing. Meanwhile politicians of all parties were being forced to realize that there were good economic and political reasons for ensuring the provision of decent homes. The First World War exacerbated bad housing conditions by diverting resources from both building and maintenance, and it also provided an example of state intervention, both more generally through the war industries and specifically in the provision of housing for war workers.

RENT STRIKES AND REVOLUTION

There has been a lot of debate on the significance of the rent strikes for the decision, realized through the 1919 Addison Act, to bring in state-funded municipal housing. This reflects broader debates on working-class agency. The rent strikes demonstrably forced the introduction of rent control, and although this was intended to be temporary, it proved impossible to remove. With housing in short supply, it was argued that removal of the restrictions would bring immediate and devastating rent rises, but the low rents were discouraging private investors from developing further rented housing (see the 1918 Committee on the Increase of Rent, Daunton 1984, 9). State-subsidized housing was welcomed as a temporary solution that would breach this impasse.

Beyond this specific and pragmatic argument, government was responding to the pressures of a restive working-class movement for whom appalling housing conditions were a highly visible focus of discontent. Indeed, the influential Royal Commission on the Housing of the Industrial Population of Scotland, which was set up in 1912 and completed in 1917, regarded housing conditions as a 'legitimate cause of social unrest', and even recorded their 'satisfaction' that workers were refusing to tolerate those conditions (Royal Commission 1918, para 2223). From 1917, housing was at the centre of plans for postwar reconstruction, with increasing recognition of the need for state funding. And there are no shortage of quotes—from the king downwards[1]— putting forward the provision of housing as a solution to unrest; or in the words of the Parliamentary Secretary to the Local Government Board, 'an insurance against Bolshevism and revolution' (Quoted in Swenarton 1981, 94).

WHY PUBLIC OWNERSHIP?

The main forces in this history will be familiar to those who have looked at housing histories elsewhere, but what is unusual in the British case is the allocation of the leading role to the local authorities. Many other European countries turned instead to other forms of social housing, especially various types of housing association. The reasons for this difference lie in the nature of the British labour movement and its emphasis on parliamentary socialism; the development of British local government, which was already involved with many areas of planning, building control and service provision, and to some extent with housing; the limits of Britain's early housing associations; and the unpopularity and lack of organization of Britain's urban landlords, which made them unlikely recipients for government subsidies. Many European socialists, who were more wary of state involvement, set up their own organizations, including organizations for providing working-class housing, and in countries where housing associations have played a more significant historical role, the associations were founded by broad-based community groups.

The United Kingdom appeared to have little need for housing associations; however, a government-subsidized supplementary community-based housing association movement developed in the 1960s and 1970s. This was championed as an alternative to state bureaucracy, but many associations grew and merged into large businesses with new and even less accountable bureaucracies, high rents and remote management practices—especially after the transfer of former council-housing stock. Housing associations have become increasingly dependent on private finance and subject to the commercial models of their financial lenders (Malpass 2000; Smyth 2018). Government preference has ensured that housing associations are now the main providers of the UK's much diminished social housing stock,[2] but despite the undoubted problems of council bureaucracies, council housing has the potential to be a much more democratic way of running social housing[3] and has also been shown to be considerably better value for money as it is not subject to commercial norms (House of Commons Council Housing Group 2005, 8).

A RELUCTANT CONSENSUS

As with rent control, so with state-subsidized public housing: a temporary
measure became recognized as a long-term necessity. Council housing
became an increasingly important part of British life—especially in urban
Scotland—but, even as they congratulated themselves on their house-build-
ing statistics, few politicians saw council housing as anything other than a
second-class tenure making up for deficiencies in the private market for those
who could not aspire to the ideal of homeownership. It was a rare politician
who, like John Wheatley and Nye Bevan, saw public housing as more than
a necessity.

Bevan, who was in charge of housing as Minister of Health from 1945
to 1951, famously had a vision of good quality council homes rented by
people from all walks of life. However, this was not shared by everyone
in the postwar Labour government. He limited private housing to one-fifth
of new homes, but a thoroughgoing nationalization (or municipalization)
of housing was never attempted, increased subsidies were not enough
to make rents affordable for the worst off and when pressures grew for
cuts in public expenditure, housing was particularly vulnerable. More
radical proposals never made it onto the statute book, including public
ownership of the construction industry, which was supported by the 1944
Labour Party conference, and the transfer of private-rented homes to the
local authorities, which was proposed in 1949 and later adopted as party
policy for a period while Labour was in opposition. By the time of the
next Labour government, the party was clear that it regarded the expansion of public housing as a temporary measure to meet exceptional needs,
whereas the expansion of owner occupation was 'normal' and a 'social
advance' (1965 White Paper, quoted in Community Development Project
1976, 22). For most of the time that council housing was enlarging its
share of the British housing stock—peaking at just under a third of the
total in 1979—it was being increasingly confirmed by governments of
both main parties as a residual tenure for those who could not afford to
own their own homes.

This helps to explain not just the current dismantling of this huge public
asset but also some of council housing's much publicized failures. Quality
was sacrificed for quantity, and this was made worse by a fixation on relatively untested industrial system building methods, and the insistence, from
1955, that money borrowed by councils had to be at commercial interest
rates. Second-class status also resulted in second-class treatment in the form
of top down and insensitive bureaucratic management, poor maintenance
and perpetual cuts. The dice were loaded against achieving anything better.
Local-authority housing schemes made sure that millions of families had a

decent affordable place to live, but when, in 1976, workers from the government-sponsored Community Development Projects wrote a report in support of the case for proper investment in council housing, its title took the form of a question: *Whatever Happened to Council Housing?* And their answer was unforgiving:

> First, from creditable and idealistic origins it has descended to a miserly output of often poorly designed and constructed homes for 'underprivileged' groups. . . . Second, most of the public subsidies and rents which fund council housing go not to adding to the housing stock or further improving conditions, but back to the money-lenders in the form of interest charges. (1976, 28)

The resulting problems have been used not so much to criticize inadequacies of execution as to condemn the very idea of public housing. Even in Scotland, where, under devolution, there is still a significant level of government support for public and other social housing, this is seen as part of a multitenure system where homeownership is the tenure of aspiration, and private letting has an increasingly important role. In England, under the current Tory government, there is a question mark over how social housing in any meaningful form can continue to exist at all.

BACK TO THE FUTURE

In the course of the twentieth century, the proportion of households in private-rented housing saw a huge drop. In England and Wales it dropped from three-quarters of all homes in 1918 to just 9 percent in 1991. In Scotland the proportion fell to less than 6 percent. Private renting seemed to be becoming permanently marginalized, but recent years have confounded earlier predictions. In 2016 the figures for private renting were more than 15 percent of households in Scotland and over 20 percent in England. Margaret Thatcher's Conservative government removed rent control for new private tenancies in 1989, with the aim of encouraging people to become private landlords, but it was the loss of the social-housing alternative that allowed private renting to increase again. More recently, this has been combined with a decline in homeownership. Financial deregulation and consequent property speculation has forced many households to turn to private lets, first because of the spiralling price of ownership and then in response to financial difficulties consequent of the 2007 financial crash and subsequent austerity economics. Both house-price inflation and crash were the result of government policies to encourage property speculation.

This renewed dependence on private renting has drawn parallels with a 100 years ago, so should we be dusting down those old banners for municipal housing? Certainly all the forces that made private renting a problem in the past are still there. Market pressures tend to reduce quality of repair and security of tenure and to drive up rents. Even if all these things were regulated, and in Scotland we have seen a few small steps in that direction helped by a large Living Rent campaign (see Living Rent, this volume), landlordism remains an intrinsically exploitative system that acts as a major vehicle for transferring further wealth to the rich. Rent paid for private tenancies comes from the pockets of some of the poorest in our society—and, through housing benefit, from the public purse—and it goes to owners of extra properties as unearned income. By contrast, rent paid for council housing returns to local government for reinvestment in the community (figure 11.1).

Figure 11.1   Against Landlord Tyranny. Sarah Glynn.

WHAT DO WE WANT?

As a housing activist, I am very aware of how easy it is to become totally absorbed in the urgency of immediate struggle. There does not seem to be time to look beyond individual, often defensive, campaigns to imagine and work out what better system we could be aiming for. And most academic research concentrates on criticizing actually existing processes rather than proposing alternatives. The purpose of this chapter is to step out into the void and put forward some coherent long-term goals as socialist groups were doing in 1915 and as was done by the mass-housing movement of the late 1930s that laid the ground for postwar investment in council housing (Glynn 2005). Activists need to articulate not only what they are against but also what they want and how to get there, so as to supplement immediate struggles with campaigns for real substantial change. A key stage of any such campaign is to get these different ideas onto the wider agenda, to open current housing practices up to discussion and debate and to enable people to begin to realize that another way of doing things is possible.

As with any effective movement, campaigners can build support, strength and understanding by combining the types of grassroots actions described in this book with wider analysis and long-term visions for change. Ideas have to be shown to be desirable, practical and firmly founded on real ground: no mere back of an envelope rhetorical wish for x thousand more council houses but a considered and realizable proposal. It is this that will give people the ammunition to move beyond isolated battles and push for a better system with the same confidence shown by the generation who brought in the Welfare State. As before, struggles against the immediate problems of exploitative private renting need to be linked to the campaign for a publicly funded, publicly owned alternative. And this time activists need to ensure the creation of places that communities can engage with and be proud of.

TOWARDS A NEW KIND OF SOCIALISM

Neoliberal hegemony has acted on the public imagination to equate socialism and public ownership with the worst forms of uncaring bureaucracy. Stalinist Russia is regarded as the inevitable conclusion of any more wholehearted socialist ambitions, and in the field of housing, public housing has become equated with the worst examples of a troubled housing scheme. It is important to address this rewriting of history and examine public housing's many—often unobtrusive—successes, as well as its more notorious failures. But campaigners also need to make clear that they are not arguing for a return to the bureaucratic systems of the past; that they want to go forward to a different and better future.

Socialist visions of 100 years ago were forged at a time of industrialization and increasing mass production. Along with taking control of the productive forces, they embraced growth and economies of scale as the route to produce enough to meet everyone's needs. Today, productive forces can already generate more than enough for everyone, but capitalism continues to work against more equal distribution. We still need to ensure fair distribution of labour and of the products of that labour through common ownership and control of production, but we do not need further growth; indeed, in a world of finite resources, an economic model based on growth is unsustainable. Instead, we should be looking towards a system with different social and organizational forms, based not on 'growth' but on creating a better society in tune with our environment. Demands for social and environmental sustainability are mutually reinforcing. Both require a shift from a system driven by short-term profit to one that prioritizes long-term social and environmental values—a system that is reinforced through maximizing community ownership and bottom-up democratic control of basic resources (Bookchin 1999; Löwy 2015).

Ideas that can be grouped under the banner of ecosocialism call for a grassroots democracy, where most people can live and work as part of a local community integrated into their environment. They envisage a decentralization of jobs and services to local areas that function as local communities both socially and politically, with community ownership of major industries so that they can be run for the common good. Public or community-owned housing has a vital part in this system. Despite the overwhelming threat posed by climate change, a threat that can serve as a driver towards a social economy and a better type of society, we have to acknowledge that the political climate is not yet ready for such a wholesale shift of outlook, but we can still fight for every change that takes us in this direction. As in the past, the provision of public housing serves important functions in itself, and it is also a transitional step towards a fairer future.

ARGUING THE CASE FOR PUBLIC HOUSING—AND SOME SUPPORTING CHANGES TO TAXATION

After almost four decades of neoliberal housing policies, the case for public housing has never been stronger. The drive for short-term profit has intensified the UK's endemic housing crisis, fuelled inequalities of wealth and opportunity and destroyed the economy. Capitalism will always leach money to the finance sector, as well as to other owners of capital.[4] But following financial deregulation, the flow to finance has become a flood, fuelling unrestrained property speculation. The Office for National Statistics calculated in 2015 that dwellings accounted for £5.5 trillion, or 63 percent of the UK's total net worth.[5] Our economy is built on a giant Ponzi scheme that relies on there being always more buyers for houses at ever increasing prices. When buyers run out and prices fall, the current housing bubble will burst like the last one did ten years ago. In addition, money speculated is not being spent on other things, such as building and improving homes and infrastructure. Housing costs have generated unsustainable levels of personal debt, and the recent revival of private renting has proven to be a vehicle for renewed exploitation.

Although the growth in household formation—itself a function of our atomized socioeconomic model—along with net migration has generated the need for additional homes, the main driver of the housing crisis remains the systemic failure to address issues of affordability and fair distribution (Dorling 2014). For a propertied elite, their share of wealth is extending off the scale, while, for a growing portion of the population, poor-quality expensive housing is impacting every aspect of their lives. The result of regarding housing as a commodity rather than as homes is being etched on a generation. The underlying demands of any housing campaign—or wider social movement—need to be predicated on reversing this position and regarding housing in terms of social and environmental needs.

A housing policy that focuses on housing as homes, and on promoting housing equality, has to marginalize the use of housing for speculation. Although this could be achieved by taking all property into public ownership, today's politics is not ready for such a step. However, it is possible to move towards similar goals through a transitional, more evolutionary, approach that would combine the expansion of public housing with an effective convergence of different types of housing tenure (Glynn 2014). If private owners were increasingly restricted from using their homes to make private profit, while social tenants were given greater security of tenure and freedom to personalize their homes, and all homes were subject to socially driven planning and regulation, then in the long run, the differences between ownership and social tenancy would tend to diminish. Fiscal changes to reduce speculation could include land value tax (LVT), raising the rate of capital gains tax and extending it to include the main home, a tax on inheritance and ending all subsidies for private ownership (Murphy 2017). Some of these would be more easily introduced than others, but all could be brought in at a low level and subsequently increased. Persuading people to abandon the curious British obsession with house price rises might be harder, but if prices were to fall and stabilize at a lower level, most people actually living in their homes would not suffer from the drop in their paper value, as long as all mortgages were made portable to other properties so they were not prevented from moving. (In Germany, by comparison, the last forty years of housing policy kept prices relatively stable with a slow overall decline.) For those finding difficulties in meeting their mortgage payments or other costs associated with owning a home, or who would simply prefer to rent, existing mortgage to rent schemes could be extended to offer the alternative of converting their existing home into a local authority tenancy.

The simplest way to ensure that land use is in the public interest is through public ownership. An evolutionary policy model needs to include ways both to increase public ownership and to regulate the use of land that is not publicly owned so as to minimize speculation and maximize social and environmental benefits. When land is brought into public ownership this raises issues of compensation. This could be helped by the reintroduction of the law, abolished in 1959, that allowed councils to purchase land for development at current use-values. The introduction of LVT, combined with a strong, democratic and transparent planning system, would have even wider impact. It would promote the most beneficial use of privately owned land, enable increases in land value to bring public benefit and reduce land speculation, which is the major element of property speculation (Jones 2008). An initial low-level LVT could be brought in as a much more progressive replacement for council tax, as advocated by the Scottish Greens, and included as a possibility in the 2017 Labour Manifesto. As LVT levels increase, so possibilities for land speculation diminish, and ownership moves towards being nothing more than the right to use the land, in accordance with planning guidelines.

At the same time, a major investment in new and upgraded genuinely affordable public housing would allow such housing to become a tenure of choice. We have been conditioned in the United Kingdom to find this surprising, but postwar Swedish housing policy came close to its ideal aim that homes of different tenures should be of similar standard and that there should be no intrinsic financial advantage in living in one type of tenure over another, with the result that ownership patterns did not vary much between different social classes (Kemeny 1981, 102–106). Ultimately, there is no practical, as distinct from political, reason why we could not have a system where everyone who wanted it was entitled to affordable public-rented housing as a universally available service, with no need for rationing or means testing. Universal services need to be paired with a progressive-taxation system so that beneficiaries who are better off make their contribution through higher taxes, and wealth is redistributed. Decent housing is a basic requirement for a well-functioning society, and investment in public housing is investment in a social good, like investment in health, education or transport infrastructure. The postwar welfare state never fully took on the problem of housing—especially after Nye Bevan's resignation in 1951—but a new approach to housing can learn from past mistakes and ensure policy works in the interest both of better homes and of greater equality in housing and beyond. This means not being afraid to invest in building, buying and upgrading public housing.

The provision of social goods should be a major function of government expenditure, and that ought to be sufficient reason in itself for investing in housing. When Birmingham City Council took over the city's waterworks in 1876, the mayor, Joseph Chamberlain, told a House of Commons Committee, 'We have not the slightest intention of making profit. . . . We shall get our profit indirectly in the comfort of the town and in the health of the inhabitants' (quoted in Marmot 2010). It would be a sad day if we cannot aspire to be at least as progressive as a nineteenth-century Liberal. But this does not mean we can ignore the financial costs of such public investment and nor should we fail to recognize the economic benefits of good affordable public housing. The lack of decent housing has financial as well as social costs, and the financial gains from the provision of better homes are potentially huge, even if they are difficult to measure. Good homes and a more equitable housing provision would form the foundation for better health and life chances and better social cohesion. In addition, the building, upgrading and maintenance of the homes would create a major stimulus to the economy, bringing money and jobs to local areas and helping to counter the impact of the economic cycle.

Money in a modern economy is not a physical thing, like a bar of gold, but a promissory note for future payment, which means that theoretically there is no limit on government expenditure so long as this generates sufficient future returns and does not stimulate inflation by putting more money into the economy than there is increase of things to buy. (The idea that government spending can be compared to that of a household is a dangerous fallacy.) Sufficient returns would be what is needed to pay a low-interest loan such as could be made available from a national investment bank. The financial returns from investment in public housing are both direct (from the rents) and induced (recovered by the government as taxes on the economic benefits arising from construction and from better housing). The cost of public services and infrastructure—which should include housing—can also be partially refunded through taxation in other areas, and even with very favourable borrowing rates, it is clear that such contributions would continue to be needed. Wealthy elites always try and persuade the less well-off that taxes are equally an attack on everyone who earns an income or owns even the tiniest bit of property. The argument has to be made, and remade, that when progressive taxation is used to fund public investment and services, the majority of people benefit, especially when wealth distribution has become so skewed in favour of the super-rich 1 percent.

BOTTOM-UP DEMOCRACY

We need public housing. We can afford public housing, but how can it be made to work better? Activists also have to consider how to avoid distant and inflexible bureaucracies and instead develop locally based management that can respond quickly to needs and keep regular checks on maintenance—perhaps even encompassing the function of concierge. For this to succeed in meeting the needs of tenants, they have to be given the opportunity to play an active part. This can be achieved through tenant management coopera-tives. Despite some successful examples in the late 1970s and 1980s (Power 1988; Scott 2000), and a legal 'right to manage' since 1994, these have so far only been taken up by a small proportion of tenants, usually as a result of dissatisfaction with existing management and repairs. Such organizations demand a major commitment from the tenants involved, and any tenant management system needs to strike a careful balance between facilitating the setting-up process and retaining necessary checks and safeguards. An evalu-ation of English Tenant Management Organizations carried out for the UK government in 2002 found that they were generally well managed and were especially effective in dealing with small repairs, cleaning and general maintenance (Cairncross et al. 2002). Many of the organizations extended their remit beyond basic housing functions.

Of course not all groups of tenants will want, or be able to cope with, such active involvement, especially before the implementation of other social changes (such as a universal basic income) that could give them more time and fewer pressures. In other places, tenant management might be wanted initially, but fail later; however, when that happens, homes can be taken back into full council management. At the same time, care has to be taken that this kind of tenant involvement does not replace and exclude more campaigning forms of tenant organization. Anyone who has been involved with community groups will be familiar with pressures to co-opt and incorporate independent organizations and close down criticism; and tenant groups have proved particularly susceptible through schemes for registration and grant funding (Glynn 2010). Beyond and separate from management organizations of the kind described here, tenants need to be free to arrange their own independent tenant-controlled campaigning organizations, which can act in a comparable manner to a trade union with active local branches. The 1930s housing movement provides a powerful and effective example (Glynn 2005), while organizations such as the Radi-cal Housing Network, Acorn and Living Rent are marking out similar paths today.

Public-sector houses are every bit as much people's homes as are privately owned houses and should feel that way. This means, besides security of tenure, the freedom for tenants to make alterations to suit their household and tastes. They would still be restricted from disadvantaging their neigh-bours or damaging the value of what remains publicly owned property, but private owners are also required to conform to a degree of neighbourliness by planning and environmental regulations and would not generally make changes that devalue their home.

Finally, although local authority ownership already ensures a measure of democratic control, if public housing is to respond fully to local needs, it would have to be developed as part of a wider reappraisal of local democracy—a reappraisal that devolved many more decisions to local communities. Although governments pay lip service to local devolution, local democracy in the United Kingdom remains extraordinarily centralized. Radical ideas for a participative grassroots democracy have been developed in Bookchin's writings on 'Libertarian Municipalism' (Bookchin 1999).

PLANNING FOR THE LONG TERM

Public ownership alongside real devolved democracy should enable more sensitive design and planning, with priority given to social and environmental considerations. Developments do not have to be subservient to volume housebuilders' requirements to squeeze in the most cost-effective configuration of homes and reap the quickest reward. 'Regeneration' can be designed for existing communities rather than displacing them for more profitable gentrification. Even now, the more holistic and long-term approach possible within the social-housing sector has allowed it to take a lead in creating energy saving homes.

Campaigns for better housing and well-planned places mesh with campaigns for environmental and energy protection and the objectives of environmentally friendly living, strong communities and a better quality of life are mutually reinforcing. Achieving these goals calls for a proactive approach to planning that is guided by the public interest and not reduced to reactive responses to the wishes of developers. Regional planning is needed to coordinate homes and jobs and ecological concerns, so as to make the best use of land and resources and enable a more community-focused way of life.[6] And at a local level, communities can be directly involved, alongside planners and architects, in designing and developing the places where they live. Attention can then be given to the spaces between buildings and not just to individual houses; provision can be made for local services, efficient and cheap public transport and community spaces; sheltered housing and elderly friendly outdoor spaces can be integrated into communities with proper facilities for children and young adults; and developments can be laid out to maximize natural light and sunshine and access to the outdoors and green space. The improved environment, as well as people's involvement in its creation, can help to reinforce community structures.

None of these changes will be handed down to us. Every improvement will have to be fought for, and to do this we need clear positive agendas for worked out and workable alternatives. The fight for better housing is a fight for better housing quality, for greater housing equality and for genuine environmental sustainability. These will not be fully achieved until we have created a more equal, community-centred society, driven by social rather than simply economic criteria; but the fight for better housing—based on demo-cratic public housing—is part of the bigger campaign for that better society. Every gain will not only be valuable in itself but will also contribute to that greater aim.

NOTES

1. In a speech to the local authorities given in April 1919, George V observed: 'If 'unrest is to be converted into contentment, the provision of good homes may provide one of the most potent agents in that conversion' (quoted in Burnett 1978, 215).

2. Scotland still has a higher proportion of social housing than the rest of the United Kingdom and more owned by local authorities than by housing associations.

3. Although housing associations include tenants on their board, these are not there as tenant representatives and have to act in the interests of the association.

4. This even applies to council housing whenever money is borrowed in the open market or construction is carried out by private contractors.

5. www.ons.gov.uk/news/news/ukworth88trillion.

6. A major factor in the current housing crisis is the lack of any significant attempt to bring investment and jobs to areas where homes are available, and so stem migra-tion to an ever-more crowded London and southeast England. This also results in socially and environmentally unsustainable commuting.

REFERENCES

Bookchin, Murray. 1999. *The Murray Bookchin Reader*, edited by Janet Biehl. Montréal: Black Rose Books.

Burnett, John. 1978. *A Social History of Housing 1815–1970*. Newton Abbot: David and Charles.

Cairncross, Liz, Caroline Morrell, Jane Darke and Sue Brownhill. 2002. *Tenants Managing: An Evaluation of Tenant Management Organisations in England.* Office of the Deputy Prime Minister.

Community Development Project. 1976. *Whatever Happened to Council Housing?* Nottingham: Russell Press Limited. http://www.imaginenortheast.org/download/ CDP_Whatever_Happened_to_Council_Housing_Report.pdf

Daunton, Martin J., Ed. 1984. *Councillors and Tenants: Local Authority Housing in English Cities. 1919–1939*. Leicester: Leicester University Press.

Dorling, Danny. 2014. *All That Is Solid: How the Great Housing Disaster Defines Our Times, and What We Can Do about It*. London: Allen Lane.

Glynn, Sarah. 2005. "East End Immigrants and the Battle for Housing: A Comparative Study of Political Mobilisation in the Jewish and Bengali Communities." *Journal of Historical Geography* 31: 528–45.

———. 2010. "The Tenants' Movement: Incorporation and Independence." In *The Glasgow Papers: Critical Perspectives on Community Development*, edited by Akwugo Emejulu and Mae Shaw, 53–57. Edinburgh: Community Development Journal.

———. 2014. *Housing for a Better Nation*. http://allofusfirst.org/library/housing-for-a-better-nation.

House of Commons Council Housing Group. 2005. *Support for the 'Fourth Option' for Council Housing: Report on the Enquiry into the Future Funding of Council Housing 2004–2005*. Nottingham: Russell Press.

Jones, Jerry. 2008. *Land Value . . . For Public Benefit*. Highcliffe-on-Sea: Labour Land Campaign. www.labourland.org/downloads/papers/land_value_for_public_benefit.pdf.

Kemeny, Jim. 1981. *The Myth of Homeownership: Private Versus Public Choices in Housing Tenure*. London: Routledge.

Löwy, Michael. 2015. *Ecosocialism: A Radical Alternative to Capitalist Catastrophe*. Chicago: Haymarket Books.

Malpass, Peter. 2000. *Housing Associations and Housing Policy: A Historical Perspective*. Basingstoke: Palgrave Macmillan.

Marmot, Michael. 2010. Foreword to *Social Capital, Human Capital and Health. What Is the Evidence*. OECD. www.oecd.org/edu/research/45760738.pdf.

Murphy, Richard. 2017. "Homes Should Not Be Tax Havens, But That's Exactly What They Are Right Now." *Tax Research UK*, October 7. www.taxresearch.org.uk/Blog/2017/10/07/homes-should-not-be-tax-havens-but-thats-exactly-what-they-are-right-now/.

Power, Anne. 1988. *Under New Management: The Experience of Thirteen Islington Tenant Management Co-operatives*. London: Priority Estates Project.

Royal Commission. 1918. *Report of the Royal Commission on the Housing of the Industrial Population of Scotland Rural and Urban*. Edinburgh: His Majesty's Stationary Office.

Scott, Suzie. 2000. "The People's Republic of Yoker: A Case Study of Tenant Management in Scotland." *Journal of Co-operative Studies* 33(1): 15–38.

Smyth, Stewart. 2018. "Embedding Financialisation: A Policy Review of the English Affordable Homes Programme." *Housing Studies*: 1-20. doi: 10.1080/02673037.2018.1442561.

Swenarton, Mark. 1981. "An 'Insurance against Revolution': Ideological Objectives of the Provision and Design of Public Housing in Britain after the First World War." *Historical Research* 54: 86–101.

Chapter 12

Beyond the Rent Strike, Towards the Commons

Why the Housing Question Requires Activism That Generates Its Own Alternatives

Tim Joubert and Stuart Hodkinson

The 1915 Glasgow Rent Strike arguably represents the most successful housing struggle the United Kingdom has ever seen. By collectively withholding payments to the landlord and resisting evictions, tenants multiplied their power to win their immediate urban struggle for rent controls, which would remain in place until January 1989, while forcing the state to effectively nationalize housing policy that laid the foundation for mass public housing during the twentieth century. Throughout this period, the rent strike was arguably *the* tactic of the housing movement within a relatively clear terrain of struggle between the mass working class and exploitative monopoly landlordism. After a notable hiatus, rent strikes are very much back in vogue among debt-racked students, generating new enthusiasm for their wider redeployment in other housing struggles. In this chapter we critically reflect on where the rent-strike tactic stands today in the armoury of UK housing struggles, making two provocations.

First, the rent strike should no longer be viewed as the go-to tactic for addressing the contemporary housing question in the United Kingdom. Although rent strikes can still work, the conditions that made the Glasgow Rent Strike successful bear little resemblance to today's housing realities. Our second provocation, however, is that the rent strike's core principle of breaking the circulation of money to the landlord remains relevant but must be reinvented as part of the construction of a cross-tenure movement that develops tactics of resistance based on *generating its own alternatives.* Our reinvented rent strike idea builds on recent theoretical discussions of the concept of 'commons' (De Angelis 2017) to argue that different housing struggles need to be politically articulated into what Dyer-Witheford (2006) has called the 'circulation of the common': the production and extension of collective sharing processes beyond market exchange. We conclude by arguing that a reinvented rent strike is essential for ensuring all have the 'right to the city'.

THE POTENCY OF THE GLASGOW RENT STRIKE

As the Introduction to this book shows, the Glasgow Rent Strike transformed a simple idea into mass direct action. Led by socialist and labour militants, tenants organized to collectively withhold the increased rent demanded by landlords with full support from trade unions and left-wing parties. These actions were supplemented by a campaign of defence actions to resist eviction and large street demonstrations, bringing grievances to national attention and explicitly articulating demands for a new state housing policy (Castells 1983; Melling 1983). The rent strike resulted in a clear victory after a few months with the 1915 Increase of Rent and Mortgage Interest (War Restrictions) Act that froze rents and mortgages at their 1914 levels until the early 1920s (Damer 2000; McLean 1983), and 'led to the rapid retreat of the private landlord and the emergence of council housing' (Power 1993, 179).

The rent strike took place against the background of an appalling housing crisis. Glasgow and the wider Clydeside area was a core node of capitalist urbanization, and rapid industrial and population growth had long outpaced housing construction. The already high cost of housing was exacerbated by both the collapse of private housing construction because of rising building costs (Melling 1983, 7), and the accelerated demand for industrial labour at the beginning of the war, leading to both massive overcrowding and spiralling rents over previous decades. These conditions were further compounded by harsh laws, such as the 'Law of Urban Hypothec', that enabled landlords to not only evict tenants withholding rent but also to confiscate their property; landlords and their collectors also conducted illegal evictions and extracted rents through harassment and intimidation (Castells 1983; Englander 1983). In Scotland, after 1911, tenancies moved from being set annually and paid quarterly in arrears to a monthly basis, allowing landlords to evict tenants in only seven days of arrears at forty-eight hours' notice. These summary eviction powers were exploited by landlords as a means of forcing up rents (Hughes and Lowe 1995, 13).

Added to this housing crisis were increasingly exploitative workplace conditions. The government's wartime disciplinary measures, which temporarily stifled growing unrest in shipbuilding and munitions factories, shifted the terrain of class struggle to the arena of social reproduction. This enabled workers to express legitimate grievances over exploitation by landlords, making the issue a visible threat to the wartime industrial effort. A key factor here was the proximity and relative homogeneity of class and place: the shared experience of a crisis in social reproduction fostered a common identity across class factions and militant mobilization took place in closely-knit communities in geographical proximity to one another 'where work, home, leisure, industrial relations, local government and home-town consciousness were inextricably mixed together' (Hobsbawm 1987, 40; Griffin 2015).

A final element in the rent strike's potency was the political economy of rental housing itself. With the typical owner of working-class housing from the lower middle class, 90 percent of Glasgow housing was purchased by bond mortgage, making thousands of landlords dependent on regular cash flow from their housing investments to service their own debts (Melling 1983, 8–9). Thus, rent strikes could seriously hurt the landlord at a time when industrial capital and the state were desperate to ensure that workers' unrest over housing conditions—at a time of emerging communist movements—did not reverberate back into the factory and sink the war machine (Castells 1983). The rent strike was thus born out of a particular kind of class consciousness in which workers recognized their class power and the unique leverage it had within this confluence of historical factors (Damer 2000). In the next section, we argue that such conditions no longer hold in today's political economy because neoliberalism has displaced dweller power.

THE RENT STRIKE NEUTERED:
THE DISPLACEMENT OF DWELLER POWER
UNDER NEOLIBERALISM

Although rent strikes were waged with mixed success against local councils throughout the twentieth century, they gradually faded away from tenant activism during the neoliberal decades as the private-rental sector shrank to less than 10 percent of the housing stock, and homeownership reached new levels, flanked by a diminishing social-housing sector. Over the past few years, however, the return of a housing crisis marked by a growing private-rental market has prompted the return of rent strikes, particularly among students. The extraordinary Cut the Rent campaign at University College London (UCL) has led the way, protesting huge recent rent increases that make student life unaffordable for many (Cant 2016) and winning concessions of more than £2million in three years (UCL Cut the Rent n.d.). This has reopened for many housing activists the possibility of promoting the rent strike as the way to fight the housing crisis and the wider crisis of social reproduction under neoliberal austerity (Beach 2015). However, an analysis of the historical transformation of the housing system since 1915, and especially since 1979, reveals a number of ways in which the rent-strike tactic has been confronted with more difficult obstacles and limitations.

First, the organic class and geographical fusion of workplace and homeplace struggles against exploitation that underpinned the rent strike on Clydeside has been undermined not only by restrictive legislation and the decline of trade unions but also by the increasingly splintered spatial composition between workplace and homeplace in postindustrial Britain, making the collectivizing glue of production and reproduction struggles against capital far less sticky. Glasgow in effect represented a generalized class condition of landlord exploitation: around 90 percent of the UK population at this time were private tenants and subject to overcrowding, unpayable rents, intimidation and eviction (Englander 1983). Today, a far more fragmented tenure picture exists: around 62 percent of households live in owner occupied housing of which more than half own outright without a mortgage, 20 percent are private renters and less than 18 percent are social tenants (Department for Communities and Local Government Live DCLG n.d., 101). Although this tenure diversity is geographically uneven both across the United Kingdom and within local authority boundaries, the effect has been to fundamentally recompose the city into a patchwork quilt of tenure and condition that cuts through streets, estates, tower blocks and neighbourhoods. This tenure fragmentation not only mitigates any clear class consciousness and solidarity generated by common experience, but also makes the rent strike far less possible as a generalizable tactic as the majority of households now own their own home and thus have no monopoly landlord to collectively organize against.

Second, the landlord-tenant relation itself has also fundamentally changed along this diversifying spectrum of experience. Glasgow's tenants paid rent directly from their wages, other earnings or borrowing; there was no housing benefit to cover all or part of the cost. Today, slightly less than half of all renters receive housing benefit towards all or part of their rent, which for a significant proportion—around a third—goes straight from one part of the state to another in the form of their municipal landlord, so *they never have any rent to withhold*. Should the rest of those 4.8 million renters on housing benefit decide to go on rent strike, their landlord will be able to apply to have the benefit paid directly to them, neutering that rent strike. Then there is the fear of taking action caused by the potential dire consequences of withholding rent. This did not deter the Glasgow rent strikers given the barbarism of their conditions, but today's renters do have something to lose as precarious citizens disciplined by economic insecurity amid the ongoing shift from the 'welfare state' that the Glasgow Rent Strike helped win to the neoliberal 'workfare state' (Peck 2001). State policies such as the bedroom tax, the benefit cap, and the so-called 'right to rent' that require landlords to check migrants' immigration status have merely accentuated this housing precarity. Landlords' heap further conditionality onto those forced to rent, requiring credit checks, references or guarantors and hold the power to discriminate against welfare recipients. Such an environment poses a serious threat not only to their ability to cling on to an existing home that might, if they are lucky, be near their job, their kids' schools, their family or friends, but also to their right to access benefits or ability to rent in the future.

Third, the Glasgow Rent Strike as a generalized tactic cohered with a generalized housing crisis of the vast majority of industrial urban dwellers at the hands of the monopoly power of private landlordism. Although such structural dynamics are clearly in play in the speculation-driven property machine of London and its southern commuter belts where student housing militancy has grown, today's housing crisis is also marked by a swathe of apparently different problems experienced by specific groups. For instance, a new kind of urban struggle is unfolding on London's housing estates as both homeowners and social tenants battle to stop their homes from being bulldozed under so-called regeneration and other development projects (Watt and Minton 2016). Elsewhere, the crisis of unaffordable housing is experienced more in the context of barriers to social and spatial mobility created by the dysfunctional mortgage finance market faced by current or prospective homeowners (Forrest and Hirayama 2015). The worst conditions are affecting migrants and the poorest of the poor, struggling to meet mortgage or rental payments to stay in their homes. Mass coordinated rent or mortgage strikes make little sense given this general picture of fragmented housing crises, especially when such experiences have been individualized and pushed firmly into the private sphere between the individual household and its landlord or lender.

REINVENTING THE RENT STRIKE
FOR THE TWENTY-FIRST CENTURY:
BREAKING THE CIRCUIT, BUILDING THE COMMONS

Nevertheless, if the rent-strike *method* and *target* are increasingly outmoded, the rent-strike *idea* remains core to housing struggles today. By temporarily shutting off the circulation of interest-bearing capital in the urban environment, the rent strike stopped the flow of money to landlords, while also enabling people to remain in their homes as a right claimed against the encroachment of capitalist enclosure. It was a perfect example of 'self-reduction' of the social costs of living, which would later become common in Italian Workerism in the 1970s (Cherki and Wievorka 2007). The twenty-first-century housing crisis needs a new kind of rent strike: a form of collective action that not only blocks the flow of money to rentier capitalism—public and private landlords, landowners, banks and other financial interests—but switches the collective labour that generates rents into alternative forms of housing provision based on need, not profit. That is, rather than break the circuit of capital in the hope that the state will intervene to solve our housing needs, we need to create our own collective housing solutions that can withstand the neoliberal state's inevitable backlash.

Drawing on Hodkinson (2012a), the reinvented rent strike starts from political ideas inspired by the 'commons', which are often expressed through the example of how land was held and utilized in common before its violent enclosure and transformed into individual private property (Linebaugh 2008). Here we see the twin notions of *natural resource commons* gifted by the planet such as soil, water and vegetation, and *common property regimes* in which people collectively use and manage these natural commons (Ostrom 1990). These principles can be extended to the wider *public or social commons* of goods and services, typically provided free at the point of use by the state, to primarily meet need instead of profit (Dyer-Witheford 2006) and to the *relational commons* that emphasizes how producing and managing commons relies on cooperation and mutual aid in everyday life (Gibson-Graham 2006, 82). The enclosure of these commons has been a continuous feature of capitalism over many centuries, separating people from the means of production while closing off our ability to socially reproduce outside capitalist market relations by turning common resources into privatized commodities (De Angelis 2007).

Applying this analysis to the fractured housing movement today, it is the common struggle against new rounds of capitalist *enclosure* and 'accumulation by dispossession' (Harvey 2003) that potentially unites those currently struggling against what appear to be very different problems in the realm of housing. But recognizing the wider enemy is not enough to win change; creating alternatives based on that common interest must also be part of this shared struggle. In what follows, we spell out four strategic coordinates that might guide and push those struggles into common articulation with each other.

Ending the False Binary between Ideal-Type and Actually Existing Housing Commons

What kind of housing do we want *and* need in ideal terms? By answering 'housing in common', we are emphasizing two simultaneous qualities: first, the *use-values* of housing as spaces of shelter, autonomy and social reproduction that satisfy material and emotional needs, and not its *exchange-value* as asset, income stream, investment or commodity; and second, the collective means of *producing and reproducing* those use-values that are nonhierarchical, directly democratic, egalitarian and affordable in our every-day lives. In the ideal-type housing commons, therefore, we would not want the hierarchical, bureaucratic and impersonal neoliberal state managing a national housing stock on behalf of the public. Following Hardt (2010), the commons is instead more properly conceptualized as 'the abolition of not only private property but *property as such*' (2010, 352, our emphasis). To guarantee secure access to that commons, housing must be provided as a guaranteed right irrespective of wealth or income. Housing as commons offers other use-values such as providing protections from market forces and external control, thus curtailing capitalist power in the workplace.

The ideal-type housing commons is arguably reflected in Colin Ward's anarchist manifesto for dweller control and self-help housing, *Tenants Take Over* (Ward 1974). Instead of defending state housing, which he called 'municipal serfdom—based on paternalism, bureaucratic social control, segregation and substandard housing, Ward argued for housing that simul-taneously enabled three freedoms denied by the state: to move at will, to stay put and to control one's own home (Ward 1985, 41). All three could be found in the model of 'mutual homeownership', which allowed for a form of collective ownership that simultaneously recognized individual autonomy and control. Tenants would become members of a housing society that pur-chased existing dwellings (or land to build new homes) and would be directly involved in the collective management of their own homes. Rent levels would be set to service any debts incurred and build up an equity share in the property so that when a tenant left, they would receive capital returns, which Ward (1974, 131) argued was necessary to make mutuality as attractive as individual homeownership.

However, the neoliberal assault since 1979 that has seen the re-privatiza-tion of housing through the progressive selling off of the historic stock of public housing has had a particularly devastating effect on housing condi-tions in all sectors (Hodkinson 2012b). Millions of households can no longer access a quasi-secure housing space that once constrained the exploitative power of capital through its mix of low rents and legal protections. Instead, they are forced into the private-housing market where, through fear of mort-gage defaults or evictions, they are more susceptible to capitalist exploitation. Pushing for the ideal-type housing commons at the expense of existing public housing thus risks losing sight of what Harvey (2012) correctly highlights as the strategic need to defend existing or new commons against (re)enclo-sure. Local autonomous commons do not inherently escape capitalist social relations just because we collectively own and manage them. Nor is local self-management always necessarily anti-capitalist; neoliberalism, after all, loves localism and local control, and unless it specifically disrupts capitalist social relations, the commons as self-organized social reproduction could work in capital's favour by relieving capital or the state of responsibility for the 'social wage'. This is what De Angelis (2013) has called capital's 'commons fix'.

What Harvey helps us to see, beyond the blinkered idealism of ideal-type commons, is that *all* housing, irrespective of tenure and ownership, constitutes an *actually existing housing commons* when we recognize its collective use-value as social infrastructure that benefits us all when everyone can access it. The existing stock of homes in the United Kingdom currently stands at slightly more than 28 million dwellings (DCLG n.d., 101), of which more than three-quarters is privately owned by either owner-occupiers or private landlords. This is a national resource of residential buildings that will be with us for hundreds of years into the future, thus representing important sites of resistance to enclosure. For example, individual homeownership, and the mortgage-bondage it usually requires, might form an essential pillar supporting capitalism, but when a household is repossessed for failing to meet mortgage payments or is compulsory purchased by the state to make way for a new development, a new round of enclosures are taking place that can only be resisted by defending the homeowner. Similarly, state housing may well be bureaucratic, paternalistic and subject to neoliberalization, but for those unable to access a home they can control, it remains a vital resource pool that should always be defended from attack given that the alternatives in such a context will always be worse.

Combining Defensive and Offensive Commoning

What is at stake, therefore, is both the preservation of an existing stock of commons (*defensive commoning*) and the production of new housing commons (*offensive commoning*). *Defensive commoning* resists enclosure of the actually existing housing commons, recognizing it as forms of protection against the market, however 'corrupted' (Hardt and Negri 2009). It involves defending everyone's 'right to housing' and their 'right to stay put' (Hartman 1984), through resistance to the privatization of public housing, the further marketization of social-rented housing, the demolition of homes and estates regardless of tenure and the repossession and eviction of both homeowners who have defaulted on their mortgage payments and tenants of social or private landlords (see figure 12.1).

Offensive commoning means actively creating new spaces of shelter and home that embody the ideal-type commons. For instance, existing homeowners can create new housing commons by turning their existing individual properties into a mutual homeownership society that is run on a more collective basis. Alternatively, existing public ownership can be democratized through Nevitt's (1971) 'communal tenant ownership' vision in which public tenants are made joint-legal owners of public housing in a social contract variation of Ward's mutual homeownership model. This would give tenants legal rights to security of tenure, to modify and improve their homes, to be represented in local housing management and to enjoy the lowest possible rents based on collective sharing of costs and risks via the state.

A cross-tenure housing movement, however, must go further than supporting isolated acts of resistance and creation or isolated strikes against enclosure. We must fuse defensive and offensive commoning together wherever possible as part of the same struggle. In the moment of struggle to defend the existing housing commons, we must seek to transform it along the principles of living-in-common wherever possible but without weakening the protective shield that strategic housing commons provide. Similarly, in the moment of creating cooperative forms of housing, we should ensure that these new spaces of commons actively support existing housing commons and undermine enclosure. In our approach, commoning takes place at the apex of such acts of resistance and creation. This approach can be illustrated by three examples of creative resistance:

1. *The London Squatters Campaign.* Born in 1968 as an act of resistance to the problems of homelessness and slum landlords, the London Squatters Campaign mainly targeted luxury flats, hotels and empty public buildings to house the homeless and pressure the government to change its priorities. Beginning with short-lived, tokenistic occupations that put the scandal of

Figure 12.1   Defending the existing housing commons from enclosure. Stuart Hodkinson.

empty property and homelessness onto the political agenda, the squatters soon learned the art of squatting and how to handle the law, police, media and public bodies. Once occupied, the squatters would seek to negotiate for the right to stay with a tenancy agreement or to be rehoused elsewhere within the local authority. Within months new groups were forming and families from across London were contacting the group, keen to squat. One outcome was the establishment of a legal precedent that landlords could not evict squatters themselves (often through intimidation and violence) but had to seek a court order, making evictions less straightforward and generating important bargaining power. In many London boroughs, councils handed over thousands of empty homes, some destined for demolition, to squatters on short-term licences. Squatting also politicized the problem of homelessness to the extent that the Labour government was forced to amend homeless legislation (see Bailey 1973).

2. *Transforming real estate into housing coops in Montreal.* In 1968, in response to plans to evict them for a $250-million redevelopment project, residents of Milton Park in Montreal organized, holding protest marches and street festivals to campaign against the demolition of the neighbourhood and culminating in 1972 when fifty-six protesters were arrested during a protest sit-in as bulldozers moved in. However, partly as a consequence of this militant activity, the development project floundered and in 1977 the developer sought to sell the unbuilt two-thirds of its stake in the neighbourhood. Under pressure from a resurgent neighbourhood movement, the city passed a zoning bylaw limiting building heights in the district, effectively ending the original project, and in 1979 the Canadian government bought the six hundred homes that had not been demolished so that they could be renovated and handed over to cooperative housing associations. The Milton Park story has inspired housing cooperatives across Quebec, with about thirteen hundred cooperatives administering sixty thousand residents in thirty thousand units, while the community members have continued to improve the neighbourhood through both direct action and cooperative production, securing new green spaces, pedestrianized roads and community centres (see Kowaluk and Piché-Burton 2012).

3. *Resisting mortgage repossession, creating social rent in Spain.* Since the 2008 financial crisis, a wing of the Spanish housing movement, the PAH (Platform for People Affected by Mortgages), has been successfully resisting the wave of mortgage repossessions through collective actions, including large protest demonstrations and direct action. There are now well over two hundred PAHs and local housing assemblies, operating according to values of mutual aid and collectivism and creating leverage over banks with coordinated militant resistance against evictions, occupations of bank offices and squatting in buildings at risk of eviction, which

pressures lenders into negotiating on debt and repossession. Importantly, the PAH is also seeking the creation of new housing commons through the transformation of empty houses owned by banks (some of which are owned by the Spanish taxpayer since the postcrisis bailout) into social or cooperative housing. Some occupied buildings are currently functioning as living spaces for families, according to cooperative principles, while under threat of re-enclosure and eviction. The PAH's success and popularity has seen one of its most prominent figures, Ada Colau, elected as mayor of Barcelona in May 2015 with the platform *Barcelona en Comú* winning minority control of the municipal government (see García-Lamarca 2017b).

Circulation of the Housing Commons

Here we see how different acts of resistance to enclosure in different parts of the housing struggle generate new forms of commons that themselves support the creation of further commoning projects. These are clear examples of what Dyer-Witheford (2006) calls 'circulation of commons', a process by which people organize themselves into collectives that generate a common that is then able to produce more associations and commons. If we want to expand the housing commons at a faster rate than it is being enclosed, we must make these singular, one-off acts of commoning become, like the circulation of capital itself, 'aggressive and expansive: proliferating, self-strengthening and diversifying' until they become socially hegemonic (Dyer-Witheford 2010, 110). De Angelis (2017) conceptualizes this circulation and expansion of the commons in terms of 'boundary commoning', whereby different commons systems are put into productive relations with each other, building new kinds of expanded commons based on communication and sustained cooperation. Forms of 'structural coupling' between different commons could make one system's complexity available to another and so allow 'the boundaries of one system to be included in the operational domain of the other' (Luhmann 1995, 217). Such forms of linkage and cooperation might thus '[give] shape to commons at larger scales, pervading social spaces and intensifying the presence of commons within them' (De Angelis 2017, 287).

We can imagine these processes of expanded reproduction by bringing separate acts of generative resistance outlined into circulation with each other. In each of these examples, new knowledge, finance, housing and activism are being created that can feed into other projects. For example, squatting collectives can not only be useful in occupying empty homes but the activists and their acquired knowledge can also be invested in other struggles when the occupation of homes is needed to resist demolitions or evictions. Similarly, anti-privatization campaigns can provide support and advice to homeowners trying to mobilize their own campaign against demolition. The homes that are saved, brought into forms of common ownership or newly constructed within these projects, can also be vital additions to the actually existing commons that could at any point become an important source of shelter for communities resisting enclosure.

The concept of commoning thus enables us to imagine a *cross-tenure platform* for the creation of a 'common housing movement' that brings together public tenants, homeowners, private renters, squatters and the homeless around a common political agenda. Alongside campaigns against evictions or mortgage repossessions, for regulation of rents and conditions and for security, the common housing movement would also support all forms of cooperative and mutual homeownership schemes as long as they do not involve the undemocratic privatization of public housing or a net loss of affordable housing in a locality. The long-term aim of such a strategy would be to create a critical mass of diverse strategic and tactical interventions, from blocking privatization and gentrification, stopping the closure of community facilities, occupying land, or standing in local elections to force periodic concessions from state and capital, re-energize housing campaigns, create and defend housing commons, and bring them into articulation with strategic commoning in other spheres of production (e.g., cooperative food growers), exchange (e.g., shops) and reproduction (e.g., community schools).

Coordination of the Housing Commons

Finally, the most important question raised by our argument is how does all this happen? Who will make this expanded circulation of commoning happen and how does it get coordinated? Most autonomist Marxist thinkers conceive of commoning as the formation and self-management of autonomous spaces and new value practices that exist beyond the reaches not only of capital but also the state apparatus (see De Angelis 2017). Hardt and Negri (2009), for instance, argue that new commons continually emerge through new associations of human activity—knowledge, communication and creativity—in ways that a state neither could nor should have control of because that complexity exceeds its capacity to act as a controlling force.

Although we share this politics of autonomy and rejection of state-centrism, we also share Harvey's (2012) concerns about the democratic limits of scale brought up by horizontalism and localism; 'scaling-up' requires some form of nested hierarchical structure that can link together local commons into a citywide or regional commons infrastructure in an egalitarian, democratic and socially just way. There are a number of reasons such a structure might be necessary: local communities can produce externality effects that cannot be controlled by them and might have detrimental effects on others (see Purcell

2006); the accrued social benefit of distinct local commoning projects will likely be uneven, and a more just outcome would require those benefits to be distributed more evenly; the commons at the metropolitan or regional level requires certain technologically intensive resources—such as housing, transport, waste and energy infrastructures—to be integrated and centralized in ways that coordinated local actions are unlikely to achieve; and finally only some form of external pressure towards openness can counter the tendency for boundaried autonomous communities to become exclusionary. Harvey's main point here, however, is that assuming this can be accomplished without some sort of hierarchical organizational structure is wishful thinking: 'when it comes to bundling together issues of this kind, left-analysis becomes vague, gesturing hopefully towards some magical concordance of local actions' or noting but ignoring the problem (2012, 80).

In response, we see real potential in the current networked vertical and horizontal practices of the Spanish housing movement, which builds on neighbourhood housing assemblies to coordinate and circulate struggles and ideas (García-Lamarca 2017b). The PAH model, for instance, begins from the direct involvement in housing assemblies of those affected by the housing crisis, who share experiences and strategies, plan acts of resistance and creation and link with other local nodes in a wider housing movement that scales up to coordinated regional and state level meetings (PAH 2016; Youngman 2015). Although the PAH has tended to focus on repossessed and evicted homeowners, mobilizing on the ensuing moral affect of homeowners as a betrayed generation, our approach demands that neighbourhood housing assemblies are always cross-tenure. Potentially, there could be dozens of assemblies of different tenure compositions and geographies, each self-managing their own autonomous local housing activism, which circulates through a wider assembly that self-organizes at the scale of the city, neighbourhood or territory in question, and in turn, coordinates with other assemblies as part of a national (or transnational) movement.

Finally, following Lefebvrian-inspired ideas of planetary urbanization (Lefebvre 2003 [1970]; Merrifield 2014) in which the metropolis has become the key site of struggle against capitalist enclosure of the common (Hardt and Negri 2009), we also need to ensure that the housing commons becomes one node articulated into a broader ecology of urban commoning and the right to the city (see Harvey 2012). This movement would be comprised of different assemblies working with each other to create commons within the various urban systems underpinning our everyday social reproduction: energy, transport, education, public space, waste, food and so on. Such a model has the potential to reproduce another key dimension of the Glasgow Rent Strike: a wider urban and national struggle against injustice under capitalism.

CONCLUSION

Glasgow showed how successful rent strikes require not only organization, courage and solidarity, but the urban proletariat recognizing and deploying its own class power. It was an urban struggle, not just a housing issue, in which the city's grassroots were lined up against their industrial and financial overlords as a cohesive social force. The rent strike was therefore a strategic strike at the heart of empire, class rule and profit, in which a perfect storm of circumstances meant landlords could be sacrificed to keep the social peace, conditions that currently do not exist. However, the key function of the rent strike—stemming the circulation of capital through the built environment—must be reinvented for today's conditions if we are to gain leverage against the power of state and capital in a new terrain of struggle marked by neoliberalism, splintered class and tenure geographies and the precarity of everyday social reproduction. Without allying demands to the real power to create blockages in the flow of money, landlord, lender or state will not listen or act. This power must proceed from a project of building our own alternative housing options in the form of a commoning movement that brings together new and existing housing resources with new associations built on alternative value practices. Such a commons would work towards providing for our housing needs in the here and now by simultaneously defending the existing housing commons and actively supporting new alternatives in ways that would create blockages in the circulation of capital while simultaneously reducing our reliance on the private market and the state. But these alternatives also need to hold out against re-enclosure by capital, meaning they need to expand and become hegemonic through complex circulatory articulations between and among each other and other systems. Coordinating this circulation can find a starting point in the housing assembly, as a means of democratic organization that can scale up the capacity of the movement to act without compromising principles of grass-roots democracy and self-governance. The circulation of the commons here takes place not through the invisible hand of the market, but through the very visible body of the housing commoners, the groups of activists and individuals who are resisting and creating. Each action to commonize housing cannot by itself mean the end of capitalism and thus the end of the housing question, but they can help to circulate and expand the commons to improve life in the present and provide the basis for an exit from capitalism in the future.

REFERENCES

Bailey, Ron. 1973. *The Squatters*. London: Penguin.
Beach, Ben. 2015. "Is It Time for London to Go on a Rent Strike?" *Vice*, June 16. https://www.vice.com/en_ca/article/vdxdb9/rent-strike-ben-beach-839.

Cant, Callum. 2016. "Students in the UK Prepare for a New Wave of Rent Strikes." *Roar Magazine*, October 17. https://roarmag.org/essays/uk-student-rent-strike/.

Castells, Manuel. 1983. *The City and the Grassroots*. Berkeley: University of California Press.

Cherki, Eddy, and Michel Wievorka. 2007. "Autoreduction Movements in Turin." In *Autonomia: Post-Political Writings*, edited by Sylvere Lotringer and Christian Marazzi, 72–79. Los Angeles: Semiotexte.

Damer, Sean. 2000. "'The Clyde Rent War!' The Clydebank Rent Strike of the 1920s." In *Class Struggle and Social Welfare*, edited by Michael Lavalette and Gerry Mooney, 71–95. London: Routledge.

Department for Communities and Local Government (DCLG). n.d. "Table 101: By Tenure, United Kingdom (Historical Series)." https://www.gov.uk/government/uploads/system/uploads/attachment_data/file/609286/LT_101.xls.

De Angelis, Massimo. 2007. *The Beginning of History: Value Struggles and Global Capital*. London: Pluto Press.

———. 2013. "Does Capital Need a Commons Fix?" *Ephemera: Theory and Organization in Society* 13(3): 603–15.

———. 2017. *Omnia Sunt Communia: On the Commons and the Transformation to Postcapitalism*. London: Zed Books.

Dyer-Witheford, Nick. 2006. "The Circulation of the Common." Paper presented to the Conference on Immaterial Labour, Multitudes, and New Social Subjects: Class Composition in Cognitive Capitalism, 29–30 April 2006, King's College, University of Cambridge. http://www.fims.uwo.ca/people/faculty/dyerwitheford/Commons2006.pdf.

———. 2010. "Commonism." In *What Would It Mean to Win?* edited by Turbulence Collective, 81–87. Oakland, CA: PM Press.

Englander, David. 1983. *Landlord and Tenant in Urban Britain, 1838–1918*. Oxford: Oxford University Press.

Forrest, Ray, and Yosuke Hirayama. 2015. "The Financialization of the Social Project: Embedded Liberalism, Neoliberalism and Homeownership." *Urban Studies* 52(22): 233–44.

García-Lamarca, Melissa. 2017b. "Reconfiguring the Public through Housing Rights Struggles in Spain." In *City Unsilenced: Urban Resistance and Public Space in the Age of Shrinking Democracy*, edited by Jeffery Hou, 44–45. New York: Routledge.

Gibson-Graham, J. K. 2006. *A Post-Capitalist Politics*. Minneapolis: University of Minnesota Press.

Griffin, Paul. 2015. *The Spatial Politics of Red Clydeside: Historical Labour Geographies and Radical Connections*. PhD diss., University of Glasgow.

Hardt, Michael. 2010. "The Common in Communism." *Rethinking Marxism* 22(3): 346–56.

Hardt, Michael, and Antonio Negri. 2009. *Commonwealth*. Cambridge: Harvard University Press.

Hartman, Chester. 1984. *Between Eminence and Notoriety: Four Decades of Radical Urban Planning*. New Brunswick, NJ: CUPR Press.

Harvey, David. 2003. *The New Imperialism*. Oxford: Oxford University Press.

———. 2012. *Rebel Cities: From the Right to the City to the Urban Revolution*. London: Verso.

Hobsbawm, Eric. 1987. "Labour in the Great City." *New Left Review*, 1/166 November–December: 39–51.

Hodkinson, Stuart. 2012a. "The Return of the Housing Question." *Ephemera: Theory and Politics in Organization* 12(4): 423–44.

———. 2012b. "The New *Urban* Enclosures." *City: Analysis of Urban Trends, Culture, Theory, Policy, Action* 16(4): 500–18.

Hughes, David, and Stuart Lowe. 1995. *Social Housing Law and Policy*. London: Butterworths.

Kowaluk, Lucia, and Carolle Piché-Burton, eds. 2012. *Communauté Milton-Parc: How We Did It and How It Works Now*. Montreal: Communauté Milton-Parc. http://www.miltonparc.org/English.pdf

Linebaugh, Peter. 2008. *The Magna Carta Manifesto: Liberties and Commons for All*. California: University of California Press.

Lefebvre, Henri. 2003 [1970]. *The Urban Revolution*. Minnesota: University of Minnesota Press.

Luhmann, Niklas. 1995. *Social Systems*. Redwood City: Stanford University Press.

Merrifield, Andy. 2014. *The New Urban Question*. London: Pluto Press.

McLean, Iain. 1983. *The Legend of Red Clydeside*. Edinburgh: John Donald.

Melling, Joseph. 1983. *Rent Strikes: Peoples' Struggle for Housing in West Scotland 1890–1916*. Edinburgh: Polygon Books.

Nevitt, Della. 1971. *Fair Deal for Householders*. London: Fabian Society.

Ostrom, Elinor. 1990. *Governing the Commons: The Evolution of Institutions for Collective Action*. New York: Cambridge University Press.

Plataforma de Afectados por la Hipoteca (PAH). 2016. *The PAH's Green Book: A Basic Guide to the PAH*. http://afectadosporlahipoteca.com/wp-content/uploads/2016/06/GreenBook-PAH-21juny.pdf.

Peck, Jamie. 2001. *Workfare States*. London: Guilford Press.

Power, Ann 1993. *Hovels to Highrise: State Housing in Europe since 1850*. London: Routledge.

Purcell, Mark. 2006. "Urban Democracy and the Local Trap." *Urban Studies* 43(11): 1921–41.

UCL, Cut The Rent. n.d. Facebook Group. Accessed July 15, 2017. https://www.facebook.com/uclcuttherent/.

Ward, Colin. 1974. *Tenants Take Over*. London: The Architectural Press Ltd.

———. 1985. *When We Build Again: Let's Have Housing that Works!* London: Pluto Press.

Watt, Paul, and Anna Minton. 2016. "London's Housing Crisis and Its Activisms: Introduction." *City: Analysis of Urban Trends, Culture, Theory, Policy, Action* 20(2): 204–21.

Youngman, Tom. 2015. "Housing Gains in Spain." *Red Pepper*, August 25. http://www.redpepper.org.uk/houyoungsing-gains-in-spain/.

Afterword

The Futures of Housing Activism

Neil Gray

This book has combined a reappraisal of a key moment in housing history and a critical affirmative engagement with contemporary housing agitation in Britain and Ireland. It has re-examined the 1915 Glasgow Rent Strikes in light of new empirical research and new theoretical understandings and considered its continuing relevance at a time when housing issues have forcefully reappeared at the forefront of political-economic life. The 1915 Rent Strikes, along with housing unrest across Britain, forced government intervention through rent restrictions, and eventually, necessarily, public housing, generating a legacy of progressive improvements in tenants' rights in Britain through much of the twentieth century. But these achievements were progressively undermined from the late 1970s with the virtual decimation of public then social housing[1] through deregulation and privatization, a massively subsidized material-ideological homeownership drive, the increasing financialization of the housing market and the resurgence of the rentier landlord, resulting in a contemporary housing situation mired in crises of affordability, tenure security and quality.

All this should come as no surprise. As Engels (1942 [1872]) made clear in *The Housing Question*, housing crisis, augmented by housing shortage, is no temporary inconvenience or partial failing of the market but a deliberate, systemic and perennial feature of capitalist relations. In this regard, the current British housing crisis is an exemplary creature of state policy, involving the ideological promotion of debt-financed homeownership backed by a raft of subsidies and tax breaks, the privatization and deregulation of the housing sector and drastic reductions in social-housing construction alongside static or declining private housing construction levels (Meek 2014; Robertson 2015). Such is the efficiency of the market and the vaunted equilibrium of supply and demand. Ireland's housing crisis, meanwhile, was built on the privatization of social housing, the deregulation of mortgage markets, the mis-selling of subprime mortgages and an oversupply of private housing for sale predicated on ever-expanding consumer debt levels and the hubristic dream of eternal growth (McCabe 2011; Norris and Coates 2014; Byrne and Norris 2017). When such policies converged with the Great Financial Crisis (GFC), 2007–2009, what resulted was a landscape peppered with 'ghost estates' that existing owners could no longer afford to maintain, and prospective buyers could no longer afford to access (Kitchin et al. 2014; O'Callaghan et al. 2014).[2]

The mass public housing built through the auspices of the British postwar Fordist-Keynesian consensus between capital, labour and the state—evident to a lesser extent in Ireland (Byrne and Norris 2017)—can now be seen historically as a relatively brief hiatus in an ongoing series of housing crises dominated by the private market and regulated by the state in the interest of housing speculation (Madden and Marcuse 2016). The diagnostic is grim, but the question as ever for those seeking to preserve the use-value of housing over its exchange and asset value, remains: what can be done about this state of affairs? This book has invoked the successful tenants' organization of the 1915 Rent Strikes to tease out continuities in the housing question between then and now, while being attentive to profound political-economic transformations in the interim period. It has examined the diverse aims, tactics and strategies of historic and current modes of housing agitation with the aim of making a partisan contribution to the contemporary housing question in a time of exacerbated housing crisis. Here, I summarize some of the main themes, while suggesting some new issues that demand attention from contemporary housing movements.

HISTORY AGAINST THE GRAIN

Rent strikes and housing unrest have been key features of political struggle in Britain and Ireland from the late nineteenth century. Yet the tenants' movement has largely been hidden from history: 'rarely able to represent itself, or to make itself heard as a subject' (Bradley 2014, 18). Historically, housing movements have received little institutional funding or support from labour movements and trade unions, which typically prioritize the formal workplace over social reproductive struggles (Bunge 1977; Damer 2000a; Gray 2017; Moorhouse et al. 1972). Moreover, as Grayson (1996) observes, labour history has been predominantly male history, with tenant associations and housing campaigns, often led by women, typically seen as secondary to workplace struggles. Tenants' movements also receive inadequate attention from the media because of their relatively autonomous working-class character, which conforms neither to the patronising image of a sheeplike working class being led into misadventure by extreme Leftist leaders, nor to the cult of homeownership underwritten by Conservative ideology (Sklair 1975, 250).[3]

Such inattention is to be expected from mainstream sources, but from the labour movement and trade unions, it is inexcusable, especially in an era when housing is now more central to national political economies than ever (Aalbers and Christophers 2014; Harvey 2012; Gray, this volume). But if housing struggles and housing movements in Britain and Ireland have too often been marginalized, many tenants and residents have understood the centrality of the housing question in their everyday lives and the necessity of struggling across both productive and reproductive spheres (Bunge 1977; Bradley 2014; Damer 2000a; Grayson 1996; Johnstone 1992, 2000). Considered in this light, this hidden history deserves to be uncovered in more systemic fashion to flesh out the continuum of housing agitation that has been central to defending rent controls and the principle of public housing in the twentieth and twenty-first centuries.

Foregrounding the meaning and extent of such struggles in the British and Irish context, contributors to this book help rectify the historical erasure that housing movements have been subject to, while affirming the ongoing relevance and necessity of housing as a crucial vector of political struggle in both historical and contemporary contexts. Yet, there is significant room to deepen and expand this project, from radical local histories to international solidarities, traversing relations of gender, class and race. Concerted efforts to erase or ignore particular histories, including revisionist reconstructions of official archives and ways of remembering, require contestation. Archival retrieval has often been mobilized to foster nostalgia, historicism or the ghosts of repetition, but the aim should be to 'brush history against the grain' to detonate the slumbering time of the present with the fractious and contentious constellations of the past (Benjamin 1999, 248).

THE FINANCIALIZATION OF HOUSING

In their survey of rent strikes in the early 1970s, Moorhouse et al. (1972) suggest that future housing struggles may demand of participants greater theoretical knowledge of the complexities of housing finance and policy. Nowhere is this complexity more manifest than in the nexus between financialization and housing, which has become a compelling issue, if largely inscrutable, for tenants and residents (Christophers 2011; Fields 2017). As Bhandar and Toscano (2015, 8) observe, the blizzard of abbreviations related to economic activities such as mortgage-backed securities (MBSs), collateral debt obligations (CDOs) and structured-investment vehicles (SIVs), have generated a 'violent irruption' into the home, the primary site of social reproduction and everyday life. What is required, they argue, is mapping the relation between capital's abstractions and the everyday life of tenants so that resistance can be just as fluid as finance's attacks on housing. This dialectical approach to the housing question corresponds with the notion of a 'relational articulation' of housing struggles offered by Hearne at al. (this volume), and that of 'spatial composition' offered by Gray (this volume). The expansion of financialization in housing via securitized primary and secondary mortgage markets, predatory private equity firms and global corporate landlords, and the centrality of housing speculation to contemporary capitalism, necessitates new and immanent responses from tenants.

Fields (2017) usefully draws out the antagonism between those who privilege the liquid exchange value of housing and those who privilege its use value with the conception: 'unwilling subjects of financialization'. On the one hand, the term reflects on how opaque forms of financialization constitute tenants and residents as subjects, without their knowledge or consent, and on the other, how tenants and residents resist and contest enclosure, forming oppositional practices against the financialization of their homes. In particular, Fields focuses on private equity funds, which provide a vehicle for investment banks, private firms and other property investors and developers to manage investor funds by aggregating money from institutional investors and leveraging high-risk credit capital from banks (Fields and Uffer 2016, 1489). Typically operating with comparatively little equity, but leveraging substantial credit capital, private equity firms make investments based on the outlay of fictitious capital, which represents the net present value of future cash flows (Fields 2015, 2017). The term *fictitious* arises because it pertains to a realization of future revenues, which as the subprime mortgage crisis violently disclosed, can never be fully guaranteed. When private equity firms mobilize extremely high-risk investments in mainly 'distressed' properties in low-income areas, the gap between overleveraged loan debt and unreasonably ambitious projected returns is typically closed by raising rents dramatically and drastically reducing maintenance costs. If these tactics fail, foreclosure is a real possibility, with tenants often being evicted for financial practices over which they have no control (Fields 2015).

It would be easy to characterize housing financialization as inexorable, closing off potential for resistance and contestation (Fields 2017), but such processes have generated organized, collective resistance from tenants. For instance, Fields (2015) shows how tenant organizations in New York generated critical narratives about private equity firms by coining the term *predatory equity*, circulating the phrase via opinion formers in the media, local communities and the local council, which started recycling the critical terminology in policy documents and media statements. Housing groups also began producing investigative databases about predatory equity, with mapping projects surveying 'distressed buildings' in New York as well as money flows and legal documents related to predatory equity activity. Such databases provide a vast knowledge resource about predatory activity for housing campaign groups, researchers, journalists and sympathetic public figures (Fields 2015, 155–56). Finally, New York housing and community activist and campaign groups have traced the international capital flows involved in predatory equity, initiating intranational and international solidarity actions with housing groups in Britain and Spain, and with shack dwellers in South Africa, communities occupying buildings in Mexico and those affected by Hurricane Katrina in New Orleans. In this way, tenants used 'the spatial form of capital flows to develop and maintain new political alliances' (161). Predatory equity firms and the 'global corporate landlord' have not yet made the same progress in Britain as they have in the United States, Spain, Ireland and Greece, but they are knocking on the door (see Beswick et al. 2016). Should such processes become more common, as is likely, the New York examples of immanent tenant organization against financialization described by Fields, shows that the old adage, 'follow the money', can also be rebooted for complex new processes of housing financialization (Fields 2015, 2017). In this way, the abstractions of capital can be understood in relation to the lived experience of everyday life, and tenant and resident resistance to financial enclosure.

GENDER AND HOUSING POLITICS

As Grayson (1996) contends, a narrow political focus on worker-employer and capital-labour relations has tended to relegate or even ignore tenants' and residents' movements, which have often been led by women. Such neglect has simultaneously downplayed the significance of housing politics, women's material and ideological struggles across private and public spheres, and the politics of social reproduction more generally. However, the 1915 Rent Strikes, and the direct action militancy of women organizers, marked a stellar challenge to this hierarchical precedence, even if this history has too often been considered secondary to workplace contradictions (Gray, this volume). This collection provides a close engagement with women's struggles in this period, considering the relation between class and gender in political mobilization, and women's role as active political subjects, from the suffrage movement, to wartime, to the interwar years (Currie, this volume; Hughes and Wright, this volume).

Since 1915, women have been central to marking out and contesting the terrain of social reproduction as a political and politicized arena, challenging two primary characteristics of Fordist-Keynesian capitalism: the separation of private (domestic) and public spheres, and of unpaid feminized domestic labour from predominantly male wage labour in the formal workplace (Dalla Costa and James 1972; Federici 2012; Fortunati 1995; Gonzalez 2010; Mitchell et al. 2003). Despite the relative advance of women in waged work, the domestic sphere remains overwhelmingly managed by women in an entrenched 'sexual division of labour'. Ultimately, the incursion of women into the workforce has not precluded 'double work', encompassing both paid labour in the workplace and unpaid domestic labour (Federici 1984). Where that fate is avoided, it is largely because *other women*, predominantly non-white and working class, are 'forced to care' via low-paid domestic labour positions, such as as cleaners, chambermaids, child minders, care-workers and au pairs (Glenn 2012). Indeed, the amount of domestic and care work undertaken by women, against a narrative of women's emancipation through the workplace, has likely increased at a global level since the 1970s (Federici 2012, 108).

Women's leading role in the 1915 Rent Strikes has been duly incorporated into the history of the women's movement (see Currie, this volume). Yet, the significance of the specific material relation between gender and housing often remains obscured (but see Grayson 1996; Gonzalez 2010; Gray 2017). Because wage gains in the workplace are routinely undermined through inflation at the level of consumption, a sphere largely allocated to and managed by women, struggles in this sphere should be understood as central to maintaining wage levels. Moreover, it is routinely women who face the bailiff, the debt collector, the police, the sheriff officer and the social worker at the point of social reproduction, thus directly confronting intrusive state intervention in everyday life (Gray 2017). As Smyth (1992) argues, it is precisely because women in the 1915 Rent Strikes revealed and confronted this relation with such clarity that their struggle has such important ramifications (see Gray, this volume). There is a long, if hidden, continuum of such militant gendered housing contestation, which should not be lost on contemporary housing movements (Grayson 1996; Marcuse 1999; Hughes and Wright, this volume). Grasping the arena of social reproduction as a general immanent concern, linked to the reproduction of labour and the relations of production and to the defence of the 'social wage', can help break down existing hierarchies and divisions between public and private spheres, and between women and men, building genuine collective social force and unity across the false separation of productive and reproductive spheres (James 1975; Gonzalez 2010; Gray 2018).

RENT CONTROL

The 1915 Rent Strikes were the main catalyst for rent control in Britain through the Rent and Mortgage Interest (War Restrictions) Act 1915. The issue of rent control indexes the major contradiction between those who view housing as a vehicle of exchange and those who defend housing's use-value as a home. As several commentators have shown, it has required continual housing struggle throughout the twentieth century to retain rent controls in the face of ardent rent deregulation lobbies (Damer 2000a; Johnstone 2000; Madden and Marcuse 2016). Despite these efforts, British rent controls were slowly undermined and finally repealed in the Housing Act 1988. In Ireland, they were repealed in 1982. As Fields and Uffer (2016) note, in a comparative study of New York and Berlin, the repeal of rent controls in each city has provided a new urban frontier for speculative investors and predatory private equity firms, resulting in inflated rents, insecure tenancies and the erosion of repairs and maintenance. Similarly, in Britain and Ireland, the decontrol of rent dovetails quite precisely with the rapid development of the private-rental sector (PRS) and the privatization, deregulation and immiseration of public and social housing, leading to dramatic rent escalation (Byrne and Norris 2017; Hodkinson 2012b; Robbins 2017).

As Kallin and Slater show (this volume), figures like Friedrich Hayek and Milton Freidman—classical liberal economists and fierce critics of socialism—have intervened historically to give their predictably negative verdict on rent control. This line has since been tirelessly recycled by various right-wing think tanks, becoming a kind of common sense for policy makers, economists, financial investors and speculators, and landlord and construction lobbies, who know that rent control is a major barrier to rental profits. Given the inextricable relation between the deregulation of rent controls and escalating rents across both private- and public-housing sectors, the political significance of tenant and resident campaigns for rent control is explored by Mick Byrne and Living Rent in this volume, with regard to Ireland and Scotland, respectively. In both cases, the introduction of rent control legislation in the form of 'Rent Pressure Zones' (RPZs) represents a significant discursive and material intervention by tenants into prevailing mainstream orthodoxies in the housing market (see also Fields 2015). Lobbied for and won by tenants, the attainment of RPZ legislation puts rent control back on the agenda for the first time since the 1980s, providing a vital pivot for both publicizing and politicizing rental tyranny. Similar controls are currently being demanded by tenants and residents in England and Wales (see Living Rent, this volume).

Yet RPZs, as they currently stand, have serious limits. Calling for an RPZ to be designated in Scotland involves a formidably Byzantine process requiring the local authority to make a claim for an RPZ zone to the national state, which must then consider whether the designated zone will be permitted. At a time when asset wealth creation through housing is viewed as the only game in town at both local and national levels, an adequate intervention by local councils and the national state seems improbable. Moreover, RPZs in both countries make provision for only a percentage cap on rising rents with none for *decreasing* rents (a vital necessity because rents have escalated exponentially in the last decade); in Scotland, rent control under RPZs is limited in duration to five years and also limited to sitting tenants, so that rents can easily be jacked up between changes in tenure; in Ireland, newly built properties are exempt from the legislation. With such restrictions in mind, the way forward is surely to expose the timid limits of current RPZ legislation, stressing the need for stronger powers of intervention, while using the discursive opportunity that RPZs represent to push the rent question into mainstream discourse. If rent controls are one of the major means by which the further financialization of housing can be arrested (Beswick et al. 2016; Fields and Uffer 2016; Madden and Marcuse 2016), then every opportunity to politicize RPZs and similar legislation must be tested to its limits by recalcitrant housing movements.

THE MYTH OF HOUSING ASSOCIATIONS

Housing associations (HAs), or registered social landlords (RSLs), heavily promoted as an affordable and viable social rent solution to the housing question and the problems associated with monolithic state landlordism, increasingly function to exacerbate the hyper-commodification of public housing. Alongside Right-to-Buy (RTB), which has been responsible for the loss of around 2.7 million public homes in Britain since 1980, 'stock transfer' from public housing (or 'council housing' in Britain) has been responsible for the loss of around 1.5 million public homes in an epochal housing privatization process (Hodkinson 2012b, 510). Following initial loss-leading preferential funding allocation treatment via a public-private model rather than direct state investment in public housing—which has been frozen out of the equation—HAs have latterly seen massive budget cuts, making them even more dependent on the private market than they were already. Now acting as large corporate organizations, increasingly funded by mergers and bond funding, HAs typically produce homes for market rent, market sale, 'affordable rent' (80 percent of market rent) and 'affordable homeownership', rather than genuine 'social rent'. This is the norm rather than the exception and is not a moral question but a material one. Regardless of whether HAs are charities or follow a 'community model' with social obligations, as defenders claim, with dwindling state funding they must submit to the prerogatives of the banks and the market. The figures are damning: in England, only 8.4 percent of HA housing completions during Q2 of 2017 and 2018 were for 'social rent', the rest were for market or intermediate rent or sale (National Housing Federation 2017b). In the financial year 2016–2017 fewer homes for social rent were built with government funding than in any other year on record, with completions down by 96 percent in seven years (Barrat 2017).

HAs have cornered the market in the devil's lexicon of duplicitous terms such as 'social housing', 'urban regeneration', 'community ownership', 'participation', 'transformational regeneration areas' and 'affordable housing'. The reality of HA tenure output, and widespread privatization in the social-housing sector, gives credence to Madden and Marcuse's (2016, 138) observation that the term *affordable* is an ideological tool used to legitimize private development: 'a strategy of the real estate machine rather than a relief from it'. The promise once held out for HAs as models of community ownership, based on their emergence from the housing cooperative movement, is fundamentally compromised by funding cuts, corporate management structures and increasing commodification. But the narrative of HAs as a bold new experiment in local control was always hyperbolic because 'community-based housing associations' were already being characterized as 'the tool of central government' in the early 1970s, and a Trojan Horse for the privatization of public housing (quoted in Collins and Jones 2006, 60).

The incorporation of tenants into largely toothless and depoliticized HA tenant committees, in practice representing the interests of increasingly corporatized HAs rather than tenants, has drastically undermined the independent tenants' movements in Britain. That HA tenant representation would be 'primarily symbolic' was predicted very early on by Defend Council Housing[4] and other commentators. In Glasgow for instance, Mooney and Poole (2005, 31–32) stressed that tenants had no role in the preparation and process of 'housing stock transfer' and thus any 'tenant participation' was deeply circumscribed by decisions already made. Such abuse of power should come as no surprise: parity of participation is neither 'synonymous with collectivism' nor 'inherently opposed to capitalism' (see Bishop 2012, 4), as evidenced by the top-down invocation of 'participation' that is now practically compulsory in 'regeneration' (aka gentrification) strategies (Gray 2018). In terms of obscuring genuine solutions to the housing question, which is necessarily bound up with wider capitalist relations, the 'myth of Housing Associations' should be added to ongoing myths around the efficiency of the market (see Kallin and Slater, this volume) and the allegedly 'benevolent state' (see Madden and Marcuse 2016, 119). Long subject to eulogies about the merits of HAs, tenants and residents must undertake a critical 're-education process'[5] to arrive at genuine, rather than symbolic, tenant-led solutions to the housing question.

PUBLIC HOUSING DEMANDS

Public housing was a central demand for the 1915 rent strikers, and subsequent rent restrictions were instrumental in forcing government subsidy for public housing through the Addison Act 1919 and the Wheatley Act 1924. This book has re-examined the case for public housing following intensive ideological campaigns that have elevated homeownership as the 'common sense' tenure of choice, whilst denigrating publichousing as a Stalinist relic propped up by a 'meddling state' (Madden and Marcuse 2016, 143). Yet, homeowners receive far more public subsidy than public-housing tenants in the United States, with four times as much spent on homeowner subsidy than affordable housing subsidy (Collinson et al. 2015). In Britain the long-held Conservative narrative of oversubsidized public housing is equally premised on a disavowal of public subsidy for private profit. Not least is the RTB policy introduced in the Housing Act 1980—the central plank of the Conservative government's promise of a 'property owning democracy'—which involved state-funded discounts, ranging from 33 percent to 50 percent, for more than 2.7 million homes (Ginsburg 2005; Hodkinson 2012b). State subsidies via debt write-off for housing stock transfer, Help-to-Buy schemes for first-time buyers, capital gains tax relief for homeowners, stamp duty relief, renovation grants for private housing, housing benefit paid to private landlords rather than local authorities and the staggering state bank bail-out related to the mortgage market crash in the Great Financial Crisis of 2007 to 2009—all of these direct and indirect subsidies for private housing are rarely, if ever, acknowledged when public housing is castigated for being 'over-subsidized' (see Perry 2012).

As Madden and Marcuse (2016, 142) observe, 'all housing is in a sense public housing', since the housing system, public or private, 'is inextricably tied to the state, law, and public authority'. Indeed, what we have seen since the Housing Act 1980 is not only privatization and deregulation, but *re-regulation* in the form of multiple policies and subsidies to service property speculation and the ambitions of the propertied asset class. On the one side, the forces of real estate and property speculation line up to attack housing, on the other side, groups like Defend Council Housing, and numerous independent tenants' and residents' groups across Britain and Ireland, challenge the privatization and decimation of local authority housing (Ginsburg 2005; Watt 2009a; Hodkinson 2012b). Notably, such campaigns, and the choices of tenants in multiple local authorities across Britain, have prevented 'housing stock transfer' in more than one hundred of the three hundred or so stock transfer ballots undertaken in Britain since the late 1980s (see Robbins 2002; Mooney and Poole 2005; Watt 2009a; Watt, this volume), an under-acknowledged counternarrative of tenant resistance, that awaits a systematic overview.

Given the correlation between the erasure of public housing from 1980 and enormous increases in house prices and rent since that point, the argument for public housing is compelling. Public housing has been, and remains, the most simple, direct and universal way to challenge gentrification, decom-modify housing and provide affordable housing for all (see Madden and Marcuse 2016, 203–206). Surely, then, public housing should be a minimum demand from organizations seeking to challenge the tyranny of private property? But there is a certain amount of paralysis on this question. As Madden and Marcuse (2016) observe, public housing models from the twentieth century cannot be uncritically readopted because they were created within very different conditions than those we face today. Such models were always closely, and problematically, linked with the reproduction of the labour force for industrial development, and thus reflected particular political-economic dynamics in the Fordist-Keynesian era. Public housing was built to defuse conflicts between capital, the state and labour; facilitate construction companies and private developers; and generate economic growth through large-scale labour intensive construction projects. The chapters by Glynn and by Joubert and Hodkinson (this volume) recapitulate many of the main debates about the merits or demerits of demands for public housing in Britain.

Undercutting the liberal myth of consistent progressive policies geared towards alleviating the housing problem, Madden and Marcuse (2016) argue that the state has historically intervened in housing primarily to preserve political stability and the existing order in the face of housing unrest. Yet, there is a danger that such a narrative, however accurate, obscures how tenants' and residents' movements have forced housing policy in more progressive and affordable directions, facilitating the development of political consciousness and wringing concessions on the 'social wage' (Damer 1980, 2000a; Johnstone 2000; Grayson 1996; Gray, this volume). At the same time, alternative hopes for local control, community ownership and 'autonomy' by way of allegedly 'community-based housing associations', as we've seen, have been unmasked as a Trojan Horse for privatization (Collins and Jones 2006; Hodkinson 2012a; Robbins 2017). All in all, despite these qualifications, public housing affords a generalized, potentially universal material barrier to housing privatization that must be defended with urgency until a more radical approach to housing can be found (Hodkinson 2012a; Joubert and Hodkinson, this volume; Madden and Marcuse 2016), especially because it appears as one of the last bastions protecting tenants and residents from the hyper-financialization of housing markets (Beswick et al. 2016; Fields and Uffer 2016).

Madden and Marcuse (2016) ultimately argue that defending, improving and expanding public housing, as long as it is 'radicalized and democratized', with a critique of the status quo foregrounded, provides the best opportunity to defend tenants in both the public- and private-housing sectors because improving and expanding the public sector provides an attractive and affordable option that reduces overheating in the private sector. In this volume, Joubert and Hodkinson offer the concepts of defensive and offensive 'commoning' to capture the relation between housing struggles that defend essential forms of protection against the market, albeit compromised, such as public and social housing, and those that generate new forms of shelter and home that break with the market and present anti-capitalist solutions to the housing question. Defensive and offensive housing strategies must be fused together, they argue, to protect previous gains while creating new housing praxis and movements from the shell of the old.

CROSS-TENURE HOUSING STRUGGLES

A key theme to emerge in this volume is the need for cross-tenure housing organization and resistance. The emergence of housing organizations addressing the PRS—as well as social housing in some cases—such as the Dublin Tenants Association (Byrne, this volume), Living Rent in Scotland (this volume) and London Renters Union (see Byrne 2017), has been both necessary and inevitable given the dramatic tenure shift towards the PRS in the last two decades. As Byrne (2017) notes, such emergent initiatives in the PRS aim to de-individualize the often alienating experience of renting, while simultaneously politicizing that experience by showing how tenants working together can change their reality. The challenge, he contends, is to create a shared sense of being a private tenant, so that a culture of mutual organizing and political practice can be developed. Against the decomposition of tenants' movements, this is precisely the kind of effort at *political recomposition*, despite attendant difficulties, that is required both within and between tenures. The dramatic decline of the public and social housing demographic, and the resultant complexity of tenure in Britain and Ireland, means that older forms of tenant organization restricted to public housing are no longer adequate or representative. Such organizations must instead be part of a broader housing movement, aiming to recompose tenant unity from the wreckage of a deliberately fragmented and privatized housing landscape.

The London Radical Housing Network (RHN) provides a working example in this regard, with a 'group of groups' or 'movement of movements' approach active across the public housing sector, a complex social-housing sector involving multiple HA landlords, the PRS, homeownership, student housing, homelessness and benefit agencies, and alternative housing models such as self-build, cooperative housing and squatting. Such movements, paralleling Joubert and Hodkinson's advice (this volume), begin from, but go beyond, isolated acts of resistance and creation, which can easily, though not inevitably, become the preserve of more affluent, specialist groups or become reintegrated into the circuits of accumulation (Gray 2018; Madden and Marcuse 2016). Instead they fuse defensive and offensive housing struggles together within the same struggle to produce generalized modes of political organizing against capitalism (see Joubert and Hodkinson, this volume). A larger scale of influence is crucial to avoid the allure of the interesting exception (Madden and Marcuse 2016), the 'local trap' (Purcell 2006) or the fate of 'autonomous' practices that are in fact imposed from above via austerity processes of devolved governance, downloaded responsibility and externalized risk (Böhm et al. 2010; Gray 2016; Peck 2012). Moreover, as Fields notes (2015, 2017), resistance to new modes of housing financialization must be both as intranational and international as housing finance itself. Such resistance must also be relational and connected to broader processes of urbanization and gentrification to capture the centrality of housing to contemporary political economy, and thus the centrality of housing struggle to anti-capitalist organizing (Gray, this volume; Harvey 2012; Robertson 2015).

CONCLUSION

This book has contended that the urbanization of capital, the resurgence of the rentier landlord, and the increasing financialization of housing, means that housing must necessarily be a key frontier of anti-capitalist organizing (see Aalbers and Christophers 2014; Gray 2018; Harvey 2012; Robertson 2015). It has charted a raft of hidden, and not-so-hidden, housing struggles in the past and in the contemporary era to argue that a continuum of direct action struggles by tenants and residents in housing movements has been the sine qua non of progressive change in housing policy historically and that such struggles must necessarily be central to any movement for housing transformation in the present. Overall, the contributors to this book show that the solution to the housing question must involve tenants and residents centrally, or there will be no solution at all. Joubert and Hodkinson (this volume) stress the politicizing and potentially transformative aspects of organized housing praxis, arguing that in the very act of defending the existing 'housing commons', tenants and residents must become conscious of the limits of the housing system as it stands, and the wider set of socioeconomic relations of which it is a part, necessitating what Madden and Marcuse (2016) call 'system-transforming' rather than 'system-maintaining agitation'. Revisiting the perennial housing question, Smith notes:

All in all, the point is not to focus on particular forms or solutions to the housing problem. The solution is to build the power politically so that at a future point, when it is a viable and feasible possibility that solutions to the housing problem can be created, the people are in a position to push them through. (2016, 682)

In this way, housing movements might start from where they are with what they have, avoiding the quagmire of 'transitional demands' and the hubris of 'blueprints' without mandate, to construct and develop insurgent, constitutive movements that seek radical social change via collective 'social force' rather than promoting vain hopes for recognition from the very institutions that have created, and continue to escalate, housing crises in the first place (see Gray 2018).

NOTES

1. I have argued that this distinction is vital throughout this volume because it equates to quite different models of funding and expresses dramatic shifts in state redistributive models and the relation between public and private financing of housing.

2. The housing market has since picked up again but the underlying problems remain.

3. The political function of homeownership in securing obedience and submission to government has long been observed. It increases the economic profitability and stability of the system by ensuring that debt-encumbered mortgage holders work overtime or take additional jobs, fearing job loss and the consequences of being unable to make payments and losing one's home. It privatizes experience and dampens desire for collective social services and the social conflict necessary for such services, instead producing subjects with an individual stake in increasing asset wealth that benefits capital in its totality while reproducing socioeconomic inequality.

4. http://www.defendcouncilhousing.org.uk/dch/dch_infopage.cfm?KWord=transfer.

5. Personal communication with London-based writer, trade unionist and housing activist Glyn Robbins, who is planning an edited book in his *Red Roof* self-publishing imprint, provisionally titled *Whatever Happened to Housing Associations*.

REFERENCES

Aalbers, Manual B., and Brett Christophers. 2014. "Centring Housing in Political Economy." *Housing, Theory and Society* 31(4): 373–94.

Barrat, Luke. 2017. "New Social Rented Homes at Lowest Level than any Other Year on Record." *Inside Housing*, June 20. https://www.insidehousing.co.uk/news/news/new-social-rented-homes-at-lowest-level-than-any-other-year-on-record-51020

Benjamin, Walter. 1999. "Theses on the Philosophy of History." In *Illuminations*, edited and with an Introduction by Hannah Arendt, 245–55. London: Pimlico.

Beswick, Joe, Georgi Alexandri, Michael Byrne, Sònia Vives-Miró, Desiree Fields, Stuart Hodkinson and Michael Janoschka. 2016. "Speculating on London's Housing Future: The Rise of Global Corporate Landlords in 'Post-Crisis' Urban Landscapes." *City* 20(2): 321–41.

Bhandar, Brenna, and Alberto Toscano, A. 2015. "Race, Real Estate and Real Abstraction." *Radical Philosophy* 194 (Nov/Dec). https://www.radicalphilosophy. com/article/race-real-estate-and-real-abstraction.

Bishop, Claire. (2012). *Artificial Hells: Participatory Art and the Politics of Spectatorship*. London: Verso.

Böhm, Steffen, Ana C. Dinerstein and Andre Spicer. 2010. "(Im)possibilities of Autonomy: Social Movements in and beyond Capital, the State and Development." *Social Movement Studies* 9(1): 17–32.

Bradley, Quintin. 2014. *The Tenants' Movement*. London: Routledge.

Bunge, William. 1977. "The Point of Reproduction: A Second Front." *Antipode* 9(2): 60–76.

Byrne, Mick. 2017. "Organizing Tenants in the Rentier Society." *ROAR*, November 8. https://roarmag.org/essays/organizing-tenants-rentier-society/.

Byrne, Michael, and Michelle Norris. 2017. "Procyclical Social Housing and the Crisis of Irish Housing Policy: Marketization, Social Housing, and the Property Boom and Bust." *Housing Policy Debate* 28(1): 1–14.

Christophers, Brett. 2011. "Revisiting the Urbanization of Capital." *Annals of the Association of American Geographers* 101(6): 1347–64.

Collins, Chik, and Peter E. Jones. 2006. "Analysis of Discourse as 'a Form of History Writing': A Critique of Critical Discourse Analysis and an Illustration of a Cultural-Historical Alternative." *Atlantic Journal of Communication* 14(1–2): 51–69.

Collinson, Robert, Ingrid Gould and Ellen Jens Ludwig. 2015. "Low-Income Housing Policy (No. w21071)." National Bureau of Economic Research (NBER), Working Paper series. Cambridge, Massachusetts. http://www.nber.org/papers/w21071.pdf.

Dalla Costa, Mariarosa, and Selma James. 1972. *The Power of Women and the Sub-version of the Community*. Bristol: Falling Wall Press.

Damer, Seán. 1980. "State, Class and Housing: Glasgow 1885–1919." In *Housing, Social Policy and the State*, edited by Joseph Melling, 73–112. London: Croom Helm.

———. 2000a. "'The Clyde Rent War!' The Clydebank Rent Strike of the 1920s." In *Class Struggle and Social Welfare* edited by Michael Lavalette and Gerry Mooney, 71–95. London: Routledge.

Engels, Friedrich. 1942 [1872]. *The Housing Question*. London: Lawrence and Wishart.

Federici, Silvia. 1984. "Putting Feminism Back on Its Feet." *Social Text* 9/10: 338–46.

———. 2012. *Revolution at Point Zero: Housework, Reproduction, and Feminist Struggle*. New York: PM Press/Autonomedia/Common Notions.

Fields, Desiree. 2015. "Contesting the Financialization of Urban Space: Community-Based Organizations and the Struggle to Preserve Affordable Rental Housing in New York City." *Journal of Urban Affairs* 37(2): 144–65.

———. 2017. "Unwilling Subjects of Financialization." *International Journal of Urban and Regional Research* 41(4): 588–603.

Fields, Desiree, and Sabina Uffer. 2016. "The Financialization of Rental Housing: A Comparative Analysis of New York City and Berlin." *Urban Studies* 53(7): 1486–1502.

Fortunati, Leopardi. 1995. *The Arcane of Reproduction: Housework, Prostitution, Labor, and Capital*. New York: Autonomedia.

Ginsburg, Norman. 2005. "The Privatization of Council Housing." *Critical Social Policy* 25(1): 115–35.

Glenn, Evelyn N. 2012. *Forced to Care: Coercion and Caregiving in America*. Cambridge, Massachusetts: Harvard University Press.

Gonzalez, Maya. 2010. "Notes on the New Housing Question." *Endnotes 2: Misery and the Value Form*, 52–66. Glasgow: Bell & Bain Ltd.

Gray, Neil. 2016. "Neither Shoreditch nor Manhattan: Post-Politics, 'Soft Austerity Urbanism' and Real Abstraction in Glasgow North." *Area*. Doi:10.1111/area.12299.

———. 2017. "Beyond the Right to the City: 'Territorial Autogestion' and the Take over the City Movement in 1970s Italy." *Antipode* 50(2): 319–39.

Grayson, John. 1996. *Opening the Window: Revealing the Hidden History of Tenants Organizations*, edited by Maggie Walker. Manchester: TPAS and Northern College.

Harvey, David. 2012. *Rebel Cities: From the Right to the City to the Urban Revolution*. London: Verso.

Hodkinson, Stuart. 2012b. "The New *Urban* Enclosures." *City: Analysis of Urban Trends, Culture, Theory, Policy, Action* 16(4): 500–18.

James, Selma. 1975. "Sex, Race and Class." https://libcom.org/files/sex-race-class-2012imp.pdf.

Johnstone, Charles. 1992. *The Tenants' Movement and Housing Struggles in Glasgow, 1945–1990*. PhD diss., University of Glasgow.

———. 2000. "Housing and Class Struggles in Post-war Glasgow." In *Class Struggle and Social Welfare*, edited by Michael Lavalette and Gerry Mooney, 139–54. London: Routledge.

Kitchin, Rob, Cian O'Callaghan and Justin Gleeson. 2014. "The New Ruins of Ireland? Unfinished Estates in the Post-Celtic Tiger Era." *International Journal of Urban and Regional Research* 38(3): 1069–80.

Madden, David, and Peter Marcuse. 2016. *In Defense of Housing*. London: Verso.

Marcuse, Peter. 1999. "Housing Movements in the USA." *Housing, Theory and Society* 16(2): 67–86.

McCabe, Conor. 2011. *Sins of the Father: The Decisions that Shaped the Irish Economy*. Dublin: History Press Ireland.

Meek, James. 2014. "Where Will We Live?" *London Review of Books* 36: 7–16.

Mitchell, Katharyne, Sally A. Marston and Cindi Katz. 2003. "Introduction: Life's Work: An Introduction, Review and Critique." *Antipode* 35(3): 415–42.

Mooney, Gerry, and Lynne Poole. 2005. "Marginalized Voices: Resisting the Privatization of Council Housing in Glasgow." *Local Economy* 20(1): 27–39.

Moorhouse, Bert, Mary Wilson and Chris Chamberlain. 1972. "Rent Strikes—Direct Action and the Working-Class." *Socialist Register* 9(9): 133–56.

National Housing Federation. 2017b. "How Many Homes Did Housing Associations Deliver in Quarter Two 2017/18?" November 22. London: National Housing Federation.

Norris, Michelle, and Dermot Coates. 2014. "How Housing Killed the Celtic Tiger: Anatomy and Consequences of Ireland's Housing Boom and Bust." *Journal of Housing and the Built Environment* 29(2): 299–315.

O'Callaghan, Cian, Mark Boyle and Rob Kitchin. 2014. "Post-Politics, Crisis, and Ireland's 'Ghost Estates.'" *Political Geography 42*: 121–33.

Peck, Jamie. 2012. "Austerity Urbanism: American Cities Under Extreme Economy." *City* 16(6): 626–55.

Perry, John. 2012. "Who Really Gets Subsidized Housing?" *Public Finance*, January 27. http://www.publicfinance.co.uk/2012/01/who-really-gets-subsidized-housing.

Purcell, Mark. 2006. "Urban Democracy and the Local Trap." *Urban Studies* 43(11): 1921–41.

Robbins, Glyn. 2002. "Taking Stock—Regeneration Programmes and Social Housing." *Local Economy* 17(4): 266–72.

———. 2017. *There's No Place: The American Housing Crisis and What It Means for the UK*. London: Red Roof.

Robertson, Mary. 2015. "Re-asking the Housing Question." *Salvage* (1): 161–72.

Sklair, Leslie. 1975. "The Struggle against the Housing Finance Act." *Socialist Register* 12(12): 250–92.

Smith, Neil. 2016. "The Housing Question Revisited." *ACME: An International Journal for Critical Geographies* 15(3): 679–83.

Smyth, James. 1992. "Rent, Peace, Votes: Working Class Women and Political Activity in the First World War." In *Out of Bounds: Women in Scottish Society 1800–1945*, edited by Esther Breitenbach and Eleanor Gordon, 174–96. Edinburgh University Press: Edinburgh.

Watt, Paul. 2009a. "Housing Stock Transfers, Regeneration and State-led Gentrification in London." *Urban Policy and Research* 27(3): 229–42.

References

PRIMARY SOURCES

Ewart, Mr. Scottish Oral History Centre Archive (SOHCA/019/031/Glasgow).
Crawfurd, H. n.d. *Autobiography*.
Dundee Advertiser, 9 October 1915, 25 October 1915.
Dundee Courier and Argus, 25 September 1915.
Forward, 1907–1918; 7 November 1922.
Glasgow Herald, 1915–1916.
Govan Press, 1915.
Hawick Women's Section, 7 April and 23 September 1924.
Labour Leader, 1916–1918.
Labour Women, "Report of WLL Conference at Glasgow, January 26 1914." February 1914, 1(10).
Partick and Maryhill Press, 1915–1916.
Peoples Journal, 16 October 1915, 23 October 1915, 27 November 1915.
SCWG, *Minute Books of the Central Council*, CWS1/39/1/8, 4 August 1920, 1 September 1920, 6 February 1924, 28 August 1929, 25 September 1929.
Textile Workers' Guide (no. 2), April 1916.
The Scotsman, 10 March 1936, p. 9; 10 November 1937, p. 7.
Votes for Women, 1915.
Women's Dreadnought, 1916.

BIBLIOGRAPHY

Aalbers, Manuel B. 2015. "The Great Moderation, the Great Excess and the Global Housing Crisis." *International Journal of Housing Policy* 15(1): 43–60.
Aalbers, Manual B., and Brett Christophers. 2014. "Centring Housing in Political Economy." *Housing, Theory and Society* 31(4): 373–94.

Adonis, Andrew, and Bill Davies. 2015. *City Villages: More Homes, Better Communities*. London: IPPR.

Allcock Tyler, Debra. 2016. "In Four Years There Will Be No Grants for Charities—It Will Destroy Communities." *The Guardian*, February 11. https://www.theguardian.com/voluntary-sector-network/2016/feb/11/grants-local-charities-campaign-appeal-government-cuts.

Anas, Alex. 1997. "Rent Control with Matching Economies: A Model of European Housing Market Regulation." *Journal of Real Estate Finance and Economics* 15: 111–37.

Attuyer, Katia. 2015. "When Conflict Strikes: Contesting Neoliberal Urbanism outside Participatory Structures in Inner-city Dublin." *International Journal of Urban and Regional Research* 39(4): 807–23.

Bailey, Ron. 1973. *The Squatters*. London: Penguin.

Barrat, Luke. 2017. "New Social Rented Homes at Lowest Level than any Other Year on Record." *Inside Housing*, June 20. https://www.insidehousing.co.uk/news/news/new-social-rented-homes-at-lowest-level-than-any-other-year-on-record-51020.

BBC. 2014. "Housing Benefits: Changes See 6% of Tenants Move." March 28. http://www.bbc.com/news/uk-26770727.

———. 2016. "The Sheriffs Are Coming." Accessed November 5. http://www.bbc.co.uk/programmes/b01q1j5d/episodes/guide.

Beach, Ben. 2015. "Is It Time for London to Go on a Rent Strike?" *Vice*, June 16, 2015. https://www.vice.com/en_ca/article/vdxdb9/rent-strike-ben-beach-839.

Beauregard, Robert A. 1994. "Capital Switching and the Built Environment: United States, 1970–89." *Environment and Planning A* 26(5): 715–32.

Benjamin, Walter. 1999. "Theses on the Philosophy of History." In *Illuminations*, edited and with an Introduction by Hannah Arendt, 245–55. London: Pimlico.

Bentley, David. 2015. "The Future of Private Renting." *Civitas*, January. http://civitas.org.uk/pdf/thefutureofprivaterenting.

———. 2016. "The Housing Question: Overcoming the Shortage of Homes." *Civitas*, March. http://www.civitas.org.uk/content/files/thehousingquestion.pdf.

Bernstock, Penny. 2014. *Olympic Housing: A Critical Review of London 2012's Legacy*. Farnham: Ashgate Publishing Ltd.

Beswick, Joe, Georgi Alexandri, Michael Byrne, Sònia Vives-Miró, Desiree Fields, Stuart Hodkinson and Michael Janoschka. 2016. "Speculating on London's Housing Future: The Rise of Global Corporate Landlords in 'Post-Crisis' Urban Landscapes." *City* 20(2): 321–41.

Berry, Kate, and Anouk Berthier. 2015. "SPICe Briefing: Private Rents." 15/66, October 15. Edinburgh: Scottish Parliament. http://www.parliament.scot/ResearchBriefingsAndFactsheets/S4/SB_15-66_Private_Rents.pdf.

Bhandar, Brenna, and Alberto Toscano, A. 2015. "Race, Real Estate and Real Abstraction. Radical Philosophy." 194 (Nov/Dec). https://www.radicalphilosophy.com/article/race-real-estate-and-real-abstraction.

Bishop, Claire. 2012. *Artificial Hells: Participatory Art and the Politics of Spectatorship*. London: Verso.

Bissett, John. 2008. "Regeneration: Public Good or Private Profit?" Dublin: Tasc at New Island.

Böhm, Steffen, Ana C. Dinerstein and Andre Spicer. 2010. "(Im)possibilities of Autonomy: Social Movements in and beyond Capital, the State and Development." *Social Movement Studies* 9(1): 17–32.

Bologna Sergio. 1992. "The Theory and History of the Mass Worker in Italy: Part 2." *Common Sense* 12: 52–78.

———. 2007 [1977]. "The Tribe of Moles." In *Autonomia: Post-Political Writings*, edited by Sylvere Lotringer and Christian Marazzi, 36–61. Los Angeles: Semiotext(e).

BOLEYNDEV100. 2016. "Campaign for 100% Social Housing for the Boleyn Ground Development." https://boleyndev100.wordpress.com

Bone, John, and Karen O'Reilly. 2010. "No Place Called Home: The Causes and Social Consequences of the UK Housing 'Bubble'." *British Journal of Sociology* 61: 231–55.

Bookchin, Murray. 1999. *The Murray Bookchin Reader*, edited by Janet Biehl. Montréal: Black Rose Books.

Bourne, Ryan. 2014. *The Flaw in Rent Ceilings*. London: Institute of Economic Affairs.

Bowman, Anna. 2004. "Interim Spaces: Reshaping London—the Role of Short Life Property, 1970 to 2000." PhD diss., University of Bristol.

Bradley, Quintin. 2014. *The Tenants' Movement: Resident Involvement, Community Action and the Contentious Politics of Housing*. London: Routledge.

Brenner, Neil, and Theodore Nik. 2002. "Cities and the Geographies of 'Actually Existing Neoliberalism.'" *Antipode* 34(3): 349–79.

Brooksbank, Mary. 2009. *Sidlaw Breezes*. Dundee: David Winter & Son Ltd.

———. 2017. *No Sae Lang Syne*. Dundee: Dundee Printers Ltd.

Bryant, Richard. 1982. "Rent Strike in the Gorbals." *Community Development Journal* 17(1): 41–46.

Bunge, William. 1977. "The Point of Reproduction: A Second Front." *Antipode* 9(2): 60–76.

Burness, Catriona. 2015. "Remembering Mary Barbour." *Scottish Labour History Review* 50: 81–96.

Burnett, John. 1978. *A Social History of Housing 1815–1970*. Newton Abbot: David and Charles.

Butler, Patrick. 2016a. "Benefit Cap Will Hit 116,000 of Poorest Families, Say Experts" *The Guardian*, Nov 1. www.theguardian.com/society/2016/nov/01/extended-benefit-cap-hit-116000-families-housing-experts.

———. 2016b. "Appeal Court Rules Bedroom Tax Discriminatory in Two Cases." *The Guardian*, January 27. http://www.theguardian.com/society/2016/jan/27/appeal-court-rules-bedroom-tax-discriminatory-in-two-cases.

Butt, John. 1978. "Working-Class Housing in Glasgow, 1900–1939." In *Essays in Scottish Labour History: A Tribute to W. H. Marwick*, edited by Ian MacDougall, 143–70. Edinburgh: John Donald.

Byrne, Michael. 2016. "'Asset Price Urbanism' and Financialization after the Crisis: Ireland's National Asset Management Agency." *International Journal of Urban and Regional Research* 40(1): 31–45.

Byrne, Michael, and Michelle Norris. 2017. "Procyclical Social Housing and the Crisis of Irish Housing Policy: Marketization, Social Housing, and the Property Boom and Bust." *Housing Policy Debate* 28(1): 1–14.

Byrne, Mick. 2017. "Organizing Tenants in the Rentier Society." *ROAR*, November 8. https://roarmag.org/essays/organizing-tenants-rentier-society/.

Caird, Trish. 2013. "Mary Barbour and the Glasgow Rent Strike". *Counterfire*, March 8. http://www.counterfire.org/women-on-the-left/16331-mary-barbour-and-the-glasgow-rent-strike.

Cairncross, Liz, Caroline Morrell, Jane Darke and Sue Brownhill. 2002. *Tenants Managing: An Evaluation of Tenant Management Organisations in England*. London: Office of the Deputy Prime Minister.

Callen, Kate M. 1952. *History of the Scottish Co-operative Women's Guild: Diamond Jubilee 1892–1952*. Glasgow: Scottish Co-operative Women's Guild.

Campbell, Alan. 2000. *The Scottish Miners 1874–1939, Volume One*. Aldershot: Ashgate.

Cant, Callum. 2016. "Students in the UK Prepare for a New Wave of Rent Strikes." *ROAR*, October 17. https://roarmag.org/essays/uk-student-rent-strike/.

Castells, Manuel. 1983. *The City and the Grassroots: A Cross-Cultural Theory of Urban Social Movements*. Berkeley: University of California Press.

Central Bank. 2016. "Residential Mortgage Arrears and Repossession Statistics." https://www.centralbank.ie/docs/default-source/statistics/credit-and-banking-statistics/mortgage-arrears/gns-6-2-2-4-2016q1_ie_mortgage_arrears_statistics.pdf?sfvrsn=8.

Central Statistics Office (CSO). 2012. "Profile 4: A Roof Over Our Heads." http://www.cso.ie/en/media/csoie/census/documents/census2011profile4/Profile_4_The_Roof_over_our_Heads_Full_doc_sig_amended.pdf.

———. 2015. "Residential Property Price Index." http://www.cso.ie/en/releasesandpublications/er/rppi/residentialpropertypriceindexdecember2015/.

———. 2017. "CSO 2016 Profile 1: Housing in Ireland." Dublin: CSO.

Charnock, Greig. 2010. "Challenging New State Spatialities: The Open Marxism of Henri Lefebvre." *Antipode* 42(5): 1279–303.

Cherki, Eddy, and Michel Wievorka. 2007. "Autoreduction Movements in Turin." In *Autonomia: Post-Political Writings*, edited by Sylvere Lotringer and Christian Marazzi, 72–79. Los Angeles: Semiotexte.

Christophers, Brett. 2011. "Revisiting the Urbanization of Capital." *Annals of the Association of American Geographers* 101(6): 1347–64.

Citylets. 2015. "Oil Cooled Market." *Quarterly Report*, Issue 33. https://www.citylets.co.uk/research/reports/pdf/Citylets-Rental-Report-Q1-15.pdf?ref=reports.

Clark, Helen, and Elizabeth Carnegie. 2003. *She Was Aye Workin'*. Oxford: White Cockade Publishing.

Cleaver, Harry. 1979. *Reading Capital Politically*. Brighton: Harvester Press Limited.

Colau, Ada, and Adria Alemany. 2012. *Mortgaged Lives. From the Housing Bubble to the Right to Housing*. Barcelona: Cuadrilatero Libros.

Collins, Chik, and Peter E. Jones. 2006. "Analysis of Discourse as 'a Form of History Writing': A Critique of Critical Discourse Analysis and an Illustration of a Cultural-Historical Alternative." *Atlantic Journal of Communication* 14(1–2): 51–69.

Collinson, Robert, Ingrid Gould and Ellen Jens Ludwig. 2015. "Low-Income Housing Policy (No.w21071)." National Bureau of Economic Research (NBER), Working Paper series. Cambridge, Massachusetts.

Community Development Project. 1976. *Whatever Happened to Council Housing?* Nottingham: Russell Press Limited. http://www.imaginenortheast.org/download/ CDP_Whatever_Happened_to_Council_Housing_Report.pdf.

Cooper, Anne E. 2017. *306: Living under the Shadow of Regeneration.* London: Devotion Press.

Cooper, Vickie, and Kirsteen Paton. 2015. "Tenants in Danger: The Rise of Eviction Watches." *OpenDemocracy*, April 17. https://www.opendemocracy.net/ourkingdom/ kirsteen-paton-vickie-cooper/tenants-in-danger-rise-of-eviction-watches.

Cowley, John. 1979. *Housing For People or For Profit?* London: Stage 1.

Cox, Anthony. 2013. *Empire, Industry and Class: The Imperial Nexus of Jute, 1840–1940.* Abingdon: Routledge.

Credit Strategy. 2016. "High Court Enforcement Group Acquires Sheriffs Office." *Credit Strategy*, February 1. https://www.creditstrategy.co.uk/news/news/high- court-enforcement-group-acquires-sheriffs-office-339.

Daft. 2016. "The Daft.ie Rental Price Report 2016". http://www.daft.ie/report/2016- q4-rental-daft-report.pdf.

Dalla Costa, Mariarosa, and Selma James. 1972. *The Power of Women and the Sub- version of the Community.* London: Falling Wall Press.

Damer, Seán. 1980. "State, Class and Housing: Glasgow 1885–1919." In *Housing, Social Policy and the State*, edited by Joseph Melling, 73–112. London: Croom Helm.

———. 1982. *Rent Strike! The Clydebank Rent Struggles of the 1920s.* Clydebank: People's History Pamphlet.

———. 1989. *From Moorepark to 'Wine Alley': The Rise and Fall of a Glasgow Housing Scheme.* Edinburgh: Edinburgh University Press.

———. 1990. *Glasgow: Going for a Song.* London: Lawrence and Wishart.

———. 1997. 'Striking Out on Red Clyde' in *Built to Last? Reflections on British Housing Policy*, edited by John Goodwin and Carol Grant, 35–40. London: ROOF Magazine.

———. 2000a. "'The Clyde Rent War!' The Clydebank Rent Strike of the 1920s." In *Class Struggle and Social Welfare*, edited by Michael Lavalette and Gerry Mooney, 71–95. London: Routledge.

———. 2000b. "'Engineers of the Human Machine': The Social Practice of Council Housing Management in Glasgow, 1895–1939." *Urban Studies* 37(11): 2007–26.

Daunton, Martin J. 1984. *Councillors and Tenants: Local Authority Housing in Eng- lish Cities, 1919–1939.* Leicester: Leicester University Press.

Department for Communities and Local Government (DCLG). "Table 101: By Tenure, United Kingdom (Historical Series)." https://www.gov.uk/government/ uploads/system/uploads/attachment_data/file/609286/LT_101.xls.

———. 2017. "Government Action to Ban Letting Agent Fees." https://www.gov.uk/ government/news/government-action-to-ban-letting-agent-fees.

De Angelis, Massimo. 2007. *The Beginning of History: Value Struggles and Global Capital*. London: Pluto Press.

———. 2013. "Does Capital Need a Commons Fix?" *Ephemera: Theory and Organization in Society* 13(3): 603–15.

———. 2017. *Omnia Sunt Communia: On the Commons and the Transformation to Postcapitalism*. London: Zed Books.

Dennis, Norman, Fernando Henriques and Clifford Slaughter. 1971. *Coal Is Our Life: An Analysis of a Yorkshire Mining Community*. London: Tavistock Publications.

Di Feliciantonio, Cesare. 2016. "Subjectification in Times of Indebtedness and Neoliberal/Austerity Urbanism." *Antipode* 48(5): 1206–27.

———. 2017. "Social Movements and Alternative Housing Models: Practicing the 'Politics of Possibilities' in Spain." *Housing, Theory and Society* 34(1): 38–56.

Dorling, Danny. 2014. *All That Is Solid: The Great Housing Disaster*. London: Penguin Books.

Douglas, Pam, and Jo Parkes. 2016. "'Regeneration' and 'Consultation' at a Lambeth Council Estate." *City* 20: 287–91.

Downey, Daithi. 2014. "The Financialization of Irish Homeownership and the Impact of the Global Financial Crisis." In *Neoliberal Urban Policy and the Transformation of the City*, edited by Andrew MacLaran and Sinead Kelly, 120–38. London: Palgrave Macmillan UK.

Dublin Region Homeless Executive. 2016. Homeless Accommodation Use. http://www.homelessdublin.ie/accommodation-usage.

———. 2017. Families Who are Homeless in the Dublin Region. http://www.homelessdublin.ie/homeless-families.

Dundee Social Union. 1905. *Report on Housing and Industrial Conditions in Dundee*. Dundee.

Duxbury, Nick, and Jess McCabe. 2015. "The Rise of the Housing Activist." *Inside Housing*, May 1. http://www.oceanmediagroup.co.uk/features/housingprotests/.

Dyer-Witheford, Nick. 2006. "The Circulation of the Common." Paper presented to the Conference on Immaterial Labour, Multitudes, and New Social Subjects: Class Composition in Cognitive Capitalism, 29–30 April 2006, King's College, University of Cambridge.

———. 2010. "Commonism." In *What Would It Mean to Win?* edited by Turbulence Collective, 81–87. Oakland, CA: PM Press.

Edwards, Brian. 1999. "Glasgow Improvements, 1866–1901" In *The Forming of the City*, edited by Peter Reed, 84–103. Edinburgh: Edinburgh University Press.

Elmer, Simon, and Geraldine Dening. 2016. "The London Clearances." *City: Analysis of Urban Trends, Culture, Theory, Policy, Action* 20: 271–77.

Engels, Friedrich. 1942 [1872]. *The Housing Question*. London: Lawrence and Wishart.

Englander, David. 1981. "Landlord and Tenant in Urban Scotland—The Background to the Clyde Rent Strikes." *Journal of Scottish Labour History Society* 15: 4–14.

———. 1983. *Landlord and Tenant in Urban Britain, 1838–1918*. Oxford: Oxford University Press.

Federici, Silvia. 1975. *Wages against Housework*. Bristol: Power of Women Collective and Falling Wall Press.

————. 1984. "Putting Feminism Back on Its Feet." *Social Text* 9/10: 338–46.

————. 2012. *Revolution at Point Zero: Housework, Reproduction, and Feminist Struggle*. New York: PM Press/Autonomedia/Common Notions.

Fields, Desiree. 2015. "Contesting the Financialization of Urban Space: Community-Based Organizations and the Struggle to Preserve Affordable Rental Housing in New York City." *Journal of Urban Affairs* 37(2): 144–65.

————. 2017. "Unwilling Subjects of Financialization." *International Journal of Urban and Regional Research* 41(4): 588–603.

Fields, Desiree, and Sabina Uffer. 2016. "The Financialization of Rental Housing: A Comparative Analysis of New York City and Berlin." *Urban Studies* 53(7): 1486–1502.

Fitzpatrick, Suzanne, and Hal Pawson. 2014. "Ending Security of Tenure for Social Renters: Transitioning to 'Ambulance Service' Social Housing?" *Housing Studies* 29(5): 597–615.

Flynn, Jerry. 2016. "Complete Control." *City: Analysis of Urban Trends, Culture, Theory, Policy, Action* 20: 278–86.

Forrest, Ray, and Yosuke Hirayama. 2015. "The Financialization of the Social Project: Embedded Liberalism, Neoliberalism and Homeownership." *Urban Studies* 52(22): 233–44.

Fortunati, Leopardi. 1995. *The Arcane of Reproduction: Housework, Prostitution, Labor, and Capital*. New York: Autonomedia.

Foster, John. 1976. "British Imperialism and the Labour Aristocracy." In *1926: The General Strike*, edited by Jeffrey Skelley, 3–58. Southampton: Lawrence and Wishart.

————. 1990. "Strike Action and Working-Class Politics on Clydeside, 1914–1919." *International Review of Social History* 35(1): 33–70.

Gait, Edward A. 1984. *Imperial Gazetteer of India: Bengal, Vol. I*. New Delhi: Usha.

García-Lamarca, Melissa. 2017a. "From Occupying Plazas to Recuperating Housing: Insurgent Practices in Spain." *International Journal of Urban and Regional Research* 41(1): 37–53.

García-Lamarca, Melissa. 2017b. "Reconfiguring the Public through Housing Rights Struggles in Spain." In *City Unsilenced: Urban Resistance and Public Space in the Age of Shrinking Democracy*, edited by Jeffery Hou, 44–55. New York: Routledge.

García-Lamarca, Melissa, and Kaika, Maria. 2016. "'Mortgaged Lives': The Biopolitics of Debt and Housing Financialization." *Transactions of the Institute of British Geographers* 41(3): 313–27.

Gauldie, Enid. 1976. "The Middle Class and the Working Class Housing in the Nineteenth Century." In *Social Class in Scotland: Past and Present*, edited by Allan MacLaren, 12–35. Edinburgh: John Donald Publishers Ltd.

Gibson-Graham, J. K. 2006. *A Post-Capitalist Politics*. Minneapolis: University of Minnesota Press.

Gillespie, Tom, Hardy, Kate, and Paul Watt. 2018. "Austerity Urbanism and Olympic Counter-Legacies: Gendering, Defending and Expanding the Urban Commons in East London." *Environment and Planning D: Society and Space*. DOI: http://journals.sagepub.com/doi/full/10.1177/0263775817753844

Gilmartin, Mary. 2014. "Immigration and Spatial Justice in Contemporary Ireland." In *Spatial Justice and the Irish Crisis*, edited by Gerry Kearns, David Meredith and John Morrissey, 161–76. Dublin: Royal Irish Academy.

Ginsburg, Norman. 1979. *Class, Capital and Social Policy*. Basingstoke: Macmillan.
———. 2005. "The Privatization of Council Housing." *Critical Social Policy* 25(1): 115–35.
Glasgow City Council. 2017. *Glasgow's Housing Strategy 2017–2022*. Glasgow: Glasgow City Council.
Glenn, Evelyn N. 2012. *Forced to Care: Coercion and Caregiving in America*. Cambridge, Massachusetts: Harvard University Press.
Glynn, Sarah. 2005. "East End Immigrants and the Battle for Housing: A Comparative Study of Political Mobilization in the Jewish and Bengali communities." *Journal of Historical Geography* 31: 528–45.
———. 2009. *Where the Other Half Lives: Lower Income Housing in a Neoliberal World*. London: Pluto Press.
———. 2010. "The Tenants' Movement: Incorporation and Independence." In *The Glasgow Papers: Critical Perspectives on Community Development*, edited by Akwugo Emejulu and Mae Shaw, 53–57. Edinburgh: Community Development Journal.
———. 2014. "Housing for a Better Nation." *Commonweal*. http://allofusfirst.org.
Gonzalez, Maya. 2010. "Notes on the New Housing Question." *Endnotes 2: Misery and the Value Form*, 52–66. Glasgow: Bell & Bain Ltd.
Gordon, Eleanor. 1991. *Women and the Labour Movement in Scotland, 1850–1914*. Clarendon: Oxford.
Gotham, Kevin F. 2009. "Creating Liquidity out of Spatial Fixity: The Secondary Circuit of Capital and the Subprime Mortgage Crisis." *International Journal of Urban and Regional Research* 33(2): 355–71.
Gould, Mark. 2015. "Local Residents Angry at Lack of Social Housing at West Ham's Ground." *The Guardian*, February 24. https://www.theguardian.com/society/2015/feb/24/newham-residents-social-housing-west-ham.
Gray, Neil. 2018. "Neither Shoreditch nor Manhattan: Post-Politics, 'Soft Austerity Urbanism' and Real Abstraction in Glasgow North." *Area*. Doi: http://onlinelibrary.wiley.com/doi/10.1111/area.12299/full.
———. 2018. "Beyond the Right to the City: 'Territorial Autogestion' and the Take over the City Movement in 1970s Italy." *Antipode* 50(2): 319–39.
Grayson, John. 1996. *Opening the Window: Revealing the Hidden History of Tenants Organisations*, edited by Maggie Walker. Manchester: TPAS and Northern College.
Greater London Authority (GLA). 2016. *Planning Report D&P/3399/02, 28 April 2016: West Ham Stadium, Boleyn Grind, Green Street, Upton Park, London E13 9AZ*. London: GLA.
Griffin, Paul. 2015. *The Spatial Politics of Red Clydeside: Historical Labour Geographies and Radical Connections*. PhD diss., University of Glasgow.
Hannam, June, and Karen Hunt. 2002. *Socialist Women: Britain: 1880s to 1920s*. London: Routledge.
Hansard Online. 2011. "Short-life Homes (Lambeth)." *Hansard Online*, December 6. https://hansard.parliament.uk/Commons/2011-12-06/debates/11120680000002/Short-LifeHomes(Lambeth).

Hardt, Michael. 2010. "The Common in Communism." *Rethinking Marxism* 22(3): 346–56.

Hardt, Michael, and Antonio Negri. 2006. *Multitude*. London: Penguin Books.

———. 2009. *Commonwealth*. Cambridge: Harvard University Press.

Hartman, Chester. 1984. *Between Eminence and Notoriety: Four Decades of Radical Urban Planning*. New Brunswick, NJ: CUPR Press.

Harvey, David. 1982. *The Limits to Capital*. Oxford: Blackwell.

———. 1985. *The Urbanization of Capital: Studies in the Theory and History of Capitalist Urbanization*. Baltimore: John Hopkins University.

———. 2003. *The New Imperialism*. Oxford: Oxford University Press.

———. 2007. *The Limits to Capital*, 3rd ed. Oxford: Blackwell.

———. 2012. *Rebel Cities: From the Right to the City to the Urban Revolution*. London: Verso.

Hayek, Friedrich von. 1972. "The Repercussions of Rent Restrictions." In *Verdict on Rent Control*, 1–16 London: Institute of Economic Affairs.

Hearne, Rory. 2011. *Public Private Partnerships in Ireland: Failed Experiment or the Way Forward for the State*. Manchester: Manchester University Press.

———. 2014. "Achieving a Right to the City in Practice: Reflections on Community Struggles in Dublin." *Human Geography* 7(3): 14–25.

———. 2015. "The Irish Water War." *Interface: A Journal for and about Social Movements* 7(1): 309–21.

———. 2017. "A Home or a Wealth Generator? Inequality, Financialization and the Irish Housing Crisis." Dublin: TASC. https://www.tasc.ie/download/pdf/a_home_or_a_wealth_generator_inequality_financialisation_and_the_irish_housing_crisis.pdf.

Hearne, Rory, and Kenna, Padraic. 2014. "Using the Human Rights Based Approach to Tackle Housing Deprivation in an Irish Urban Housing Estate." *Journal of Human Rights Practice* 6(1): 1–25.

Hilton, Alexander. 2016. "How to Repair the Housing Market Quickly—A Crisis Response." *Communication Workers Union*. http://www.devolved.org.uk/HousingReport.pdf.

HM Treasury. 2010. *Investment in the UK Private Rented Sector*. London, UK Treasury.

HMG. 1915. "Report of the Committee to Enquire into the Circumstances Connected with the Alleged Recent Increases in the Rental of Small Dwelling houses in Industrial Districts in Scotland." Edinburgh: His Majesty's Stationary Office.

Hobsbawm, Eric. 1987. "Labour in the Great City." *New Left Review* 1/166, November–December: 39–51.

HOCCHG. 2009. *Council Housing—Time to Invest*. London: House of Commons Council Housing Group.

Hodkinson, Stuart. 2012a. "The Return of the Housing Question." *Ephemera: Theory and Politics in Organization* 12(4): 423–44.

———. 2012b. "The New Urban Enclosures." *City: Analysis of Urban Trends, Culture, Theory, Policy, Action* 16(4): 500–18.

Hodkinson, Stuart, and Beth Lawrence. 2011. "The Neoliberal Project, Privatization and the Housing Crisis." *Corporate Watch* 50 Autumn/Winter.

Hodkinson, Stuart, and Glyn Robbins, G. 2013. "The Return of Class War Conservatism? Housing Under the UK Coalition Government." *Critical Social Policy* 33(1): 57–77.

Hodkinson, Stuart, Paul Watt and Gerry Mooney. 2013. "Neoliberal Housing Policy—Time for a Critical Re-appraisal." *Critical Social Policy* 33(1): 3–16.

Homeless Link. 2017. "Rough Sleeping—Our Analysis." http://www.homeless.org.uk/facts/homelessness-in-numbers/rough-sleeping/rough-sleeping-our-analysis.

Horsey, Miles. 1990. *Tenements & Towers: Glasgow Working-Class Housing 1890–1990*. Edinburgh: Royal Commission on the Ancient and Historical Monuments of Scotland.

House of Commons Council Housing Group. 2005. *Support for the 'Fourth Option' for Council Housing: Report on the Enquiry into the Future Funding of Council Housing 2004–2005*. Nottingham: Russell Press.

House of Commons Library. 2017. "Households in Temporary Accommodation (England) House of Commons Briefing Paper." *House of Commons Library*, October 23. http://researchbriefings.parliament.uk/ResearchBriefing/Summary/SN02110.

Housing Agency. 2010. "2010 National Housing Survey." http://www.housing.ie/Our-Services/Unfinished-Housing-Developments/2010-National-Housing-Survey.

Hudson, Michael. 2006a. "Real Estate, Technology and the Rentier Economy: Pricing in Excess of Value, Producing Income without Work." Speech delivered at the 'Economics of Abundance' conference, Kings College, London, July 3.

———. 2006b. "The New Road to Serfdom: An Illustrated Guide to the Coming Real Estate Collapse." *Harper's Magazine*, May, 39–46.

———. 2010. "From Marx to Goldman Sachs: The Fictions of Fictitious Capital, and the Financialization of Industry." *Critique* 38(3): 419–44.

Hughes, Annmarie. 2010. *Gender and Political Identities in Scotland, 1919–1939*. Edinburgh: Edinburgh University Press.

———. 2013. "'A Clear Understanding of our Duty': Labour Women in Rural Scotland, 1919–1939." *Scottish Labour History Review* 48: 136–57.

Hughes, David, and Stuart Lowe. 1995. *Social Housing Law and Policy*. London: Butterworths.

Jackson, J. M. 1979. "Economic Life: A General Survey." In *Third Statistical Account of Scotland: The City of Dundee*, edited by J. M. Jackson, 97–104. Arbroath: The Herald Press.

James, Selma. 1975. *Sex, Race and Class*. https://libcom.org/files/sex-race-class-2012imp.pdf.

Jameson, Frederic. 1991. *Postmodernism or the Cultural Logic of Late Capitalism*. London: Verso.

Jeraj, Esmat. 2016. "Community Demands 300 Homes on the Boleyn Development." *Citizens UK*, February 12. http://www.citizensuk.org/community_demands_300_homes.

Joannou, Maroula, and June Purvis. 1998. Introduction to *The Women's Suffrage Movement: New Feminist Perspectives*, edited by Maroula Joannou and June Purvis, 1–14. Manchester: Manchester University Press.

Jones, Jerry. 2008. *Land Value . . . For Public Benefit*. Highcliffe-on-Sea: Labour Land Campaign. www.labourland.org/downloads/papers/land_value_for_public_benefit.pdf.

Jones, Rupert. 2016. "Average Rents in UK Fall for the First Time in More Than Seven Years." *The Guardian*, June 6. https://www.theguardian.com/money/2017/jun/06/uk-rents-fall-london-brexit.

Johnstone, Charles. 1992. *The Tenants' Movement and Housing Struggles in Glasgow, 1945–1990*. PhD diss., University of Glasgow.

———. 2000. "Housing and Class Struggles in Post-war Glasgow." In *Class Struggle and Social Welfare*, edited by Michael Lavalette and Gerry Mooney, 139–54. London: Routledge.

Kearns, Kevin C. 1979. "Intraurban Squatting in London." *Annals of the Association of American Geographers* 69(4): 589–98.

Kelly, Sinead. 2014. "Light-Touch Regulation: The Rise and Fall of the Irish Banking Sector." In *Neoliberal Urban Policy and the Transformation of the City*, edited by Andrew MacLaran and Sinead Kelly, 37–53. London: Palgrave Macmillan UK.

Kemeny, Jim. 1981. *The Myth of Homeownership: Private Versus Public Choices in Housing Tenure*. London: Routledge.

King, Elizabeth. 1978. *The Scottish Women's Suffrage Movement*. Glasgow: People's Palace.

King, Peter. 2006. *Choice and the End of Social Housing*. London: Institute of Economic Affairs.

Kitchin, Rob, Cian O'Callaghan and Justin Gleeson. 2014. "The New Ruins of Ireland? Unfinished Estates in the Post-Celtic Tiger Era." *International Journal of Urban and Regional Research* 38(3): 1069–80.

Kitchin, Rob, Cian O'Callaghan, Mark Boyle, Justin Gleeson and Karen Keaveney. 2012. "Placing Neoliberalism: The Rise and Fall of Ireland's Celtic Tiger." *Environment and Planning A* 44(6): 1302–26.

Kitchin, Rob, Rory Hearne and Cian O'Callaghan. 2016. "Housing." In *Austerity and Recovery in Ireland: Europe's Poster Child and the Great Recession*, edited by William K. Roche, Philip J. O'Connell and Andrea Prothero, 272–89. Oxford: Oxford University Press.

Kowaluk, Lucia, and Carolle Piché-Burton. 2012. *Communauté Milton-Parc: How We Did It and How It Works Now*. Montreal: Communauté Milton-Parc. http://www.miltonparc.org/English.pdf.

Kutty, Nandinee. 1996. "The Impact of Rent Control on Housing Maintenance: A Dynamic Analysis Incorporating European and North American Rent Regulations." *Housing Studies* 11(1): 69–88.

Lansley, Stewart, and Mack, Joanna. 2015. *Breadline Britain: The Rise of Mass Poverty*. London: Oneworld Books.

Lees, Loretta. 2008. "Gentrification and Social Mixing: Towards an Inclusive Urban Renaissance?" *Urban Studies* 45(12): 2449–70.

Lees, Loretta, and Mara Ferreri. 2016. "Resisting Gentrification on Its Final Frontiers: Learning from the Heygate Estate in London (1974–2013)." *Cities* 57, September: 14–24.

Lefebvre, Henri. 1991. *The Production of Space.* Oxford: Blackwell.

———. 2003 [1970]. *The Urban Revolution.* Minnesota: University of Minnesota Press.

Leneman, Leah. 1991. *A Guid Cause: The Women's Suffrage Movement in Scotland.* Aberdeen: Aberdeen University Press.

Liddington, Jill. 1989. *The Long Road to Greenham.* London: Virago.

Linebaugh, Peter. 2008. *The Magna Carta Manifesto: Liberties and Commons for All.* California: University of California Press.

Liverpool Echo. 2014. "Merseyside Family Saved from Christmas Eviction after Vigil Outside their Home." *Liverpool Echo,* December 16. http://www.liverpoolecho.co.uk/news/liverpool-news/vigil-outside-home-merseyside-family-8295650.

London Co-operative Housing Group. 2017. *Co-operate Not Speculate.* London: Co-ops 4 London.

Löwy, Michael. 2015. *Ecosocialism: A Radical Alternative to Capitalist Catastrophe.* Chicago: Haymarket Books.

Luhmann, Niklas. 1995. *Social Systems.* Redwood City: Stanford University Press.

Lyons, Ronan. 2017. "Irish Rental Report Q4 2016." Dublin: Daft.ie. https://www.daft.ie/report/ronan-lyons-2016q4-rental.

Madden, David, and Peter Marcuse. 2016. *In Defense of Housing.* London: Verso.

Malpass, Peter. 2000. *Housing Associations and Housing Policy: A Historical Perspective.* Basingstoke: Palgrave Macmillan.

———. 2003. "The Wobbly Pillar? Housing and the British Post-war Welfare State." *Journal of Social Policy* 32(4): 589–606.

Marcuse, Peter. 1999. "Housing Movements in the USA." *Housing, Theory and Society* 16(2): 67–86.

Marmot, Michael. 2010. Foreword to *Social Capital, Human Capital and Health. What Is the Evidence.* OECD. www.oecd.org/edu/research/45760738.pdf.

Marx, Karl. 1847. *The Poverty of Philosophy.* https://www.marxists.org/archive/marx/works/1847/poverty-philosophy/.

———. 1848. *The Communist Manifesto.* https://www.marxists.org/archive/marx/works/1848/communist-manifesto/.

Mayer, Margit. 2013. "First World Urban Activism." *City: Analysis of Urban Trends, Culture, Theory, Policy, Action* 17(1): 5–19.

Mayor of London. 2016. *Homes for Londoners: Draft Good Practice Guide to Estate Regeneration.* London: GLA.

McCabe, Conor. 2011. *Sins of the Father: The Decisions that Shaped the Irish Economy.* Dublin: History Press Ireland.

McCárthaigh, Seán. 2016. "200,000 Homes Empty Amid Housing Crisis." *The Times,* July 15. https://www.thetimes.co.uk/edition/ireland/200-000-homes-empty-amid-housing-crisis-dvqjwprcc.

McCrone, David. 1994. "Towards a Principled Society: Scottish Elites in the Twentieth Century." In *People and Society in Scotland, Vol. III,* edited by Anthony Dickson and James H. Treble, 174–200. Edinburgh: John Donald.

McCrone, David, and Brian Elliot. 1989. *Property and Power in a City: The Sociological Significance of Landlordism.* Basingstoke: MacMillan Press.

McIntyre, Stuart. 1980. *Little Moscows: Communism and Working-Class Militancy in Interwar Britain*. London: Croom Helm.

McLean, Caitlin. 2015. "Beyond Care: Expanding the Feminist Debate on Universal Basic Income." WiSE Working Paper Series No.1, September. Available at *Basic Income Earth Network*. http://basicincome.org/news/2015/11/caitlin-mclean-beyond-care-expanding-the-feminist-debate-on-universal-basic-income/.

McLean, Iain. 1983. *The Legend of Red Clydeside*. Edinburgh: John Donald.

———. 1999. *The Legend of Red Clydeside*. Edinburgh: John Donald.

Meek, James. 2014. "Where Will We Live?" *London Review of Books* 36: 7–16.

Melling, J. (Ed.). 1980. *Housing, Social Policy and the State*. London: Croom Helm.

Melling, Joseph. 1979. "The Glasgow Rent Strike and Clydeside Labour—Some Problems of Interpretation." *Scottish Labour History Society Journal* 13: 39–44.

———. 1983. *Rent Strikes: People's Struggle for Housing in West Scotland 1890–1916*. Polygon: Edinburgh.

Memery, Clodagh. 2001. "The Housing System and the Celtic Tiger: The State Response to a Housing Crisis of Affordability and Access." *International Journal of Housing Policy* 1(1): 79–104.

Merrifield, Andy. 2014. *The New Urban Question*. London: Pluto Press.

Midnight Notes. 1992. "Introduction to Zerowork 1." In *Midnight Oil: Work, Energy, War, 1973–1992*, 108–114. New York: Autonomedia.

Milton, Nan. 1973. *John MacLean*. London: Pluto.

Ministry of Justice. 2015. "Mortgage and Landlord Possession Statistics Quarterly, England and Wales April to June 2015." *Ministry of Justice*, August 13. https://www.gov.uk/government/uploads/system/uploads/attachment_data/file/ 453265/mortgage-landlord-possession-statistics-april-june-2015.pdf.

Minton, Anna. 2017. *Big Capital: Who Is London For?* London: Penguin Books.

Mirowski, Philip. 2013. *Never Let a Serious Crisis Go to Waste*. London: Verso.

Mitchell, Katharyne, Sally A. Marston and Cindi Katz. 2003. "Introduction: Life's Work: An Introduction, Review and Critique." *Antipode* 35(3): 415–42.

Money Advice Trust. 2013. "Rent Arrears the Fastest Growing UK Debt Problem." *Money Advice Trust*, October 16. http://www.moneyadvicetrust.org/media/news/Pages/Rent-arrears-the-fastest-growing-UK-debt-problem.aspx.

Mooney, Gerry, and Lynne Poole. 2005. "Marginalized Voices: Resisting the Privatization of Council Housing in Glasgow." *Local Economy* 20(1): 27–39.

Moorhouse, Bert, Mary Wilson and Chris Chamberlain. 1972. "Rent Strikes—Direct Action and the Working-Class." *Socialist Register* 9(9): 133–56.

Morgan, Nicholas J. 1989. "'£8 Cottages for Glasgow Citizens': Innovations in Municipal Housebuilding in Glasgow in the Interwar years." *Scottish Housing in the Twentieth Century*, edited by Richard Rodger, 125–44. Leicester: Leicester University Press.

Murie, Alan. 2015. "The Right to Buy: History and Prospect." *History and Policy*, November 11 2015. http://www.historyandpolicy.org/policy-papers/papers/the-right-to-buy-history-and-prospect.

Murphy, Richard. 2017. "Homes Should Not Be Tax Havens, But That's Exactly What They Are Right Now." *Tax Research UK*, October 7. www.taxresearch.

org.uk/Blog/2017/10/07/homes-should-not-be-tax-havens-but-thats-exactly-what-they-are-right-now/.

National Housing Federation. 2014. "Stark Results in Bedroom Tax Report." London: National Housing Federation.

———. 2017a. "How Many Homes Did Housing Associations Build in Quarter Three 2016/2017?" http://s3-eu-west-1.amazonaws.com/pub.housing.org.uk/Supply_briefing_note_201718_Q1.pdf.

———. 2017b. "How Many Homes Did Housing Associations Deliver in Quarter Two 2017/18?" London: National Housing Federation.

Neate, Rupert. 2014. "Scandal of Europe's 11m Empty Homes." *The Guardian*, February 23. https://www.theguardian.com/society/2014/feb/23/europe-11m-empty-properties-enough-house-homeless-continent-twice.

Negri, Antonio. 2005. *Books for Burning*. London: Verso.

Nevitt, Della. 1971. *Fair Deal for Householders*. London: Fabian Society.

Newham Recorder. 2016. "Boleyn Ground Development Approved with Minimum of 25% Affordable Housing." *Newham Recorder*, 11 March 2016.http://www.newhamrecorder.co.uk/news/boleyn-ground-development-approved-with-minimum-of-25-affordable-housing-1-4452551.

Niemietz, Kristian. 2016. *The Key to Affordable Housing: A Critique of the Communication Workers Union's Rent Control Proposals*. London: Institute of Economic Affairs.

Norris, Michelle. 2016. *Property, Family and the Irish Welfare State*. Springer International Publishing.

Norris, Michelle, and Dermot Coates. 2014. "How Housing Killed the Celtic Tiger: Anatomy and Consequences of Ireland's Housing Boom and Bust." *Journal of Housing and the Built Environment* 29(2): 299–315.

Norris, Michelle, and Michael Byrne. 2015. "Asset Price Urbanism in the Irish and Spanish Housing Crises." *Built Environment* 41(2): 205–21.

O'Callaghan, Cian. Mark Boyle and Rob Kitchin. 2014. "Post-Politics, Crisis, and Ireland's 'Ghost Estates.'" *Political Geography* 42: 121–33.

Ó Riain, Seán. 2014. *The Rise and Fall of Ireland's Celtic Tiger: Liberalism, Boom and Bust*. Cambridge: Cambridge University Press.

Ocean Estate Tenants Association. n.d. *HATS OFF THE OCEAN*. London: Ocean Estate Tenants Association.

Olsen, Edgar. 1988. "What Do Economists Know about the Effect of Rent Control on Housing Maintenance?" *Journal of Real Estate Finance and Economics* 1: 295–307.

Orr, Lesley. 2015. "'Shall We Not Speak for Ourselves?' Helen Crawfurd, War Resistance and the Women's Peace Crusade, 1916–1918." *Scottish Labour History Review* 50: 97–115.

Osborne, George. 2015. "George Osborne's Speech in Full." *Conservative Home*, October 5. http://www.conservativehome.com/parliament/2015/10/george-osbornes-speech-in-full.html.

Osborne, Hilary. 2015. "Tenants in England Spend Half their Pay on Rent." *The Guardian*, July 16. https://www.theguardian.com/money/2015/jul/16/tenants-in-england-spend-half-their-pay-on-rent.

Ostrom, Elinor. 1990. *Governing the Commons: The Evolution of Institutions for Collective Action*. New York: Cambridge University Press.

Plataforma de Afectados por la Hipoteca (PAH). 2016. *The PAH's Green Book: A Basic Guide to the PAH*. Barcelona: PAH. http://afectadosporlahipoteca.com/wp-content/uploads/2016/06/GreenBook-PAH-21juny.pdf.

Peck, Jamie. 2001. *Workfare States*. London: Guilford Press.

———. 2012. "Austerity Urbanism: American Cities Under Extreme Economy." *City* 16(6): 626–55.

Perry, John. 2012. "Who Really Gets Subsidized Housing?" *Public Finance*, January 27. http://www.publicfinance.co.uk/2012/01/who-really-gets-subsidized-housing.

Petrie, Ann. 2008. *The 1915 Rent Strikes: An East Coast Perspective*. Dundee: Abertay Historical Press.

Piketty, Thomas. 2014. *Capital in the 21st Century*. Cambridge, MA: Harvard University Press.

Power, Anne. 1988. *Under New Management: The Experience of Thirteen Islington Tenant Management Co-operatives*. London: Priority Estates Project.

———. 1993. *Hovels to Highrise: State Housing in Europe since 1850*. London: Routledge.

Proctor, Robert, and Schiebinger, Londa. 2008. *Agnotology: The Making and Unmaking of Ignorance*. Stanford: Stanford University Press.

Purcell, Mark. 2006. "Urban Democracy and the Local Trap." *Urban Studies* 43(11): 1921–41.

Ramesh, Randeep. 2012. "Extra 10,000 Working People a Month Reliant on Housing Benefit, says Report." *The Guardian*, October 22. http://www.theguardian.com/society/2012/oct/22/working-people-housing-benefit-report.

Renshaw, Rosalind. 2015. "Agents and Landlords Mobilise in Scotland as Rent Controls Draw Nearer." *Property Industry Eye*. http://www.propertyindustryeye.com/agents-and-landlords-mobilise-in-scotland-as-rent-controls-draw-nearer/.

Richardson, Hannah. 2016. "Warning as Household Debts Rise to Top £1.5 trillion." *BBC*, November 7. http://www.bbc.co.uk/news/uk-37873825.

Robertson, Iain. 1997. "The Role of Women in Social Protest in the Highlands of Scotland, 1880–1939." *Journal of Historical Geography* 23(2): 187–200.

Robertson, Mary. 2015. "Re-asking the Housing Question." *Salvage* (1): 161–72.

Robbins, Glyn. 2002. "Taking Stock—Regeneration Programmes and Social Housing." *Local Economy* 17(4): 266–72.

———. 2017. *There's No Place: The American Housing Crisis and What It Means for the UK*. London: Red Roof.

Robinson, Mairi, 1985. *The Concise Scots Dictionary*. Exeter: Chambers.

Rodger, Richard. 1989. "Crisis and Confrontation in Scottish housing 1880–1914." In *Scottish Housing in the Twentieth Century*, edited by Richard Rodger, 25–53. Leicester: Leicester University Press.

Rolnik, Raquel. 2013. "Late Neoliberalism: The Financialization of Homeownership and Housing Rights." *International Journal of Urban and Regional Research* 37(3): 1058–66.

Ross, Ellen. 1983. "Survival Networks: Women's Neighbourhood Sharing in London before World War 1." *History Workshop Journal* 15(1): 4–28.

Ross, Kristen. 2015. *Communal Luxury: The Political Imaginary of the Paris Commune.* London: Verso.

Royal Commission. 1918. *Report of the Royal Commission on the Housing of the Industrial Population of Scotland Rural and Urban.* Edinburgh: His Majesty's Stationary Office.

RTÉ. 2017. *The Great Irish Sell Off. RTE Television*, Monday January 9.

Savills. 2017. *London's Future Homes and Workplaces—The Next Five Years.* London: Savills World Research.

Scott, Gillian. 1998. *Feminism and the Politics of Working Women: The Women's Co-Operative Guild, 1880s to the Second World War.* London: University College London Press.

Scott, Suzie. 2000. "The People's Republic of Yoker: A Case Study of Tenant Management in Scotland." *Journal of Co-operative Studies* 33(1): 15–38.

Scottish Government. 2014a. "Housing Statistics for Scotland—Key Information and Summary Tables." http://www.gov.scot/Topics/Statistics/Browse/Housing-Regeneration/HSfS/KeyInfoTables

———. 2014b. "Private Sector Rent Statistics, Scotland (2010 to 2014)." http://www.gov.scot/Publications/2014/11/2313.

Scottish Housing News. 2015. "Rent Control Plans 'Threaten Scotland's Burgeoning PRS Market.'" *Scottish Housing News*, September 2. http://www.scottishhousing-news.com/5216/rent-control-plans-threaten-scotlands-burgeoning-prs-market/.

Segerberg, A., and W. Lance Bennett. 2011. "Social Media and the Organization of Collective Action: Using Twitter to Explore the Ecologies of Two Climate Change Protests." *Communication Review* 14(3): 197–215.

Shelter. 2011. "Welfare Reform Bill—House of Lords Report Stage Joint Briefing on Clause 94: The Overall Benefit Cap." *Shelter*, January 7. https://england.shelter.org.uk/__data/assets/pdf_file/0019/410590/Welfare_Reform_Bill_Clause_94_briefing.pdf.

———. 2014. *Safe and Decent Homes: Solutions for a Better Private Rented Sector.* http://england.shelter.org.uk/__data/assets/pdf_file/0003/1039530/FINAL_SAFE_AND_DECENT_HOMES_REPORT-_USE_FOR_LAUNCH.pdf.

Shelter Scotland. 2017. *Shelter Scotland Written Evidence on the General Principles of the Child Poverty (Scotland) Bill (March 2017).* http://scotland.shelter.org.uk/__data/assets/pdf_file/0008/1357577/Shelter_Scotlands_written_evidence_on_the_Child_Poverty_Scotland_Bill.pdf/_nocache.

Shildrick, Tracy, Robert MacDonald, Colin Webster and Kayleigh Garthwaite. 2015. *The Low-Pay, No-Pay Cycle: Understanding Recurrent Poverty.* York: Joseph Rowntree Foundation.

Sirr, Lorcan. 2014. *Renting in Ireland: The Social, Voluntary, and Private Sectors.* Dublin: Institute of Public Administration.

Sklair, Leslie. 1975. "The Struggle against the Housing Finance Act." *Socialist Register* 12(12): 250–92.

Slater, Tom. 2013. "Your Life Chances Affect Where You Live: A Critique of the 'Cottage Industry' of Neighbourhood Effects Research." *International Journal of Urban and Regional Research* 37(2): 367–87.

———. 2016a. "The Housing Crisis in Neoliberal Britain: Free Market Think Tanks and the Production of Ignorance" in *The Handbook of Neoliberalism*, edited by Simon Springer, Kean Birch and Julie Macleavy, 370–382. London: Routledge.

———. 2016b. "Revanchism, Stigma, and the Production of Ignorance: Housing Struggles in Austerity Britain." In *Risking Capitalism*, edited by Susan Soederberg, 23–48. Bingley, Emerald Group Publishing Limited.

Smith, David M. 1994. *Geography and Social Justice*. Oxford: Blackwell Publishers Ltd.

Smith, Neil. 2002. "New Globalism, New Localism: Gentrification as Global Urban Strategy." *In Spaces of Neoliberalism: Urban Restructuring in North America and Western Europe*, edited by Neil Brenner and Nik Theodore, 80–103. London: Blackwell Publishing.

———. 2016. "The Housing Question Revisited." *ACME: An International Journal for Critical Geographies* 15(3): 679–83.

Smyth, James. 1992. "Rent, Peace, Votes: Working-Class Women and Political Activity in the First World War." In *Out of Bounds: Women in Scottish Society 1800–1945*, edited by Esther Breitenbach and Eleanor Gordon, 174–96. Edinburgh: Edinburgh University Press.

———. 2000. *Labour in Glasgow 1896–1936: Socialism, Suffrage, Sectarianism*. East Linton: Tuckwell Press.

Spicker, Paul. 1988. "Wrong Foot Forward." *Roof*, January–February: 42–43.

Spirit of Revolt. 2015. "Rent Strikes: 100 Years On." *Spirit of Revolt*, November 30. http://spiritofrevolt.info/rent-strikes-100-years-on-exhibition/.

Sprott, Gavin. 1996. "Lowland Country Life." In *Scotland in the Twentieth Century*, edited by Tam M. Devine and Richard J. Finlay, 170–88. Edinburgh: Edinburgh University Press.

Stafford, David C. 1976. "The Final Economic Demise of the Private Landlord?" *Social and Economic Administration* 10(1): 3–14.

Stainton Rogers, Wendy. 2003. *Social Psychology: Experimental and Critical Approaches*. Maidenhead: Open University Press/McGraw-Hill Education.

Stenhouse, David. 1931. *Glasgow, Its Municipal Undertakings and Enterprises*. Glasgow: Corporation of Glasgow.

Stewart, Bob. 1967. *Breaking the Fetters*. London: Lawrence and Wishart.

Swenarton, Mark. 1981. "An 'Insurance against Revolution': Ideological Objectives of the Provision and Design of Public Housing in Britain after the First World War." *Historical Research* 54 (129): 86–101.

Thane, Pat. 1990. "The Women of the British Labour Party and Feminism, 1906–1945." In *British Feminism in the Twentieth Century*, edited by Harold L. Smith, 124–43. Aldershot: Elgar.

———. 1991. "Visions of Gender in the Making of the British Welfare State: The Case of Women in the British Labour Party and Social Policy, 1906–1945." In *Maternity and Gender Policies: Women and the Rise of the European States, 1880s–1950s*, edited by Gisela Bock and Pat Thane, 93–118. London: Routledge.

The Mirror. 2015. "First Victims of Tory Welfare Cap: Family of 9 Evicted from their Home by Bailiffs." February 16. http://www.mirror.co.uk/news/uk-news/first-victims-tory-welfare-cap-5780398.

The Scotland Institute. 2016. *Housing Costs, Poverty and Homelessness in Scotland.* Glasgow: The Scotland Institute.

Thompson, Edward P. 1971. "The Moral Economy of the English Crowd in the Eighteenth Century." *Past & Present* (50): 76–136.

Thorpe, Caroline. 2006. "Unfair Dismissal." *Inside Housing*, January 13.

Tiesdell, Steven. 1999. *The Development and Implementation of Housing Action Trust Policy.* PhD diss., University of Nottingham.

———. 2001. "A Forgotten Policy? A Perspective on the Evolution and Transformation of Housing Action Trust Policy, 1987–99." *European Journal of Housing Policy* 1(3): 357–83.

Turner, Graham. 2008. *The Credit Crunch: Housing Bubbles, Globalization and the Worldwide Economic Crisis.* London: Pluto Press.

UCL Cut The Rent. n.d. Facebook Group. Accessed July 15, 2017. https://www.facebook.com/uclcuttherent/.

UK Parliament. 2016. *Housing and Planning Bill: Written Evidence Submitted by Crisis.* https://www.publications.parliament.uk/pa/cm201516/cmpublic/housingplanning/memo/hpb04.htm.

Vasudevan, Alexander. 2017. *The Autonomous City: A History of Urban Squatting.* London: Verso.

Vercellone, Carlo. 2010. "The Crisis of the Law of Value and the Becoming-Rent of Profit." In *Crisis in the Global Economy: Financial Markets, Social Struggles, and New Political Scenarios*, edited by Andrea Fumagalli and Sandro Mezzadra, 85–118. London: Semiotext(e) and the MIT Press.

Waldron, Richard, and Redmond, Declan. 2016. "Stress in Suburbia: Counting the Costs of Ireland's Property Crash and Mortgage Arrears Crisis." *Tijdschrift voor Economische en Sociale Geografie* 107(4): 484–501.

Watt, Paul. 2009a. "Housing Stock Transfers, Regeneration and State-led Gentrification in London." *Urban Policy and Research* 27(3): 229–42.

———. 2009b. "Social Housing and Regeneration in London". In *Regenerating London*, edited by Rob Imrie, Loretta Lees and Mike Raco, 212–33. London: Routledge.

———. 2013. "'It's Not For Us': Regeneration, the 2012 Olympics and the Gentrification of East London." *City: Analysis of Urban Trends, Culture, Theory, Policy, Action* 17(1): 99–118.

———. 2016. "A Nomadic War Machine in the Metropolis: En/countering London's 21st Century Housing Crisis with Focus E15." *City: Analysis of Urban Trends, Culture, Theory, Policy, Action* 20(2): 297–320.

———. 2017. "Gendering the Right to Housing in the City: Homeless Female Lone Parents in Post-Olympics, Austerity East London." *Cities.* Doi: http://www.sciencedirect.com/science/article/pii/S0264275116302165.

Watt, Paul, and Penny Bernstock. 2017. "Legacy for Whom? Housing in Post-Olympics East London." In *London 2012 and the Post-Olympics City: A Hollow Legacy?* edited by Phil Cohen and Paul Watt, 91–138. Basingstoke: Palgrave Macmillan.

Watt, Paul, and Anna Minton. 2016. "London's Housing Crisis and Its Activisms." *City: Analysis of Urban Trends, Culture, Theory, Policy, Action* 20(2): 204–21.

Ward, Colin. 1974. *Tenants Take Over*. London: The Architectural Press Ltd.

———. 1985. *When We Build Again: Let's Have Housing that Works!* London: Pluto Press.

Weber, Rachel. 2002. "Extracting Value from the City: Neoliberalism and Urban Redevelopment." *Antipode* 34(3): 519–40.

Wells, Herbert G. 1907. *Will Socialism Destroy the Home?* London: ILP.

Wilson, Wendy. 2017. "Private Rented Housing: The Rent Control Debate." *House of Commons Library*, April 3. http://www.researchbriefings.files.parliament.uk/documents/SN06760/SN06760.pdf.

Wood, Patricia Burke 2017. *Citizenship, Activism and the City: The Invisible and the Impossible*. Oxon: Routledge.

Woodward, Rachel. 1991. "Mobilising Opposition: The Campaign against Housing Action Trusts in Tower Hamlets." *Housing Studies* 6(1): 44–56.

Wright, Steve. 2002. *Storming Heaven: Class Composition and Struggle in Italian Autonomist Marxism*. London: Pluto Press.

Wright, Valerie. 2008. "Feminism and Women's Organizations in Interwar Scotland." PhD diss., University of Glasgow.

Young, James D. 1985. *Women and Popular Struggles*. Edinburgh: Mainstream Publishing.

Young, Jean K. 1991. "From 'Laissez-Faire' to 'Homes fit for Heroes': Housing in Dundee, 1868–1919." PhD diss., University of St. Andrews.

Youngman, Tom. 2015. "Housing Gains in Spain." *Red Pepper*, August 25. http://www.redpepper.org.uk/houyoungsing-gains-in-spain/.

Index

action trusts, 118–20, *119*
activism: for affordable housing, 182;
for alternative municipal housing,
176; culture of, 5, 37, 40–41, 45–46;
DCH, 120–21; DTA and, xxxiii,
88–91, *90*, *95*, 212; economics
of, 104–5, 174–75, *175*, 186; for
estate demolitions, 121–25, *123–24*,
131–32, *131*; evictions and, 128;
for FOQM, 126–27; in Glasgow,
43; globalization of, 89–92, *90*;
government and, 39, 117–18,
180–81, 183n1; grassroots activism,
19–20, 24, 45, 104, 118–20, *119*,
188; against HATs, 118–20, *119*,
122–23, 131–33, *131*; hecklers in,
34, 46n1; history of, 4, 13–14, 34,
80, 202–3; homelessness in, 156–58;
for housing, xxxiv, 25–28, 72,
144–45, 162–65; ideology of, 206–8;
from labour movements, 12, 52–53;
for legislation, 109–11; lobbying for,
109, 112–14, 126, 139; media and,
97, 108–9, 161–62, 203; for new
housing, 162–64; online petitions,
129–30; patriotism and, 105; policy
and, 40, 42; politics and, xxxv,
25–26, 36, 103–4, 154, 213–14; for
poverty, 163–64, 176; for public

housing, 209–12; for rent control,
206–8; #rentripoff campaign, 89–90,
90; rent strikes as, 8–9, 13–14, 17–
20, 28–29, 33–34, 75, 102–3, 186–
87, 189–97, *193*; in Scotland, 43;
Sinn Féin, 164; for social housing,
125–27; for tenant struggles, 62,
85–86, 181, 209; theory of, 28–29,
57–58, 97–98, 153, 201–2; in UK,
23–24, 79–81, 122–25, *123–24*;
unions in, 159–62; women in, 9–13,
22–23, 41–42; in World War I, 45
Addison Act. *See* Town Planning Act
(1919)
affordable housing: activism for, 182;
economics of, 125–26, 139–40, 180,
190–91, 196; politics of, 189
affordable rent, xxix
agnotology, xxv, xxxiv, 140–44
agriculture, 56–57
AHFPA. *See* Association of House
Factors and Property Agents
alternative municipal housing: activism
for, 176; ideology of, 170–71; policy
for, 182–83; politics of, 173–74, 183;
public ownership, 172; rent strikes
in, 171–72; socialism and, 176–77;
taxes for, 177–80; theory of, 169–70;
in UK, 174–75, *175*

246 *Index*

Pankhurst, Sylvia, 8
patriotism, 8–10, 38, 105
planning applications, 125–27
Platform for People Affected by
  Mortgages (PAH), 86, 89–92, 160–
  61, 197
police, 79
policy: activism and, 40, 42; for
  alternative municipal housing,
  182–83; in Britain, xiv, 207–8; class
  and, 93, 133; for economics, xxvi–
  xxvii, 73–74; in England, 212–13;
  for evictions, xxxii, 75–77, 87–88,
  110–11, 129–30, 195–96; *The Flaws
  in Rent Ceilings* (IEA), 147–48; for
  gender, 41, 45–46; for gentrification,
  210–11; *Geography and Social
  Justice* (Smith, D.), 141–42; GLA
  for, 121–22, 125–26; government
  for, 23, 43, 56, 63–64, 72, 145, 156;
  hegemony in, 147; history of, xviii–
  xxi; for homelessness, 156–58; for
  housing, xxix, xxxi, 13–14, 18, 36,
  62–64, 75–77, 139–40; *The Housing
  Question* (Engels), xxxii, 50–59, 63–
  64, 201–2; ideology and, 156, 192;
  in Ireland, xxix, 208; for landlords,
  8, 27–28, 106–7, 188–89; legislation
  and, 78; of LR, 104–6, 111–14;
  Marxism as, xxxii; morality and, 7,
  71–72; PAH, 197; for poverty, 103,
  141; REITs, xxviii; from rent strikes,
  xxi–xxii, xxxiv, 37–38, 42–43,
  203–4, 210–12; RTB, xxiii–xxiv,
  73–74; Scottish Housing Advisory
  Committee for, 27; for slums, 26;
  for squatting, 130–31; for tenant
  struggles, 98, 120–21, 183n3; theory
  and, 44–45, 96, 105; in UK, xiv,
  179, 184–85; for welfare, 93–94; for
  Women's Labour League Conference
  (1914), 9–10
politics: activism and, xxxv, 25–26, 36,
  103–4, 154, 213–14; of affordable
  housing, 189; of alternative

municipal housing, 173–74, 183;
  of apartments, 98; of austerity,
  82–83; ballots in, 132–33, 149; of
  banking, 160, 183n4, 203–4; of
  capitalism, 53, 85, 177–78, 198, 212;
  of class, 5–6, 38–39, 57–58, 131;
  of Clydebank Strikes, xxii–xxiii;
  of communism, 3–4, 20–21, 44;
  culture of, 17–18, 24–25, 37, 108,
  128–30; DCH, 120–21; of DTA,
  92–98, *95*; of economics, xxv, xxvii,
  xxxii, 26–27, 56, 141; of gender,
  9–10, 19–20, 205–6; in Glasgow,
  xxiv, 10–11; of government, 170–71;
  government in, 35–36; history of,
  140–41; of housing, xxiv–xxv,
  20–25, 90–92, *95*, 95–96; of housing
  commons, 189–98; ILP, 4, 11, 21,
  62; of industrialization, 173–74; in
  Ireland, 111; of labour movements,
  xvii–xviii, xxx–xxxi, 28, 33–34,
  120–21, 148–49, 179, 186–87; of
  legislation, xx–xxi, xxxiii–xxxiv,
  91, 122–25, *123–24*; LR in, 106–11;
  of neoliberalization, 159, 187–89;
  NGOs in, 162–65; of patriotism,
  8–9; of public housing, 159–62, 164,
  181–82, 192–93; of rent control, 40,
  74, 87–88, 140–44, 174–75, *175*;
  of rent regulation, 110–11; of rent
  strikes, 22, 63–64, 72, 145, 187–89;
  in Scotland, 13, 23–24; SCWG
  in, 19; of SLHCs, 127–30; SNP
  in, 139; of social housing, 165; of
  socialism, 169, 213; in Spain, 92;
  of stock transfers, 131–32; of tenant
  struggles, xxi–xxiii, 24, 87–88, 92–
  97, *95*; theory of, 91–92; in UK, 77,
  172; women in, xix–xx, 3–4, 17–18,
  29, 45, 60–61; WSPU, 3–5, 10
poverty: activism for, 163–64, 176; case
  workers for, 96–97; class and, 35–36;
  culture of, 110, 117–18, 141–43,
  182–83, 187; for government, 169–
  70; in Ireland, 93–94; legislation for,

About the Contributors

Michael Byrne is Lecturer in Urban Political Economy at the School of Social Policy, Social Work and Social Justice, Dublin. He publishes widely on financialization, the Irish housing crisis and tenants' movements and is actively involved in the Dublin Tenants Association (DTA).

Vickie Cooper is Lecturer in Social Policy and Criminology at the Open University. She is currently examining the relationship between welfare reforms, evictions and homelessness. She has published widely in edited books, academic journals, and magazines such as *Red Pepper* and *Open Democracy*.

Tony Cox teaches adult education with Lifelong Learning Dundee, University of Dundee. His book, *Empire, Industry and Class: The Imperial Nexus of Jute, 1840–1940* (2012), charts the appalling housing conditions and significant rent strikes of the 1910s in Dundee. He is the Dundee organizer of the Scottish Unemployed Workers Network.

Pam Currie is an activist, trade unionist, Further Education Lecturer and Associate Lecturer with Open University. Her master's thesis provided a feminist account of the 1915 Rent Strikes, and her writing includes contributions to *Scottish Socialist Voice*, *Frontline* magazine and a chapter in *Is There a Scottish Road to Socialism* (2007).

Seán Damer is Honorary Fellow at the University of Edinburgh. His interpretations of the 1915 Rent Strikes in the 1980s are principal reference points on the subject. He is currently completing a monograph on interwar housing.

Cesare Di Feliciantonio is a postdoctoral fellow in the National Institute for Regional and Spatial Analysis (NIRSA), University of Maynooth. His work lies at the intersection of social/urban geography, political economy, housing studies and urban studies with a focus on neoliberal subjectification and its contestations, urban social movements and sexuality studies.

Sarah Glynn is a welfare and housing activist, lecturer, architect and independent researcher. Her publications include *Where the Other Half Lives: Low-income Housing in a Neoliberal World* (2009), *Byker, Newcastle upon Tyne* (2015) and numerous articles in academic journals and popular media.

Neil Gray (editor of this volume) is Research Associate at the University of Glascow. He has published widely on housing, urbanization, gentrification and mega-events for academic journals and magazines such as *Variant* and *Mute*. He is active in Living Rent.

Rory Hearne is a postdoctoral researcher in Maynooth University working on social investment, human rights and homelessness. His most recent publication is *A Home or a Wealth Generator? Inequality, Financialization and the Irish Housing Crisis* (2017), and he is active in Irish housing and social-justice campaigns.

Stuart Hodkinson is Lecturer in Critical Urban Geography at the University of Leeds. He has carried out ESRC-funded research on residents' experiences of public-housing regeneration and is currently tracking the displacement effects of welfare cuts. He has published widely on housing issues and the commons.

Annmarie Hughes is Senior Lecturer in Economic and Social history at the University of Glasgow. Her book, *Gender and Political Identities in Scotland, 1919–1939* (2010), integrates class and gender history, public and private spheres, and cultural, economic and social structures in the interwar period.

Tim Joubert is a doctoral student at the University of Leeds. His research aims to understand 'the urban' as a potential site for contemporary anti-capitalist movements, and he is working on a historical study of radical municipalism and local socialism in 'ordinary cities' in the United Kingdom. He has been active in housing campaigns in Leeds.

Hamish Kallin completed his PhD, *Gentrification and the State of Uneven Development on Edinburgh's Periphery,* in 2015. He is a Lecturer in Human

Geography at the University of Edinburgh, and his research and writing focus on gentrification, housing, territorial stigma and housing-related debt.

Rob Kitchin is Professor and ERC Advanced Investigator at the National Institute for Regional and Spatial Analysis at Maynooth University. He specializes in social and urban geography broadly conceived and has published widely across the social sciences.

Living Rent emerged from the Edinburgh Private Tenants Action Group (EPTAG) in 2014 and established a Scottish national tenants' union in 2016. Kate Samuels, Dave Statham and Emma Saunders authored and edited this chapter on behalf of the campaign group.

Cian O'Callaghan is Assistant Professor in urban geography at Trinity College, Dublin. He specializes in urban political economy and cultural geography, with a particular focus on housing, vacancy and spatial justice. His IRC New Horizons funded research focuses on contestations over the reuse of vacant land in Dublin.

Kirsteen Paton is Lecturer in Sociology, Social Policy and Criminology at the University of Liverpool, publishing widely on class and housing issues. Her PhD study and book, *Gentrification: A Working Class Perspective* (2015) explores the impacts of gentrification on the working-class neighbourhood of Partick in Glasgow.

Tom Slater is Reader in Urban Geography at the University of Edinburgh. His many publications include the coauthored books, *Gentrification* (2008) and *The Gentrification Reader* (2010). He is working on a long-term study of how free-market think tanks manufacture ignorance of the causes of urban inequalities.

Paul Watt is based in Urban Studies at the Department of Geography, Birkbeck, University of London and writes widely on social housing, regeneration and gentrification. His most recent books are *Social Housing and Urban Renewal: A Cross-National Perspective* (2017) and *London 2012 and the Post-Olympics City: A Hollow Legacy?* (2017).

Valerie Wright completed her PhD, *Women's Organisations and Feminism in Interwar Scotland*, at the University of Glasgow in 2008. She has published in a range of academic journals and is currently a research associate on a Leverhulme project titled *Housing, Everyday Life and Wellbeing Over the Long Term: Glasgow 1950–1975*.